Harold Colne

London. January 1977

D0762385

VICTORIAN STATIONS

VICTORIAN STATIONS

Railway Stations in England & Wales 1830-1923

Gordon Biddle

Drawings by Peter Fells

David & Charles : Newton Abbot

0 7153 5949 5

Set in eleven on twelve point Bembo
and printed in Great Britain
by Latimer Trend & Company Ltd Plymouth
for David & Charles (Holdings) Limited
South Devon House Newton Abbot Devon

CONTENTS

5

LIST OF ILLUSTRATIONS

PLATES

7

LIST OF ILLUSTRATIONS

ELEVATIONAL DRAWINGS

LINE DRAWINGS IN TEXT

9

LIST OF ILLUSTRATIONS

PREFACE

THIS book owes so much to a group of other people that the customary acknowledgement at the end would be totally inadequate.

First and foremost is Roger E. G. Read, my friend and collaborator of some twenty years standing until his untimely death in 1970, but for which his name would have appeared with mine. Although the work has not appeared in the form we originally envisaged, I owe a great debt to his knowledge, guidance and, above all, to his fine collection of photographs taken with such painstaking care. By rights this book should be dedicated to his memory, but knowing that he would have scorned such a device I hope that these words will make an adequate substitute.

Death robbed us both of a kindly friend and mentor in Professor C. L. Mowat of Bangor University, who generously made his own valuable photographic collection freely available to us. Were he still present, his pen would be writing this preface.

To Peter Fells I am not only grateful for the excellent line drawings which grace the following pages, but also for his meticulous and patient work in preparing the index, assisting in proof reading and his helpful suggestions for improving the text.

Geoffrey Holt has been a tower of strength in checking the historical detail and for so willingly providing information on many points I had missed. To Margaret Holt I owe a debt of thanks for her patient struggling with my atrocious handwriting during her two successive typings of the manuscript.

Finally, and most important of all, I acknowledge with a deep sense of gratitude the support of my wife and family over the years, without which this book would not have appeared. My demands on their forbearance have been related to much more than time spent in research and writing; there has hardly ever been a family journey that has not included a detour and delay for Father to 'just look at a station'.

GORDON BIDDLE

INTRODUCTION AND
EXPLANATION

THE nineteenth century was a fascinating age. In it the Industrial
Revolution, the British Empire and one of the most individualistic
periods in our history reached their climax. Victorian philosophy was
an extraordinary mixture of piety, indifference, moral fervour, in-
ventive genius and *laissez faire* commercialism, all compounded
together with a supreme overriding self-confidence. These ingredients
were faithfully reflected in contemporary architecture, and although
the Victorians have gone many of their buildings remain. One of the
most entire products of the age was the steam railway system, owing
only the basic concept of the rail to an earlier period. Everything else
about it—its motive power, vehicles, management—was new. It
revolutionised social habits and outlook; no self-respecting community
could afford to be without a railway station bearing its name, however
far away it might be (and some of them were). The stationmaster was
a man of importance: in the village hierarchy he was only outranked
by the squire, parson and doctor; in the town he was on equal terms
with the mayor and local men of influence. Consequently stations
became a mirror of Victorian taste; if the railways were seldom in the
forefront of architectural development, they were never far behind,
so that the tremendous variety of station styles formed a microcosm
of nineteenth-century building.

Much has been written and rewritten about railways in the last
twenty years. In that time appreciation of the best in Victorian building
has come into its own, yet, despite the railways' large contribution,
there has been no attempt at a detailed and accurate survey. Excellent
accounts of the monumental in railway structures can be read in most

books dealing with Victorian architecture, but the majority of the 9,000-odd stations in existence at the height of railway prosperity, probably forming the largest single class of public building, have almost been ignored. Christian Barman's *Introduction to Railway Architecture* (1950), which I gratefully acknowledge as my initial inspiration, is undoubtedly the best book on the subject, but limited by its size and in any case long out of print. Carroll L. V. Meeks' *The Railway Station* (1957) is the classic standard work concerned with the development of large stations, but covers world-wide practice with considerable emphasis on Continental and North American stations. In the last few years several general books on railway history, treating the subject in a broader context than hitherto, have dealt sympathetically with smaller stations and their place in the landscape, but most of the standard railway histories give prominence only to the big well-known stations; few have related station design to changing social influences or have touched on the significance of the railway companies' own historical development and the outlook of their managements.

Roughly speaking, station design evolved in two phases, beginning with highly individualistic buildings of considerable charm and merit, deriving from an earlier age, and developing into what can be called 'line styles'—in other words a series of stations on a particular line or section having distinctive features in common. Then, after 1850–60, as railway companies grew larger, they developed 'company styles' that reflected a large and growing degree of uniformity, so forming the second phase, which ended in brief flirtations with the Domestic Revival. In between there was, of course, a gradual merging of styles, and despite standardisation a great number of individually designed stations were still produced, particularly among the larger ones.

My theme, then, is the English railway station in its various settings. This book makes no pretence of being a complete architectural or historical treatise. Its purpose is simply to present in word, photograph and drawing an account of *what was there*, in the hope that it may stimulate in fellow laymen the interest in stations that has given me twenty-five years of pleasure. At a time when so much has disappeared I hope the record will be thought worthwhile.

Now for a few words of explanation.

The main London termini have lately had a comprehensive and competent biographer in Alan A. Jackson (*London Termini*, 1969) while Professor Jack Simmons' *St. Pancras Station* (1968) is the only book so far to have dealt with a single large station. Consequently I make no apology for referring to the big London stations only in the general context of their periods and evolution, and for concentrating on the lesser known. I do apologise, however, for using the past tense throughout. This undesirable but unavoidable decision was reluctantly taken simply because of my inability to keep up with the spate of demolitions and alterations of the last ten to fifteen years; rather than fail to present an up-to-date survey of what is left I felt it better not to try. My finishing point is 1923, a year convenient not only because it saw the end of the Victorian railway companies' separate identities, but also as the end of the nineteenth-century influence on railway building. Only on the Great Western and, in London, the Metropolitan and the District Railways, which continued to exist in their old form, was there any continuity of design into the 1920s and 1930s. Because of my more limited knowledge of Scottish stations, their tendency, in any case, to develop their own characteristics, and the dictates of space, I have confined myself to England and Wales. Likewise London's tube stations—as distinct from those on sub-surface lines—are in rather a special category and have been omitted. Unfortunately space also precludes more than a passing reference to a few of the more interesting goods sheds, though it was my original intention to devote a chapter to them.

Wherever appropriate the latest station name has been used, except for places that have or had two or more stations, in which case the latest suffix has been given to assist identification. Most dates refer to the year of opening, or rebuilding in the form reviewed, as accurately as possible, using what I have conisdered to be the most reliable source, though unfortunately it has not been possible to date every building. Any errors or omissions of this or any other kind are, of course, entirely my own. It would have been useful to include a geographical or map reference, certainly for the lesser-known places, but lack of space defeated me again. I have tried to make amends, however, by adding the county to station names in the index, beyond which I must recommend readers to a pre-grouping railway map or gazetteer.

I have deliberately reduced the use of architectural terms as far as possible, though the use of a minimum number has been unavoidable in a book of this kind. A short simplified glossary of the less common terms is therefore included on p 231. As an amateur historian I am well aware of the importance of source references, but, as a mass of annotations merely serves to irritate in a book mainly intended for the general reader, I have deliberately limited the footnotes and instead have amplified some of the bibliographical information on p 227. Finally, I have tried as far as possible to maintain a reasonably chronological order, though in a number of places my good intentions in this respect have unavoidably been jettisoned in the interests of following a particular sequence in design. In apologising in advance I can only say that Victorian station architecture was like that. It is part of its fascination.

Plate 1 The early station at Wednesfield Heath, Grand Junction Railway, which was considered adequate to serve Wolverhampton; photographed in 1964

Page 17

Plate 2 Engraving of the original London & Birmingham Railway station at Coventry, showing terrace and stairs down to platform

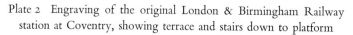

Plate 3   Florentine Italianate at Gobowen, Shrewsbury & Chester Railway, in 1955

Page 18

Plate 4   South Eastern Railway Italianate at Wadhurst, by William Tress, in 1955

CHAPTER I

THE EARLIEST YEARS

On the earliest railways passenger-carrying was non-existent, un-official or, where it was given recognition, a sideline. The prime purpose of these lines was to carry minerals, usually coal, in an England where the main population was rural and unaccustomed to travelling more than a few miles from home to the nearest market by carrier's cart or canal packet. The average townsman, for his part, rarely had need to leave his native place, and for those few who had reasons for travelling there was by 1820 a network of stagecoach services connecting all the main centres. They were helped by a growing series of tolerably good turnpike roads, but fares were high.

As the first railways were local, running from pithead to coal staith or quarry to canal, passenger traffic was not in any case on offer. The little Swansea & Mumbles Railway of 1807 remained the first and only line to carry regular fare-paying passengers until the Stockton & Darlington of 1825, which was the first to connect two sizeable and growing industrial towns; its directors realised there was a passenger-carrying potential and set out to develop it from the outset, but they did not offer a service themselves. Road practice was followed by simply providing a permanent way on which for the first few years contractors operated their own horse-drawn carriages. Stagecoach methods were followed in issuing tickets from inns near stopping places along the line. The Leicester & Swannington Railway (1832) hired a room in the Ashby Road Hotel, close to the Leicester to Ashby-de-la-Zouch road, to serve as a station. Later they bought it, and it continued in use as Bardon Hill station until its closure in 1952.

Passengers boarded trains by clambering up from the lineside, and, where covered terminal accommodation was needed, a handy goods shed was usually felt to suffice. Darlington had to put up with a converted warehouse for nine years and Stockton with a wooden coach shed for three. Just as stagecoach practice afforded the only precedent for booking arrangements, so agricultural custom was followed in designing buildings. Barn-like structures frequently served a dual purpose, like the termini of the Leeds & Selby Railway (1834). Each comprised a brick or stone shed with a triple-span timber-trussed roof on plain iron columns. Goods traffic used one side and passenger trains the other. There were no platforms and the booking offices were quite separate—at Selby in the superintendent's house. Once the future of the passenger business was fully realised, however, purpose-built stations were found to be not only necessary but desirable—in the city to impress, in the country to reassure, and in both places to attract.

The Liverpool & Manchester Railway (1830) first expressed in buildings its sense of pride in achievement. The Moorish Arch at Edge Hill was its monument, but in its modest way the plain two-storey station building at Crown Street, Liverpool, classical in concept, lent it dignity. Its Venetian windows gave on to a single platform covered by a long flat canopy on columns set close to the edge, from which sprang wooden queen-post trusses carrying an overall roof to a screen wall opposite, in contemporary illustrations looking very much like an afterthought. This first expression of the trainshed as distinct from the dual-purpose goods shed arose directly from the realisation that passenger and goods traffic must now be segregated. Hence the separate passenger shed, although it still served a double role as a shelter for trains in use and trains in store. Separate carriage sheds and sidings were still some years away.

By 1836 a new terminus had been laid out at Lime Street nearer the city centre, where John Cunningham built a simple Georgian block across the ends of the tracks, a plan which became the generally accepted layout in later years. The trainshed roof again was supported by timber trusses, this time partly glazed and carried on an arcade of iron columns whose shallow brackets formed an effective series of segmental spandrels. To front the entrance courtyard, John Foster, Jr, the city surveyor, designed a handsome classical screen embodying a pair of two-storeyed office buildings and pierced by tall Roman arches, the centre couple flanked by Doric columns and surmounted by an immense pediment to form the main entrance. The screen was completed in 1839, probably by Foster's successor, Joseph Franklin. Liverpool corporation gave £2,000 towards it, to ensure a suitably grand design to harmonise with their central development scheme, which eventually included H. L. Elmes' St George's Hall and the library and museum group. Unfortunately this early example of civic planning was soon spoilt when the screen, after surviving the first rebuilding of the station in 1846–51, was pulled down to make way for the second in 1868–71.

The contrast with Manchester could not have been more marked, for there a much poorer, even mean, stuccoed edifice was erected in Liverpool Road, graced only by some weak pilasters and a tripartite entrance. The low platform was at first-floor level beneath a pitched awning on wooden posts. These termini symbolised the difference between the two towns at that time. Both were mixtures of affluence and poverty, but Liverpool's affluence was expressed culturally: inspired by William Roscoe some thirty years before, a gracious handsome city centre was being created by civic leaders who were prepared to ensure with hard cash that the new railway entered in fitting style. Manchester, on the other hand, the growing 'cottonopolis' where 'thousands of smoking obelisks of steam engines 80 to 180 feet high destroy all impression of church steeples', was run by manufacturers, and for them a station at the bottom of Liverpool Road was good enough.

Although the Liverpool & Manchester's trains stopped at numerous places en route, stations do not seem to have been built for several years. Meanwhile the Grand Junction Railway was built to connect it with Birmingham in 1837, and two years later a handsome station with a light iron roof was opened in Curzon Street alongside the London & Birmingham's. In 1838 the latter railway had been opened throughout between terminal stations that have not been equalled since. Philip Hardwick's Doric arch at Euston was the first and finest of the monumental railway entrances, symbolising the triumph of man over nature and the beginning of a new age. There was nothing to match it in commercial architecture anywhere in England; indeed, it has been described as the finest classical monument in London. At the Birmingham end, Curzon Street station was smaller but matching in concept. The directors of the railway were proud of building the first main line out of London and were not afraid to show it.

Railway promotion was now rapidly gaining momentum, and in their larger stations the first passenger lines were early enough to catch the tail end of the great classical era of Georgian building before it was all but submerged in the Gothic Revival. The London & Southampton's Nine Elms and Southampton Terminus stations

(Chapter 3), although on a more modest scale, followed Euston; and a little later came Gosport, another exemplar of this final flourish.

Yet the grand gestures of the London & Birmingham and London & Southampton Railways were for a time isolated exceptions to the quieter dignity displayed elsewhere. Hereditary styling was best seen in the outer terminus of the London & Greenwich Railway (1838), a smaller but visually satisfying building wholly in the Georgian idiom of the town. George Smith's frontage of seven bays in stock brick was part of a simple rectangular plan, strongly Italianate in flavour, with a low-hipped roof almost hidden behind a thin but deep dentilled cornice. Stone-cased regular fenestration with flat-topped pediments and a plain string course contrasted with rusticated quoins at the ends, while the central doorway had three-quarter engaged Tuscan columns. Even Francis Whishaw was impressed. He was a civil engineer whose *Railways of Great Britain and Ireland* (1838 and 1840) contains some of the most complete descriptions of early railways. A strong advocate of economy, he was moved to say that it was 'built on a magnificent scale, and with every regard to the comfort and convenience of the public'. The trainshed was lighted by seven Venetian windows on each side, and the interior of the booking hall was in 'Grecian-Doric style' with columns. There seems to be some doubt whether the building was dismantled and rebuilt on a new site when the line was extended in 1878, as has often been stated; suffice it to say here that the new station bore a remarkable resemblance to early illustrations of the old one.

A more subtle blending of Georgian ideas with domesticity was achieved by the Lancaster & Preston Junction Railway in 1840 at Lancaster, where its restrained terminus in dressed stone looked down Penny Street in complete harmony with the town houses. Heavily corniced, it displayed a small pediment centred over a flat porch resting on coupled Ionic columns.

Soon a new generation of architects was devoting to railway stations, particularly the smaller ones, a quality of effective invention that remains an example to this day. The work of some of them is examined in Chapter 3. Unremembered local men also added their quota, though, strangely, not very many great national names were associated with extensive railway work beyond the prestige job, Sir William Tite being the notable exception (Chapter 3). Their work arose largely from the surge of belief in the great role railways would play and alongside the classical idiom, rapidly to overtake it, there appeared a leaning towards the Italianate so strong as to be nicknamed 'the railway style'. *The Illustrated London News* first used the term in its description of the South Eastern and London & Croydon Railways' joint London terminus at Bricklayers Arms in 1844. The lofty iron trainsheds had pavilions on each side joined by screens and fronted by a long, low, flat-roofed façade with Baroque touches in the scrolly brackets. Henry-Russell Hitchcock calls it 'the poor man's Barry', but the *News* thought it presented

> . . . a noble frontage . . . crowned with a bold cornice and entablature enriched in a novel and effective manner by a course of Red Venetian tiles; and in the centre is a picturesque clock and bell tower, the former of which is illuminated at night. The style has been called Italian; it might be designated more properly an English railway style, being designed by the architect, Mr Lewis Cubitt, to meet the peculiar circumstances of the case, and merely decorated with Italian forms.

Architecturally speaking, the railways had arrived, and as we shall see later Cubitt went on to propagate his 'English railway style'. Well into the 1850s it continued to be a favourite with railway stylists. Despite a disreputable train service, which remained a bad joke for over twenty years, even the Eastern Counties Railway scraped up enough money to erect a prestigious London terminus at Shoreditch, in Italianate of course (Chapter 2). It may not have vied with Euston but for a line which in 1840 had only managed to reach Brentwood it was a grand gesture, conveying a confidence that the directors could hardly have felt. The little Norwich & Yarmouth Railway was similarly moved to express itself in a degree of style at Yarmouth Vauxhall in 1844. Here Venetian first-floor windows looked out on a long flat canopy, but otherwise, apart from its size, the building was undistinguished. Behind it, twin iron trainsheds had delicately elliptical arched arcades. The first Norwich Thorpe, in the same year, was similarly equipped, with two 50ft by 360ft sheds, one serving passengers and one goods. Bramah, Fox & Co built the ironwork, which the *Norwich Mercury* considered very elegant. One side was open and the other closed by a small office building which, a year later, was augmented by a proper frontage of seven arches across the terminal end and a slim Italianate clock tower.

In 1844, too, Manchester's turn for something better arrived, although considerably muted. The Manchester & Leeds Railway, which in 1839 had opened a somewhat bleak red-brick office block (the chief ornament of which was a diamond-shaped clock) at its

Oldham Road terminus, was extended to a new station in Hunts Bank, named Victoria, allegedly but most improbably designed by George Stephenson. Oldham Road was certainly by Stephenson—a two-storey structure with a combined goods and passenger shed on the upper level and a ground-floor booking office. It was Stephenson's idea to use the arches forming the lower level as a warehouse and install hydraulic lifts to transfer wagons from one to the other. At Victoria, to which shortly afterwards the Liverpool & Manchester extended its line, the original plan for recessed arcades supported by Roman-Doric columns was scrapped in favour of cantilevered brackets in order to give free access for luggage barrows and the like, which 'in some measure destroys its architectural pretensions', said *The Builder*. There was a small central clock, and what remained of architectural pretensions was obliterated when an upper floor was added later.

In order to develop traffic it was necessary to encourage the mass of the untutored public not only to travel by the new means but to travel at all. An appealing public image was not enough; it must be reassuring, too, an expression that the architects did not have far to seek. J. C. Loudon in his *Encyclopaedia of Cottage, Farm and Villa Architecture and Furniture* (1833) was a mentor widely drawn upon, his pattern-book styles inspiring much of the highly domestic character the smaller stations assumed. Unlike the Liverpool & Manchester, the Grand Junction and London & Birmingham companies from the outset built intermediate stations that presented an air of the normal and the familiar, added to, no doubt, by such terms as 'Booking Hall' and 'Waiting Room', which were simple and direct in their meaning. Generally the smallest station building comprised the stationmaster's house, in which one room with its own entrance was set aside for station purposes—partitioned to form the booking clerk's office on one side and the waiting room on the other. The Grand Junction's intermediate stations, such as Wednesfield Heath (Plate 1), Norton Bridge and Moore were mainly like this. Dumpy and insignificant though they were, they marked an awareness of the needs of the railway traveller. Rather better stations served the more important places: Penkridge, for instance, had two floors, with the station offices including a separate waiting room on the upper one, level with the platform, and the 'house' portion below—a not uncommon arrangement where the line was on an embankment; Four Ashes and Gailey also had two-storey buildings, but arranged in the conventional manner, and all three were embellished with drip-stones over the windows. Whishaw liked them. 'It were as well if this plan was more generally attended to,' he wrote, 'it really seems on some lines as if money was the last thing thought of, the aim being evidently to make as much architectural display as possible.'

While this charge could be made at the London & Birmingham at Euston and Curzon Street, once beyond their precincts the passenger would notice similar small cottage stations but with a modicum of stone trim. Like their canal predecessors, the early railways kept to local materials—the Grand Junction and the London & Birmingham used brick, grey stocks at the London end, red in the Midlands. Generally the L & B had little to spare for frills—its resources were needed for its terminal splendours—but allowed its architect G. Aitchison a modest increase in size and styling at the more important stations. Rugby's turrets and battlements were intended to match William Butterfield's new school buildings, to the fury of that Gothic purist A. W. N. Pugin, of whom more later. Watford, Tring and Coventry were sited at the top of cuttings, each with a short, not inelegant, terrace and steps down to the line (Plate 2). A certain dignity was achieved in the same way by the Midland Counties Railway at Borrowash (1839), where the stuccoed finish, stone-framed windows beneath flat bracketed hoods, and a hipped roof formed a well pro-portioned composition. Later additions at Kegworth masked the same arrangement, which, like Countesthorpe, was a poor imitation. Again, on this line and its neighbour, the Birmingham & Derby Junction, also of 1839, local red brick was the medium. Platforms at this period were low and, at stations in this class, open to the elements. An engraving of the B & DJ's Hampton station well illustrates the complete lack of protection against the weather on the low narrow platforms as passengers waited to change to the London & Birmingham line.

East Anglia provided considerably more variety. Mild Tudor styling was adopted by the Eastern Counties Railway at Brentwood (1840), while its near neighbour, the Northern & Eastern Railway, went one better at Broxbourne and incorporated a quadrangle. Indeed, the Northern & Eastern had some curious stations altogether. Lea Bridge, Whishaw stated, was handsome in the Italian style (naturally) but had its entrance on the road bridge, probably the earliest example of this economical arrangement, which became so common later in the century. With equal frugality the waiting rooms were contained in the arches below. The junction with the ECR at Stratford had a small classical building in the angle and a characteristic flat-roofed columned awning on each of the four platforms. Ponders End comprised a pair of two-storey wooden-framed structures linked by a wooden shelter with a curved roof. Roydon (1841) embodied round-headed windows, an up-tilted platform awning and, as a façade, an extraordinary bow-fronted verandah with deep fretted valancing and coupled columns. Yet the whole place was built in timber.

Timber construction on the South Eastern Railway's original main line across Kent from Redhill to Folkestone (1842–3) started a long tradition of wooden stations that earned the company and its later rival, the London, Chatham & Dover, so much odium as to become their chief memorial. Yet, at the time they were built, wayside stations like Marden, Headcorn and Pluckley on the main line and East Farleigh on the Maidstone branch (1844) were not poor by contemporary standards, despite their economy, and in fact could show more spacious accommodation than some of their more substantial northern counterparts. What is more, they were in keeping with the clapboard tradition of the Weald.

Of lines built up to 1840, styling and the use of appropriate local materials were most apparent on the Great Western and the North Midland Railways, which are reserved for more detailed discussion in Chapter 3. By this time, as railway promotion gathered pace, there was a perceptible move to give station buildings generally more character, a development that was to burst forth into a riot of styles a few years later. Robert Dockray, the London & Birmingham's resident engineer on its newly acquired Warwick & Leamington Union Railway (1844), designed two Italianate stations. Kenilworth, described as 'elegant and very light', had its pitched roof extended over the platform on deep brackets to form an awning, a method much copied; and Warwick—later renamed Leamington (Milverton)—comprised an elegant shed covering platform and rails, a huge arched *porte cochère* and a campanile intended to house a water tank and fire pump. At many stations this *porte cochère*, or covered carriage entrance, was an important feature. It provided shelter for passengers entering and leaving their private carriages or cabs, and, much later, their motor cars and taxis and, at Brighton, even electric trams.

On the Chester & Crewe Railway (1840) *cottage orné* in the Loudon fashion, albeit very mild, began to show itself in the little homely stations at Calveley and Tattenhall Road, the former with small wooden oriels, and at the larger Beeston Castle station, which had a wooden shelter over the forecourt. All three were externally rendered and given distinctive wooden finials and bargeboards. Eastward from Crewe, the most impressive building on the Manchester & Birmingham Railway was the Queen's Hotel, Alderley Edge, begun in 1844 and one of the first railway hotels, which entirely overshadowed the humble little station. Pride of place on this line went to Heaton Norris, where three pavilions with recessed pedimental gables and a pair of stone-dressed arches apiece were linked by a lean-to verandah with iron columns. The central pavilion, higher than its fellows, sported a clock and a slender weathervane. Crewe itself, after it became a junction in 1840, is shown in a contemporary print with a Jacobean building and a remarkable platform awning on columns, the outer edge sweeping upwards in a concave curve decorated with panels.

The Birmingham & Gloucester Railway presented as complete a contrast between town and country stations as could be found any-where in 1840. The latter were small stone-trimmed brick houses with four rooms, including waiting room and booking office, mildly Tudor like Droitwich Road, with slender angled chimneys and mullioned windows. At the towns there was variety. At Bromsgrove a long low building of 'pleasing and unostentatious appearance', according to the indefatigable Whishaw, had a colonnade extending the length of the front. The building lately demolished was certainly long and low, with four curious wooden-gabled porches, two in brick and two on iron columns. Were they part of Whishaw's colon-nade? Cheltenham Lansdown station was adapted from a large town house having a longish stuccoed frontage with a shallow central pedi-ment and a Palladian window. A deep nine-bay Doric colonnade with a plain entablature gave a strong Regency flavour. The platforms were in a cutting flanked by curved retaining walls supporting a heavy overall roof, the entrance side forming a terrace with a wooden verandah. But whereas at Cheltenham aesthetic harmony was main-tained by using an existing building, the station at Tewkesbury achieved it only at considerable expense. Whishaw's description gave it full justice:

> The station house, which faces the High Street, is built of Postlip free stone and is thirty eight feet in length and thirty four feet in height. It has a fine Gothic screenwork front with oriel windows and battlements. In the centre of the building are two well proportioned gateways each twelve feet high and twelve feet six inches wide, one of which is designed for railway passengers and the other for carriages and goods. There are suitable

offices on the ground floor with cellaring underneath and four airy upper rooms forming a comfortable residence. Stone staircases lead to a light and airy booking office and there is a long paved platform for passengers beneath a substantial roof of forty foot span and upwards of one hundred and sixty feet long.

Tewkesbury was at the end of a short single-line branch from Ashchurch, on which a journey must have been considerably anti-climactic after the splendours of the station. Passengers were carried in 'a handsome and convenient carriage, drawn by one horse at a good speed'. One wonders what civic pressures were applied to the Birmingham & Gloucester to gain such architectural approbation.

Local stone was the near-universal building material north of the Mersey and the first cross-Pennine line, the Manchester & Leeds (1840), displayed a certain versatility in a region not noted for architectural display. Whishaw reacted characteristically: 'Surely the engineering works will cost quite enough without swelling the sum total by the erection of so many Elizabethan Villas'. In fact, some of the intermediate stations were far better looking than the Manchester terminus. Rochdale had a neat Italianate building with a deep rear-canted awning on iron columns, and on the opposite platform a matching shelter with end-screens. Hebden Bridge had a similar awning on a gabled block built on to the stone goods shed, and Sowerby Bridge was in 'Elizabethan Gothic' with pointed windows, a crenellated turret on either side of a projecting entrance and twin doorways below. Brighouse, the station for Bradford, was in a heavier Italianate: tripartite windows set beneath projecting eaves were in startling contrast to tall finials and a deeply corbelled turret surmounted by a spike. Wakefield was classical, with a corniced parapet and columns. Smaller places had to be content with stone cottage buildings. Whishaw pointedly commended the Manchester, Bolton & Bury—a canal company turned railway—for having 'very wisely abstained from throwing away money by the erection of costly buildings'. But even plainness could be a virtue. The dour stone building at Blackrod on the Bolton & Preston Railway (1843), with low eaves, mullioned windows and tall octagonal stacks, fitted perfectly into the moorland landscape, while the gritty cottage stations on the Blackburn & Preston Railway (1840) and later the Huddersfield–Penistone line (1850), fitted their localities well.

By the early 1840s the Liverpool & Manchester Railway had come round to building stations at its more important stopping places. A good standard was set. A. F. Tait included them in his series of litho-graphs, Newton being depicted with a three-storey Regency building flanked on each side by a small pavilion supporting a flat integral awning between—a favourite composition, which will be encountered later. The classical approach was employed at Parkside, where an imposing two-storey block faced a small matching pavilion. Each had a deep cornice on eight large scrolled brackets and a pair of widely spaced pilasters. A shallow awning matched the depth of the cornice. Identical buildings faced each other at Edge Hill in local sandstone, with separate approach roads leading down between curving walls to each platform. After the Grand Junction Railway joined the L & M at Earlestown, somewhat startling appendages were attached to an otherwise meek little structure in the angle, including three sets of octagonal chimney stacks (all different), three over-sized saw-tooth crenellations over blank shields set on a frieze, deep mullioned windows and a lean-to awning on wooden posts with curved brackets. Tait's drawing also showed a steeply pitched roof, which may have been artist's licence. Within, greater harmony reigned. An impressive hall beneath a broad flat ceiling went with heavily carved beams and doors. Only a stone fireplace was needed to complete the baronial atmosphere.

CHAPTER 2

OLD STYLES AND NEW

THE wild financial speculation in railway schemes during the 'mania' years of 1845-6 created a mushroom expansion from some 2,000 miles of line in 1844 to around 7,500 miles by 1852. Such rapid growth caused upheavals in old-established ways of life far greater than anything in the canal age. Hand-in-hand with it went heavy migration to the towns as industrialisation increased. It was a time in which the railways' finest period of building contrasted with mean streets of terraced houses spreading around every manufacturing town. The need to reassure the timid traveller with modesty and plainness gave way to a desire to impress at all levels; the pride and elaboration in the city terminals was now spreading out to humbler quarters. We shall see in the next chapter how architects like Thompson, Livock and Green translated this urge. There were others, too, many unknown, who rose equally to the challenge of the new era. What is more, until the hard times of the 1850s, the money was there to pay for it. Men might live in hovels and travel third class in open trucks—even standing up on the Manchester & Leeds Railway—but on many lines they waited for their trains at handsome stations.

The second half of the eighteenth century had witnessed a remarkable growth of romanticism in cultivated society, expressed in a desire for the 'picturesque' in domestic architecture at first associated with the landscaping of country estates and the building of rustic gate lodges, pavilions, sham ruins and follies. Although the classical style revived a century earlier by Wren was firmly established in both its Greek and Roman forms, the notion that the romantic ideal could be better achieved by Gothic forms was taking a firm hold. By 'Gothic' was meant 'medieval'—pointed arches, tracery, stone vaulting and spires. Later, Gothic came to embrace the whole range of pre-

30

Renaissance architecture from Norman castles to Tudor and Jacobean manors, and by the 1840s and 1850s a long-drawn-out 'Battle of the Styles' was in full swing, with a sharply defined division between the Gothic and classical camps, the respective protagonists indulging in ferocious wordy engagements.

Yet this intense feeling was limited to a relatively small artistic circle beyond which the booming business life of the country made up its own mind about what it wanted. By the mid-1840s most architects, builders and engineers could turn their hands to either style with equal facility anyway—certainly those whom the railways employed could—and for the next ten years or so the legacy of earlier elegance and craftsmanship, although dwindling, ensured that most of what was done was good. Classicism being the immediately traditional style, it was used far more in railway work than Gothic, although, as we have seen already, it fairly quickly gave way to various kinds of Italianate in which classical features were often incorporated. More important, at this time it was also a cheaper style to build in than Gothic, a point not lost on railway companies.

After its *debut* in London, Birmingham and Southampton, the most monumental and perfect expressions of railway classicism, surpassed only by Euston, were found in the north. Huddersfield (1847) by J. P. Pritchett, Sr, of York, superbly classical, formed one side of a handsome square, the giant Corinthian portico being flanked by long colonnades and charmingly matched terminal pavilions. Although not deliberately planned in this way, it became an integral part of its setting and an eloquent symbol of the triumph of the railway. For the Huddersfield & Manchester Railway the country's longest tunnel at Standedge was not enough; it built a magnificent classical monument as well.

Second to Huddersfield only in scale, Monkwearmouth station suffered an ignoble fate. To celebrate his election as MP for Sunderland George Hudson asked Thomas Moore of Bishopwearmouth (not John Dobson as has been popularly supposed) to design a grand terminus for the Brandling Junction Railway across the river from the town. Completed in 1848, its lofty Ionic portico and gracefully curved pilastered wings perfectly set off by arcaded walls made a noble composition. Unfortunately, after the line was extended into Sunderland it became a mere suburban station, stranded like some handsome ship in a breaker's yard.

John Dobson was one of the best architects of his time, with a particular flair for classical work, though not well known outside the north-east. He had been responsible, with Richard Grainger, for replanning the centre of Newcastle and at this time was engaged in supervising his greatest triumph, Newcastle Central station, where he took full advantage of a prominent site to produce a commanding range of buildings which, had it been completed to his original design, would have produced the finest classical station in Europe. Its clean uncluttered lines and immense length, with a series of coupled pilasters seeming to recede into the distance, were redesigned with fussier detailing to give more office accommodation on the insistence of the board. Yet still it was magnificent. When it was opened in 1850, the frontage lacked Dobson's huge central portico, which Thomas Prosser added about 1860, after Dobson's style but lacking his finesse. Newcastle was at once symbolic of Hudson and Dobson's combined vision and the short-sightedness of those who followed. Dobson's equally fine trainshed will be considered in Chapter 5.

Smaller but equally symbolic, the classical Midland Counties Railway station at Leicester Campbell Street (1840) had a portico of six Tuscan columns beneath a handsome pediment. The same company's Nottingham station had a plainer centre with lower supporting blocks.

Smaller stations could, on occasion, show equally effective classical styling. The original station at Lytham on the Preston & Wyre Railway (1846), for instance, was a charming little Doric terminus with a domed booking-hall ceiling (Plate 8), while the Grecian station at Ashby-de-la-Zouch (1849) was one part of the Midland Railway's contribution to the development of the new 'spa', harmonising with the Ivanhoe Baths and Royal Hotel opposite. (The other part was the conveyance of the 'waters' in tank wagons from Swadlincote, 6 miles away.) But pride of place, of course, must go to Newmarket.

In studying railway buildings, one is struck by the frequency with which small branch-line companies built themselves elaborate terminal stations quite out of proportion to their size, importance and capital. The Newmarket & Chesterford Railway ended its 20-odd miles of line at a station of incredible classical opulence. Composed of three buildings, it had at the end a severely practical goods shed, next an Italianate station house, and, first in line, the *chef-d'oeuvre*, what Barman so aptly called a 'Baroque orangery'—a succession of tall finely hooded windows, interspersed with coupled Ionic columns, all rising above a deep cornice to richly ornamented caps. There were seven bays in all, in ashlar stone, and nothing quite like it appeared before or after.

Prominent among the goodly selection of second-rank classical stations was Canterbury West (1846) on the South Eastern Railway, where almost identical Palladian-style buildings on both platforms produced a balanced layout, each an essay in simple dignity. Samuel Beazley, who may have designed Canterbury, used similar features for the main building at Gravesend Central (1849) on that company's North Kent line. It was larger than Canterbury, and the stucco was relieved by a modicum of brick. On the same line Beazley built the competent, quietly restrained Italianate stations at Dartford and Erith and probably the more decorative entrance building at New Cross.

The Midland Railway's brief flirtation with classicism at Ashby was preceded by two subdued but quietly effective essays at Lincoln St Marks—Grecian with fluted Ionic columns—and Newark Castle, both of 1846, the latter notable for the gracefully curved end facing the approach.

The first station at Lewes (1846) demonstrated well the link between classical and Italianate, both styles being combined to good effect. But the charm of the small classical station was best translated into Italianate at Gobowen (Shrewsbury & Chester Railway, 1846), a little Florentine essay perfect in every feature from coupled round-headed windows to the pinnacled turret (Plate 3). The round-headed window, single, coupled or triple, was a favourite device of the Italianate school—sometimes the only one—used equally effectively with the stucco of Exminster and Exeter St Thomas on the South Devon or the remarkably standardised series of sturdy grey stone stations on the East Lancashire Railway between Bury, Clough Fold and Accrington. The Florentine concept notably appeared on the North Staffordshire Railway at Trentham, with its short tower and pantiled roofs; it was built for the Duke of Sutherland, it is said, by Sir Charles Barry, which is not unlikely as he designed Trentham Hall and there was about the station a strong echo of the ducal stables.

After Bricklayers Arms (see Chapter 1) the 'English Railway Style' was best expressed in London Bridge station's 'Italian palazzo style', as *The Illustrated London News* called it, seeing in the design a suitability 'to the bustling character of a railway line'. Opened in 1844 to the design of Henry Roberts and Thomas Turner, the station was jointly owned by the London & Croydon, London & Brighton and South Eastern Railways. Two-storeyed, with a shallow pantiled roof over a cornice, and upper windows each with a small balustraded balcony, the façade's most striking feature was a large Roman-arched carriage entrance in a balustraded screen wall, which was joined to the main building by a lofty handsome campanile with clock and weathervane. The comment of the *News* on the campanile was odd: 'striking and appropriate', it wrote, adding, 'we wish it had been differently introduced'. Did it, even in a railway station, savour too strongly of Rome? After all, the Catholic Emancipation Act was only fifteen years old and feelings could still run strongly. However, when Lewis Cubitt built Dover Town station in the same year, the *News* was less inhibited. 'Imposing and appropriate . . . a beautiful adaptation of the Italianate style. The turret is remarkably effective.' And so it was, standing proudly on top of a campanile at the head of the arcaded trainshed, demonstrating that whatever horrors might lie in its hinterland the South Eastern Railway could provide a fitting gateway to England. Unfortunately London Bridge only lasted until 1851. Having abandoned the partnership, the South Eastern and the London, Brighton & South Coast Railway (which now included the Croydon line) pulled down their joint station and built two separate and larger ones side by side. Neither lived up to the previous standard. Samuel Beazley chose Italianate again for the South Eastern's, but in so debased a fashion that the *News* felt it reflected little credit on him. The Brighton's building next door was even more mundane.

There is no question that well designed Italianate lent itself admirably to that display of powerful dignity which the railways were currently trying to achieve. Full advantage was taken of sloping ground, or, as at Newcastle, a broad forecourt, to increase the effect. Nowhere was this better achieved than at Shoreditch in 1840, where Sancton Wood built the Eastern Counties Railway terminus on arches above street level. At the end of the spacious triple-arched trainshed a heavily corniced three-storey frontage block was built at the head of twin flights of balustraded stairs rising to the entrance on the first floor. In front, a broad cab-drive, also balustraded, swept round in a wide semicircle, setting off the entrance to perfection. Alongside the shed a second block was added, with a central pediment.

The balustraded staircase was used to the same effect at Tithebarn St station, Liverpool (1850), joint terminus of the Lancashire & Yorkshire and East Lancashire Railways, probably by the engineer John Hawkshaw. The arched entranceway was placed centrally in the two-storey frontage, which was given contrast by pedimented first-floor windows

Plate 5   Branch line splendour: terminus of the Stamford & Essendine
Railway at Stamford East, in 1955

Page 35

Plate 6   The ultimate in branch termini: Maldon East, Eastern Counties
Railway, from a photograph taken about 1900

Plate 7   Thurston, by Frederick Barnes, for the Ipswich & Bury Railway, in 1953

Page 36

Plate 8   Classical charm at the original Lytham station, Preston & Wyre Railway, in 1964

in ashlar and round-headed windows in rusticated stone below. The trainshed, again, was on arches, as it was at Manchester London Road (1842), another joint station used by the Manchester & Birmingham and Sheffield, Ashton-under-Lyne & Manchester Railways. Here a broad slope led up to the heavy frontage block containing the companies' boardrooms and offices. A huge door dominated it, with a flat arched opening superimposed by deep prominent voussoirs. Hooded windows were matched by square panels above. The actual station entrance was through a quietly colonnaded block alongside the platforms. Sheffield Wicker (1845), at the other end of the line, had a classically arcaded portico; and for the opening of the Lincolnshire extensions in 1849 (by which time the company had become the Manchester, Sheffield & Lincolnshire) two large Italianate stations were built at Retford and Gainsborough, with Ionic arcaded porticos and complementary end pavilions.

Most of the best railway Italianate was built between 1845 and 1860, hallmarked by heavy rusticated quoins, windows round-headed at smaller stations and pedimented at the larger, low hipped roofs, cornice, and stucco or perhaps contrasting brickwork. Tunbridge Wells Central (1845), Bury Bolton Street (1846) and North Woolwich (1847) were good examples, while Rye (1851) on the South Eastern had all these features, plus a gracefully triple-arched centrepiece, subtle touches in the window frames and an outstanding site at the head of an avenue of trees, well in keeping with the gentle flavour of the old town. Reading General may be taken as representative of the more important station, its window hoods flat, segmental and triangular, with the added feature of a pantiled clock turret rising from the middle of the almost flat roof to a ball and spiked finial. Architecturally it was well above the run of the Great Western's larger stations.

Before leaving railway Italianate for the moment, the Great Eastern's contribution deserves a glance. We shall see in Chapter 3 how the small constituent lines in Norfolk and Suffolk revived Francis Thompson's Eastern Counties style in the 1850s. It appeared, too, on the Waveney Valley Railway and at a number of individual Great Eastern stations in this and the next decade, among the best being Harleston (1855), where clever use was made of curving balustraded steps to an entrance midway between ground and first-floor platform level, creating an 'area', flanked by gabled end-sections, to give the impression of a recess in a flat wall. The close of this good period was marked by Robert Sinclair's design for Ipswich (1860), the apogee of

Great Eastern Italianate. Like Cambridge, the long single through platform required an equally long frontage, single-storeyed and symmetrical, with a large two-storey central block curiously fronted by a pair of small heavily pedimented wings, forming end pieces for a flat awning that was later extended by a standard Great Eastern canopy. Tall chimneys were complemented by no less than three belfries.

Consideration of railway Gothic must be introduced by a look at the effect of the *cottage orné* styles of the J. C. Loudon school referred to in Chapter 1, for they sprang directly from the eighteenth-century picturesque movement and were closely associated with the revival of Gothic. Many a country mansion, whether it was old classical or new Gothic, had its *cottage orné* gate lodge, to be imitated in wayside stations and crossing houses. Half timbering, thrusting gables, dormer windows, fretted bargeboards and all the other trimmings epitomised the style nowhere better than at Fenny Stratford, Woburn Sands, Ridgmont, and Millbrook on the Bedford Railway (1846), in imitation of the Duke of Bedford's neighbouring estate buildings. Straight out of Loudon was Thorpe-on-the-Hill, on the Midland Railway's Lincoln line (1846). Its curved end facing the rails and dormer-windowed roof overhanging far enough to form a Regency-style verandah on wooden pillars only needed thatch to give the complete rustic effect. Two years later more restraint was exercised in the half-timbering at Saxby and Whissendine on the line to Peterborough, and in East Anglia at Wickham Bishops. Most fascinating half-timbered stations were those built by the 'Little' North Western Railway (so called to distinguish it from the London & North Western) of 1850. Although less elaborate, their utter incongruity in the limestone country between Skipton and Lancaster, where they kept company with rugged stone farms and cottages, could not have been more marked. At the time they must have appeared flimsy indeed.

Incongruity of another sort appeared at Berwyn on the Llangollen & Corwen Railway (1865), where a massive black-and-white building overlooked an insignificant single platform. Perhaps Plas Newydd inspired it. Part of Carrog, on the same line, had timber framing, offset by random stone but spoiled by yellow brick chimneys. But the ultimate in half-timbering was at Kidderminster (1863), the more surprising for being built by the West Midland Railway, successor to the Oxford, Worcester & Wolverhampton and only slightly better off. Yet here was a large two-storey black-and-white 'magpie' building. The bargeboarding was exquisite in its intricacy, and the principal rooms and part of the platform wall had dados of decorated Minton tiles (Plate 9). It is alleged that such splendours were intended for Stratford-upon-Avon, where the Victorians would have considered them eminently appropriate, but hastily diverted to Kidderminster in a partly prefabricated state after the earlier wooden station was destroyed by fire.

Cottage orné of particular charm marked the little Caterham Railway's stations of 1856. Caterham itself had an immensely tall and steep main gable with smaller ones to match, complete with the usual decoration, quoined masonry rubble walls below and half-timbering above. In 1900 the South Eastern & Chatham Railway replaced it with a building of unrelieved banality, as was its custom, yet during its short 'good' period fifty years earlier the South Eastern built a series of *cottage orné* stations on the Redhill–Guildford line (1849) that represented the style at its best on a railway. Pick of the bunch was Dorking Town, despite suffering somewhat from largeness of scale and an excess of chimney stacks. Here the restrained styling, more 'Old English' perhaps than the 'picturesque' of its neighbours, in mellow brick relieved by exposed timbering and tiled roofs, fitted as perfectly into the Surrey hills as any railway building could.

The Gothic revivalists were led by the eccentric A. W. N. Pugin, who not only designed in the medieval style but lived in it. He passionately declared Gothic to be the only true or 'Christian' architecture, and in 1836 the style was firmly established by the decision to use it for the new Houses of Parliament. Sir Charles Barry was appointed architect for the overall plan, and Pugin the designer of the detail. Naturally contemptuous of the railways, which in the 1840s usually attempted little in Gothic beyond mild overtones to Tudor or Jacobean, Pugin did essay a design for at least one hypothetical station and even commended Brunel's wooden roof at Bristol, though he hated the mock-Tudor façade. Pugin's only other known connection with railway work, and a highly debatable one at that, was at Alton Towers station (1849) on the North Staffordshire Railway, where there appeared a Florentine design, very similar to that attributed to Barry at Trentham except that rock-faced stone replaced the stucco. Herein lies an inexplicable contradiction, for Alton Towers itself, completed two years earlier, was not only Gothic but, to quote Robert Furneaux Jordan, 'one of the most curious, most fantastic houses in England'. Pugin built it for his equally fanatical patron, the

Earl of Shrewsbury; how could they possibly have countenanced an Italianate railway station on their doorstep? Barry and Pugin's collaboration on the Houses of Parliament was at best uneasy, and that they had periods of violent disagreement is well known. Perhaps Alton Towers was a manifestation of one of them?

As an aside, Cresswell on the same company's Stoke–Derby line (1849) bore more than a hint of Trentham and Alton—three storeys tall with Italianate openings and pantiled roof. Again by Barry or, more likely, a copy?

Gothic heavily overlaid with rustic detailing—a near-turret, a quaint little dormer and two steep pointed gables forming a bargeboarded porch—were the highlights at the later Knighton (1861) on the London & North Western's Central Wales line. The gables were tripled in an otherwise much plainer Tudor building at nearby Bucknell (1860). The purest Gothic railway station—*Gothick* in the Pugin manner—was William Tress's work at Battle (1852) on the South Eastern Railway, inspired no doubt by the proximity of Battle Abbey. Tress, a pupil of Tite, went in for a deliberate essay in medieval styling (not quite '1066 and all that') in dark-faced stone sparingly trimmed with lighter Caen stone, lancet windows, tracery and a belfry. Exposed rafters and other appropriate details graced the booking-hall interior. Oddly, the place was a success. Perhaps odder, Tress's other designs on the same line were a seemly Italianate—Robertsbridge, Stonegate, Wadhurst (Plate 4), St Leonard's Warrior Square, all bearing a family likeness—except for an unhappily vague, unrelated Tudorish assemblage at Etchingham and the much smaller Frant. The only other station to approach the authenticity of Battle was Richmond, Yorkshire (see Chapter 3).

Contrasting strongly with the purists, the 'picturesque' school in the Gothic camp indulged in the most extravagant fantasies, the most fanciful railway versions appearing on the London & Croydon line in 1846–7. Like the South Devon Railway and the Dublin & Kingstown in Ireland, the London & Croydon optimistically adopted the extraordinary atmospheric system as a form of traction, but soon abandoned it in favour of conventional locomotives after having built three Gothic pumping-engine houses at Forest Hill, Norwood and West Croydon. These houses were elaborately tricked out in the intricate bargeboards, finials and all the other trimmings of the movement, narrow pointed arches, heavy buttresses and elaborate chimneystacks with crocketed steeple-like tops complete with arrow slits to let the smoke out. These last were meant to resemble Gothic bell towers, and the intention of the whole incredible design was quite solemnly stated to be to render the buildings as unobtrusive as possible. Matching station buildings were built at Forest Hill and, somewhat less riotously endowed, at Anerley, where a crenellated little dwelling house was tacked on. By way of relief New Cross was Italianate. The architect was W. H. Breakspear and the engine-house details were by Raphael Brandon.

The original Brandling Junction Railway station at Felling (c 1839) on the south bank of the Tyne had an extraordinarily tiny building with three enormously tall lancet windows almost filling a gabled projection. It was notable in an area where stations at this time were notoriously poor.

Generally, though, the railways' contribution to the Gothic revival in the 1840s and 1850s was restricted to a safe comfortable Tudor or Jacobean styling, occasionally with a mild overlay of Gothic, as at Hereford Barrs Court (1855-6) and Ripon (1848). More often Tudor was chosen for its own sake in an endeavour to set buildings of suitable size harmoniously in their surroundings. Frequently they were admirably successful. Great care would be taken in the choice of materials and the execution of detail, none better than by the North Staffordshire Railway, which at this time almost exclusively used Tudor and Jacobean styling. Congleton (1848) was an excellent example of a medium-sized Tudor station, displaying the North Staffordshire's favourite diamond brick patterns. The Churnet Valley line (1849) showed a number of excellent examples of freely treated but lovely neo-Tudor stations at Rocester, Kingsley & Froghall, Oakamoor and Rushton, all in grey ashlar with delightful little hipped platform shelters tiled and finialed to match. But for the principal station on the line, Leek, the correct degree of importance could only be given by adding an essentially classical feature, though with Tudor motifs—a five-arched colonnade.

Typical of railway Tudor, too, were the Shrewsbury & Chester Railway's stations at Ruabon, Chirk, Llangollen Road and Rossett (1846-8) in coursed stone, interspersed with *cottage orné* at Whittington and Baschurch. Although the locality was quite different, the steep-gabled stations on the Leeds, Bradford & Halifax Junction Railway (1854) were equally at home in their northern Pennine surroundings, in dark gritstone at Armley Moor, Bramley, Stanningley and Bowling. A goodly crop of satisfyingly Tudor stations was inherited by the

Lancashire & Yorkshire Railway, including Heckmondwike Central (1848), Holmfirth (1850), Whalley (presumably for the sake of the abbey) of 1850 and a set of seven identical stations between Wigan and Southport (1855–61).

Buildings of manorial appearance and proportions were built for town stations such as the Huddersfield & Manchester Railway's original building at Dewsbury Wellington Road (1849). Where there were historical associations to consider, they might be met with a tower or a turret. T. K. Penson designed a long two-storey castellated façade in the collegiate manner for Shrewsbury, in grey stone with an embattled tower and an extended oriel window (Plate 10). In 1903–8 the building was underpinned and the courtyard lowered to allow a third storey to be added underneath. Lincoln Central, where again a crenellated tower dominated the composition—featuring small angle-turrets, a near-conical roof and, in a touch of whimsy, a false rose window—suffered from lack of contrast between the grey brick and the stone detailing. Among the best of our Tudor town stations, Stamford East, by William Hurst, formed the headquarters of the little Stamford & Essendine Railway (1856). Here the manorial influence was real, for Burleigh House, not far away, was the seat of the Marquis of Exeter, principal proprietor of the railway. This charming small terminus had particularly delicate detail work and, once again, a short square tower (Plate 5). Inside, the small but airy booking hall was lit by a lofty lantern and surrounded by an exquisite wrought-iron balustraded gallery giving access to the company's offices.

The mixing of Tudor and Jacobean features produced some of our most elaborate stations before High Victorian Gothic took hold. A remarkable series was designed by the Ipswich architect Frederick Barnes for the Ipswich & Bury Railway of 1846. His free interpretation of Elizabethan styling at Needham successfully combined a varied ensemble of gables with lower corner-towers, while a totally different but equally successful marriage of three differing Jacobean blocks at Stowmarket was achieved by linking them with unobtrusive screen walls, cohesion again being given by a lower-height octagonal tower at each end. Thurston was Barnes' answer to the station on a high embankment. He built a two-storey building, with the platforms visible well above eaves level yet not allowed to obtrude by the clever addition of a taller entrance porch, triple arched *in antis* (Plate 7). Like Stowmarket, most of the detailing was not in stone but in finely moulded brick. Barnes' masterpiece was Bury St Edmunds, another embankment site. The two platforms terminated in a pair of domed towers, treated in Free Renaissance style, the one on the frontage side forming the central feature of a long façade of compelling originality. Three large entrance openings separated from blind arches above by a strong string course formed one half, the other being a large Tudor house with ogee gables and mullioned oriels. East Anglia provided stations at the other end of the scale, too, such as Downham and Swaffham, both of 1847, whose plain ogee gables and lozenge-latticed windows betokened a delightfully cosy simplicity entirely fitting in North Norfolk.

If Newmarket represented the ultimate in classical branch-line termini, Maldon East occupied pride of place on the Gothic side, where a single platform was tacked on to a superb Jacobean mansion of a building complete to the last detail (Plate 6). Even the rainwater heads bore the company's initials. The nine-arch arcaded front, open-work parapet and gabled pavilions, which were the highlights of this lavish place, had a strange story. The original company, the Maldon, Witham & Braintree, was taken over by the Eastern Counties Railway before construction started. The deputy chairman of the Eastern Counties, David Waddington, was prospective Tory candidate for Maldon and when Peel's ministry fell in 1846 he saw in the construction gangs a ready-made nucleus of supporters—suitably influenced, no doubt. Because a general election was delayed for twelve months, the story goes that he kept them in his constituency by employing them on this large ornamental station. He was duly elected, and one hopes he helped the hard-up Eastern Counties to foot the bill.

Like its Tudor work, the North Staffordshire Railway's Jacobean contributions were notably excellent, hallmarked by the patterned roof tiling typical of this company. H. A. Hunt of London (not the 'un-known' R. A. Stent often referred to) designed the pre-eminent example at Stoke-on-Trent (1850) as part of Winton Square, a pioneer effort in railway company environmental planning. The dark red brick, stone-dressed Jacobean gables and classically arched portico of the station formed a symmetrical composition on one side, rich surface ornament being sparingly applied in exact relief to the general reticence of the design. Opposite stood the complementary North Stafford Hotel, with appropriately matched railway houses on the other two sides. The square formed the best architectural group in Stoke. Smaller, but so similar as to suggest more of Hunt's work,

Stone's continuously gabled frontage was strongly assertive despite its awkward site in the angle of the junction (1848). Longport also bore restrained features in the same mould, and Sandon was unusual for the rare instance of a room above its brick *porte cochère*. This thoughtful design was completed by an avenue of beeches from the village and Sandon Hall, seat of the Earls of Harrowby, whence came more than one member of the North Staffordshire board.

The Duke of Newcastle's great house at Clumber was probably the motive behind the Manchester, Sheffield & Lincolnshire Railway's remarkable adventure in Jacobean at Worksop (1849) in light grey Steetley stone. It was very long, with a variety of gables and enrichment ranging from a broken pediment to rusticated pilasters, medallions and strapwork. It was a pity the fenestration seemed unfortunately inappropriate.

Away on the East Lincolnshire Railway (1848) were three stations having the same basic plan but clad, as it were, in different styles, so that none looked alike. A long single-storey main building with a two-storey block at each end and a central projecting arcade was dressed in different degrees of Italianate at Alford and at Firsby. The same pattern at Louth was transformed by a Jacobean veneer into quite the most handsome station on the Great Northern Railway, of which the line eventually became part. By Weightman & Hadfield of Sheffield, the light freestone of the arcade and dressings effectively contrasted with red brick gables, balustraded steep-pitched roof and ball finials.

CHAPTER 3

SEVEN RAILWAY ARCHITECTS

LIKE the engineers they worked with, the designers of many of the stations built up to the mid-1850s stand head and shoulders above those who came later. Grander stations than theirs were built, but none achieved the originality, delicacy and sense of 'belonging' inherent in the buildings of this time. As Christian Barman put it:

> The old traditions maintained their hold for about a quarter of a century after the birth of the steam railway, and it is into that quarter of a century that the golden period of railway architecture is compressed. There is nothing quite like this mixture anywhere else in our architecture, for the seventeenth-century upheaval which was so like the Industrial Revolution had provided the builders neither with a new subject matter nor with a new technique like the technique of iron buildings. It is the very subtle combinations of old and new diction that give the railway style its characterful uniqueness. In that short period something was produced the like of which we shall not see again.

In this chapter I have chosen seven men whose quality of work was unsurpassed.

Isambard Kingdom Brunel

The Great Western Railway had a unique gauge of 7ft and a unique engineer in I. K. Brunel. Like most of the major companies, it grew by acquiring smaller railways, but with the important difference that from its earliest days it had a financial interest in many of the lines connecting with it. Consequently they, too, employed Brunel and these two influences gave the Bristol & Exeter, South Devon, Cornwall, West Cornwall, Cheltenham & Great Western Union, South Wales and Oxford, Worcester & Wolverhampton Railways an extensive visual unity with the Great Western not found elsewhere. Like everything else he did, Brunel's stations added a distinctive touch throughout the West Country, west Midlands and South Wales. More, his designs were extremely long-lived, numbers being used after his death in 1859.

Although Brunel combined the roles of engineer and architect at a time that made little distinction between them, it was primarily the engineer that showed in his trim, sturdily practical wayside stations, which had none of the visionary innovations of much of his other work. Yet, as Barman has observed, the light, flat, simple continuous awning projecting from all four sides of his small station buildings— one of the most characteristic Brunel features—had a distinctive modern appearance. Tudor doors, windows, chimneys and steep gabled roofs made up the style, in brick at Twyford (1839) and Pangbourne (1840), in flint at Shrivenham (1840), and in brick again at Minety & Ashton Keynes (1841) and Culham (1844), all exactly emphasised with stone dressings (Plate 11). Matching subsidiary buildings on the opposite platforms completed the scene.

Awning valance decoration, Heyford, GWR

Unusually for the period, Brunel built detached station houses nearby, large and generously proportioned in matching style, some, as at Wallingford Road and Steventon being almost like small mansions. Westward, brick and flint gave way to Cotswold or Mendip stone at Wootton Bassett (1841), Brimscombe (1845) and Melksham (1848). Grange Court (1853) and Bradford-on-Avon (1858) perpetuated the style, although the earlier neatness was somewhat lost at the larger stations. Hipped roof variants appeared at Box (1841), St Clears (1854), Kidlington, Heyford and Aynho (all 1852), the last four having leaden bas-relief lions' masks decorating the edges of the awnings. Highbridge (1841) had a roof of each type.

Accidents of history resulted in Brunel stations appearing on two other lines which, although intended by the Great Western to come within its sphere of influence, were snapped up by rivals. One was the Bristol & Gloucester Railway (1845), which the Midland gained by an eleventh-hour coup, thus acquiring typical Brunel stations at Stonehouse, Yate, Berkeley Road, Frocester and Charfield. The other line was the Exeter & Crediton Railway of 1854, which the London & South Western Railway took by devious means from under the nose of the Bristol & Exeter. Crediton station, of typical Brunel design, remains as evidence.

As his style developed, Brunel's flat awnings gave way to a broad hipped roof extending outwards to form awnings on all sides, generally with Italianate round-headed openings—Chippenham, for example, in 1841—and later becoming widespread, ranging from Aldermaston (1847), Mortimer (1848), Bridgend, Chepstow (both 1850) and Southam Road & Harbury (1852) to Dorchester West (1857), Stratford-upon-Avon (1864-5) and Ilminster (1866) to give a selection (Plate 12). Yatton (1841) had Tudor features, while Kidwelly (1852) was two storeys high, built against an embankment with platforms at first-floor level. At least two wooden stations appeared in this style, on the penurious Oxford, Worcester & Wolverhampton Railway at Evesham and Charlbury (1853). Ivybridge and Plympton stations (both 1848) on the South Devon Railway were given pantiled roofs, presumably to match intended Italianate engine houses like those built for Brunel's abortive atmospheric traction system between Exeter and Totnes but which, in the event, never reached this far. Bridgend (1850) on the South Wales Railway and the original Solihull (1852) on the Birmingham line had the same roofs.

Brunel's essays into larger two-storey structures did not achieve the same functional simplicity. Ealing (1838) was faintly classical; Keynsham, Twerton and Cirencester Town (all 1841), although well executed in Tudor, lacked the symmetry of their smaller brethren and did not quite strike the right note found in the same theme elsewhere.

Exminster, on the South Devon (1848) was wholly Italianate and the better for it.

The ornamental wooden valancing used to decorate platform awnings, probably the most characteristic feature of the British railway station, may be attributable to Brunel. It had a function, of course, in helping to deflect driving rain, smoke and steam from the platform. The first station illustrated with decorative valancing was probably Ealing, followed by Maidenhead.

Swindon, completed in 1842, was the only early Great Western station of importance that did not incorporate a trainshed or overall roof. A large two-storey block dominated each of the two island platforms, connected by an enclosed footbridge—itself another early example of a feature later to become characteristic. At platform level the refreshment rooms were heavily decorated with arabesques; hotel rooms formed the upper floors, and the kitchens the street-level basements. Verandahs sheltered the platforms on all four sides.

Many of Brunel's principal stations were also quite different from those of other lines. For a number he chose timber structures which, like his wooden viaducts, were unique in their layout and their longevity. Oddest was his insistence on what amounted to a separate station for up and down trains, both on the same side of the line, generally the side nearer the town. As he pointed out, passengers were less likely to board a train going in the wrong direction and, more important, did not have to cross the line. The inconvenience of conflicting train movements only became apparent as traffic increased. Reading (1840), the first of this type, had separate trainsheds with elliptical roofs and a long central lantern or clerestory. Slough, of the same date, had pitched roofs; then came Taunton and Exeter (1842 and 1844), Newton Abbot and Dawlish (both 1848). Newton later acquired a third trainshed for the Torquay branch, and was actually rebuilt with a second generation of sheds in 1861. At Gloucester's second station of 1851, separate platforms and sheds were abandoned in favour of one long one with a continuous awning. The last one-sided station on the Great Western was Wolverhampton Low Level, built jointly with the Oxford, Worcester & Wolverhampton Railway in 1854, though in the meantime the idea had spread. All were later rebuilt in conventional style or had extra platforms added, Reading being the final station to be converted, in 1899. Didcot (1844) appears to have had six platforms with awnings connected across the rails by curve-topped louvred clerestories. Built of wood again, it was burned down in 1885.

The other important stations were of the usual two-sided pattern beneath a distinctive wooden pitched roof. Bristol Temple Meads was the first, followed by the slightly less ornate Bath (1840), both of great width in order to span four broad-gauge tracks. Thereafter simplicity was the order, plain roofs on massive rafters contrasting with slender iron struts and ties, wooden walls and pillars. The station building was built on to one side of the shed, usually in timber, some being replaced later in brick or stone, like Clevedon (1847) and Henley-on-Thames (1857). Clevedon had strange emphasis in timber struts and iron ties; Frome (1850) had a wholly iron truss so slender as to be barely noticeable. Other examples appeared at Tavistock South (1859), Falmouth (1863), Moretonhampstead and Cheddar (both 1869)—p 103. Chard Central (1866) was combined with one of the small Italianate station buildings. All-wooden trusses were built at Banbury (1850)—where they lasted over a century and became a byword for railway decrepitude—Truro (Newham) of 1855 and Thame (1862), among others.

Decoration crept into so much plain solidity only in the gable ends. The lower members at the original 1846 'atmospheric' station at Exeter St Thomas were curved at one end, horizontal at the other; Plymouth Millbay (1849) had narrow-spaced glazing bars vertically dividing the upper half; Swansea (1850) had three broad ones subdivided; and Leamington (1852) had graceful semi-elliptical openings divided into five vertical sections. The Great Western's first Windsor terminus of 1850, fittingly, was rather special, but, unfortunately, the effect of the pediment-like gable, cornice and frieze on stumpy pilasters made a top-heavy composition.

The frontages to the wooden trainsheds usually were quite unpretentious, with a short flat canopy over the entrance. Weymouth Town (1857) was a little more elaborate, with a long canopy on tastefully ornamented brackets. Salisbury (1856) had lions' masks.

The financial squeeze of the 1850s provided another exercise for Brunel's ingenuity. The consistent uniformity of the wooden wayside station buildings of this decade suggests so strongly that standard drawings were used that one is tempted to speculate whether they were in fact early examples of unit construction, particularly as at this time Brunel was actively planning his large wooden prefabricated hospital for the Crimea. Portable wooden cottages had already been tried in the north of England for some years, and the South Eastern Railway had been building small uniform wooden stations since 1842.

Brunel's station buildings generally were of uniform width and height, with horizontal boarding (except at Cropredy in 1852, where it was vertical) and low-pitched roofs. Lengths varied according to need. A bay window was sometimes provided for the stationmaster's office, facing the platform at Fenny Compton (1852) but on the end at Evershot (1857). A short, plain, flat awning gave platform shelter and occasionally covered the front entrance as well, as at Lostwithiel (1859). Buildings like these were found all over the West Country and in the west Midlands, some dominated by a massive central chimney-stack like the stone specimen at Chipping Campden (1853). Otherwise the keynote was well proportioned simplicity. As in most of his work, Brunel relied on pleasing proportions to achieve effect, and rarely in his wooden stations do we find embellishment. Maidenhead (1838) was an exception, an exuberant sort of place with frilly valancing and a pinnacled turret on each building.

This combination of a sense of proportion with engineering skill needed little else to produce good building, and it was only when Brunel attempted architecture for its own sake that the results were less satisfactory. His fine trainshed at Bath, for example, strongly contrasted with the awkwardly curved frontage, which was a mixture of Tudor and Italianate. Bristol Temple Meads showed even greater contrast, for the stuccoed Tudor-Gothic frontage, although interesting now as a period piece, could not compare with the magnificently cantilevered trainshed and its wooden mock hammerbeams. Indeed, it is difficult to decide whether the Temple Meads trainshed or the great iron-arched arcades of Paddington, with their cathedral-like transepts, form the greater memorial to Brunel. Both were at once daring and original, yet, like Bristol, Paddington also suffered from a less satisfactory frontage—this time P. C. Hardwick's French Renaissance hotel (Chapter 7), an overdressed prelude to the sober magnificence and vision of Brunel's interior.

These twenty-odd years of station building were not, of course, Brunel's personal work; he was far too busy on a multitude of other projects. Rather, after the first few years, were they either the products of his office or of resident engineers using his stock designs, like those built after his death. But to Brunel must go the credit for their concept.

Francis Thompson

Travellers on the North Midland Railway from Derby to Leeds in 1840 would have observed a series of newly opened stations of quality and elegance far surpassing those in the south. Even Whishaw, after his customary strictures on expense, had to admit that they were built 'on the grand scale' and considered that 'they distinguish this line from all others in the kingdom'.

Designed by Francis Thompson, an enigmatic character seemingly remembered only for his railway work, they at once proved him to be an architect of brilliant sensitivity. Little is known about him; Mr O. F. Carter, who has carried out research into Thompson's work, concludes that he may have been a fashionable London tailor with a flair for the arts who put his gifts to good use during the railway boom but dropped them in the slump of the 1850s.

On the North Midland, no two of the stone-built stations were alike yet all were delicately proportioned, from the Italian villa styles of Belper and Eckington, the latter with a charming little rotunda of an entrance having a conical 'sugar bowl' top, to the groupings at Clay Cross and Chesterfield where pump house and water tower matched the station buildings. Clay Cross was low and again Italianate, Chesterfield larger in a much gabled and finialled Tudor, with the addition of a small entrance lodge to the approach road. Swinton was classical, with columns, cornice and parapet. Finest and best known of Thompson's small stations were Ambergate and Wingfield. The original design for Ambergate (Plate 14) shows an almost riotous use of Jacobean features, yet it is perfectly symmetrical, as were all Thompson's stations, with an elaborate square central porch on the platform side embodying a pilastered doorway, cornice, decorated frieze, blind balustrade and, atop them all, a short pilastered turret and parapet. Whether the full embellishments were incorporated we do not know, as in 1863 the building was re-erected on a new site in the angle of the Rowsley line junction and enlarged to form an 'A' shape in plan. The porch and some niches in the early illustration did not appear here and the chimney positions were changed.

A feature of Thompson's North Midland designs was the emphasis he gave to the platform elevations rather than the road frontages. Wingfield, considered by Barman to be 'the most perfect of all', had a fairly plain front relying for effect on the exact proportions and restrained styling of the central pavilion and lower flanking wings, in marked contrast to the exuberance of Ambergate. The centre of the platform elevation was elaborated by the addition of a highly ornamental clock and the station name in large gilded letters. Thompson invariably completed his urge for perfect symmetry by placing his buildings centrally on the platform and flanking them by low walls of matching design interspersed with urns, finials and other features appropriate to the whole.

At Derby his famous tri-junct station, owned by three companies, had an immensely long façade screening an equally long single platform and light iron trainshed, shown in well-known contemporary engravings and often described. The Hunslet Lane terminus at Leeds, however, was smaller and has almost been forgotten, although it was well up to his standard. 'At the grand entrance,' said *Herapath's Railway Magazine*, 'the arcade is ascended by flights of stone steps and is distinguished by a row of four highly ornamental anti-pilasters, terminating in an arch at the apex, above which is placed a most beautiful piece of rich stone sculpture, exhibiting the arms of Leeds, Sheffield and Derby.' The building was two storeys high, placed across the end of the trainshed, which was 267ft long with two platforms and a four-bay roof 113ft 6in wide. 'The roof is supported by rows of neatly fluted columns; it is, with the exception of some longitudinal rafters, composed of neat and light iron rods, similar to the one at Derby. . . . The general appearance is exceedingly handsome.'

Thompson appears also to have designed the classical Wakefield station for the Manchester & Leeds Railway (1840), perhaps while he was working in the locality.

He was paid £1,103 12s a year by the North Midland, but was sacked during an economy drive twelve months after the line opened. He next turned up on the Chester & Holyhead Railway, opened 1846–50, where Italianate was his favourite style, expressed most vividly at Chester, for whose joint General station he reverted to the one-sided layout with a strong two-storey frontage block over 1,000ft long in buff brick with stone dressings, symmetrical of course, arcaded wings having stumpy angle turrets, a pierced parapet, central Venetian windows and balconies. A pantiled roof punctuated the skyline. As two companies met here end-on, the interior layout comprised a pair of 'back-to-back' bays and a through platform, all between twin iron trainshed roofs divided by an arcaded wall. Interiors were well in keeping, particularly the elaborate timber and plaster work in the refreshment room.

For his stations to Holyhead, Thompson devised two basic designs, both with similar features and both combining offices and living accommodation in a two-storey building. The larger stations comprised a central block with flat verandah roofs at front and rear between small projecting and matching pavilions. Holywell was the best, finely detailed with classical windows, moulded rose motifs on a broad frieze, and pantiles on the near-flat roof, verandah and pavilions. Mostyn (Plate 16), a larger but quieter edition of the same, had small flanking wings instead of pavilions and was decorated with coats of arms on the front. Flint, Abergele and Bangor had hipped roofs, Abergele's verandahs again being supported by pavilions, this time with a colonnade between them; Flint had single-storey wings like Mostyn. Bangor, which was longer, had pavilions and a central bell turret on the platform side. The two last-mentioned stations had decorated iron brackets to their verandahs, at Bangor interspersed by stone 'c h' monograms on the rear wall. The overriding theme of them all was Italianate except for Conway, where it would clearly have been out of place in a station adjoining the castle wall. Yet once more Thompson kept to his plan—only the styling was different, as *The Illustrated London News* noted: '. . . an extremely handsome and well designed building in the Elizabethan style, with gabled wings, rising in steps, and projecting from the main portion'.

The smaller stations, though much plainer, still had small projecting wings with the sloping roof continued between them to form a platform shelter like an 'apron' to the two-storey house behind. Examples were Aber, Bodorgan and Valley, variously in brick, rendered or in stone. The Mold Railway, too, acquired by the Chester & Holyhead in 1849, had similar stations that suggest Thompson's influence if not his hand, as at Hope & Penyfford, Llong and Broughton. Menai Bridge, junction for the Caernarvon branch, though stated to have originally been a private house, had Thompson characteristics even though it was not opened until well after his time. In weak Tudor, its first-floor level platform had a flat awning over a recessed waiting shelter and a central octagonal chimney with curved wing supports above a clock space, reminiscent of the turret at Bangor (p 54).

There is more than a suggestion that, between his North Midland and his Chester & Holyhead work, Thompson was active on the Eastern Counties Railway where many of the original stations are generally accepted as the work of Sancton Wood. Yet three contemporary sources of 1845 attribute some of them at least to 'Mr Thompson': *The Builder* said Audley End (then named Wendon), Great Chesterford and Cambridge were his; the *Guide to the Norfolk Railway*, referring to the line between London and Brandon, said 'Mr Thompson . . . was the general architect for the stations, lodges etc. . . .' and Mr

Michael Robbins has pointed out in the *Journal of the Railway & Canal Historical Society* (XV, 4 Oct 1969) that an engraving of Cambridge station in the *Cambridge Advertiser* of 30 July, despite mentioning Wood in the caption, bears the words 'Thompson, archt.' Galt's *Railway & Commercial Information* of 1850, perhaps using the same source, attributed Cambridge, Ely and Peterborough to him. Finally, Wood's obiturist in *The Builder* of 1886 does not mention Cambridge among his station work.

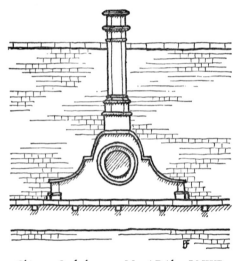

Chimney & clock recess, Menai Bridge, LNWR

What do the official records say? Certainly Sancton Wood was employed by the Eastern Counties, for on 30 October 1845 he was given three months notice, and he appears to have moved on to do work on the Leicester–Peterborough line of the Midland Railway. We know, too, that Wood designed the Eastern Counties terminus at Shoreditch. Yet an examination of Bishop's Stortford, Audley End, Great Chesterford, Shelford, Lakenheath, Waterbeach, Ely, Chettisham and Whittlesea, all built between 1842 and 1847, shows unmistakable Chester & Holyhead characteristics. Bishop's Stortford had a square flat-roofed three-storey block in blue brick with stone trim, and the familiar one-storey wings with a flat awning between. Smaller but in the same vein was Audley End, dominated at the front by a single-arched *porte cochère* for the benefit of the 'big house'. Foursquare again, Great Chesterford had a canopy carried round on all four sides on strut-like brackets, the wings being dispensed with (Plate 15). At Ely the side blocks predominated, two-storeyed and flanking a one-storey centrepiece, but again marked by the finely drawn fenestration, flat roofs and general symmetry. An early illustration shows a quaint little turret on the middle section, the forerunner of Bangor and Menai Bridge, perhaps? To the left was an Italianate house with a low tower. The other small stations had pitched roofs, pediment-gabled at Whittlesea, and hipped at Shelford, Lakenheath, Waterbeach and Chettisham. The last four each had a blank upper wall overlooking the platform decorated, (except at Shelford) with a long stone panel probably intended to bear the station name—again a Thompson characteristic that appeared either lower down or on the flanking platform walls at the Chester & Holyhead stations. Flat integral awnings marked them all, between projecting end blocks or screen walls. It is interesting to note that this general style reappeared in the 1850s between Newmarket and Bury St Edmunds and on the Harwich branch (1854), at Bealings on the Yarmouth line (1859) and on the East Suffolk Railway (1859–60).

Only Cambridge and Peterborough, of those credited to Thompson in contemporary accounts, did not bear his stamp. The attribution of Peterborough to him was probably journalistic licence anyway, as it was more probably J. W. Livock's work (see p 60); Cambridge was a striking design, with a fine fifteen-bay round-arched *porte cochère* enriched at the deep cornice and decorated in the spandrels with arms of the university colleges, while the interiors of the public rooms were equally tasteful. But it did have a Thompson feature in the long single platform beneath an elegant trainshed carried on an arched colonnade repeating the frontage idiom. What is more, it was symmetrical. Likewise, in all these buildings local materials were used, from buff East Anglian brick to flint, and the overriding style was classical in concept.

The 'apron' style sloping awning around a two-storey building seems first to have been used at Normanton in 1840, where the North Midland, the Manchester & Leeds and the York & North Midland Railways built a joint station that has been attributed to G. T. Andrews, architect to the last company (see below), even though the buildings bore the characteristics later used so extensively by Thompson. Could Thompson have picked up the idea here, where he was in any case engaged on the adjacent railway hotel, used it as a 'house-style' under Wood on the Eastern Counties, and then taken it with him to the Chester & Holyhead?

As we have just observed, Sancton Wood's movements during this period, unlike Thompson's, are known and, moreover, a station in the Eastern Counties style appeared on the Leicester–Peterborough line at Luffenham (Chapter 4). Furthermore, he had been a pupil of Sir Robert Smirke, a heavy classicist. Did, then, Thompson and Wood collaborate, with Wood, the salaried employee of the company, accounted the senior and so taking the credit? Thompson's North Midland stations were striking in their differences, his Chester & Holyhead stations striking in their similarities. He could have gained the 'house style' concept from Wood, tried it out on the Eastern Counties in fairly simple form, and then elaborated on it on the Chester & Holyhead.

Before leaving the Eastern Counties a long-standing misconception must be put right. On 20 June 1846 *The Illustrated London News* portrayed in an engraving the scene at Colchester on the opening of the extension of the Eastern Union Railway to Ipswich. On many subsequent occasions the large Italianate building and tower in the background have been described as the original station, whereas a visit will establish that they formed the station hotel, now part of the Royal Eastern Counties Hospital. The little building partly shown on the right was more likely the station.

Thompson's swansong, or at any rate his last appearance in the records so far discovered, was a design for Birmingham New Street in 1850. R. B. Dockray, resident engineer on the southern division of the London & North Western Railway, recorded in his diary on 16 December after a visit to inspect the drawings at Robert Stephenson's office: '. . . the most handsome and elegant but quite out of the question for a railway station in these times.'* Had the design been executed there is little doubt that Birmingham would have been the richer.

George Townsend Andrews

Whatever may be said about the double dealing of that first railway tycoon, George Hudson, it cannot be denied that 'The Railway King', for all his sharp practice, ensured that the lines built under his direction were given particularly meritorious stations. He may have cooked the

* From R. M. Robbins. 'R. B. Dockray's Diary I', *Journal of Transport History* (May 1965)

books to pay for them, but they were built to please and to endure. Those which eventually became part of the North Eastern Railway made a large and varied collection of high quality, numbers of them at places which many another line would have considered worth no more than a wooden hut.

Hudson was a great believer in helping those who helped him, one of whom was G. T. Andrews, architect, contractor and Sheriff of York during the 1847 general election at which he contrived to have Hudson's nominees returned to Parliament unopposed. Andrews' first job for Hudson had been to cut an arch through the city wall for the York & North Midland Railway to enter, and inside it build the first 'U'-shaped terminus to have a continuous building (three storeys) on all three sides, including a hotel (1840). The Italianate façade, in three sections, was dominated by a five-bay centrepiece with bold finely patterned windows, the upper storeys of the flanking sections receding above large Tuscan columns *in antis*. Andrews also built the elegant trainshed in iron and glass on tapering columns, with bell capitals and concentric circles in the arched ties.

For small town stations in the East and North Ridings Andrews evolved a trainshed design that became as characteristic of the North Eastern as Brunel's on the Great Western. Generally it had a hipped slated roof on light iron trusses with, at each end, slender bowstrings tied between a pair of horizontals by vertical or criss-crossed struts, as at Scarborough, Malton (both 1845), Bridlington, Filey (both 1846) and Pocklington (1847), although at Malton bowstrings were omitted. The brick side-walls had widely-spaced windows, except at Driffield (1846), which had one arcaded. Like most of his contemporaries

Iron lamp bracket, Pocklington, NER

Andrews paid careful regard to local material, so that Beverley and Driffield were in buff brick from the Wolds. Andrews placed a small single-storey office and entrance building centrally in his front wall, usually with lightly applied Italianate features and stone trim. Beverley and Driffield both had small canted awnings over the entrance door, the former with fragile-looking iron scrollwork. Market Weighton (1847) had a stone parapet to match the window casings and a central porch on a pair of coupled Doric columns. Pocklington, the best, had a five-arched arcade of considerable charm, while a similar design at the first Boroughbridge station (1847) had blind arcading incorporating a circular stone motif in the spandrels. A favourite device was to terminate these long façades with a station house at one or both ends, as at Malton; the house at Boroughbridge, a terminus, had a shallow bow window and was situated at the outer end; and at Durham Gilesgate it was at the inner.

Doubtless the more opulent venture at Whitby Town (1847) reflected Hudson's paternalistic interest in the place, where the five-arched *porte cochère* and moulded cornice in ashlar was set off by five Georgian-styled sash windows. The original Andrews trainshed at Scarborough, behind a façade in ashlar broken by three small classical pavilions and later altered (Chapter 7), was extended by converting the adjacent goods shed. At Hull Paragon (Plate 17) Andrews' classical façade of 1848 remained virtually untouched and ranked among his best. Unusually asymmetrical in grey-gold ashlar, punctuated at each end respectively by a three-storey and a two-storey block, the central feature embodied a projecting balustraded terrace at first-floor level on bold plain columns enhanced by corner pilasters, curved and angled window pediments and a corbelled hipped roof. A small porch was similarly treated but the end blocks were less lavish.

Considering Andrews' large output over a short period his consistently high standard was remarkable. The Greensfield station at Gateshead, of 1844, had a lighter roof behind an impressively long classical façade with pilastered pavilions flanking a central colonnaded Ionic portico and a deeply corniced parapet. The familiar house at one end contained the offices. For many of the smaller stations on Hudson's lines, particularly in the East and North Ridings, a simple stock pattern was favoured, notably where the site adjoined a level crossing. The plain house at right-angles to the line, with its front door to the road and a hipped bay window to the platform next to a short lean-to porch over the booking office door, whether in brick or ashlar, bore the mark of fine workmanship, and by its very simplicity was equally suited to the Wolds, the plain of York or the uplands of County Durham. The smallest ones like Bempton (1847), and Bubwith and Holme Moor (both 1848) had no embellishments, but greater importance, as at Burton Agnes, Hutton Cranswick (both 1846), Londesborough (1847), Shincliffe (c 1844) and Warthill (1847), was indicated by a corniced stone door-casing and fanlight to the road frontage. The most important stations in this series were given a classical touch in a shallow stone portico on square columns and a lean-to platform verandah, such as appeared at Stamford Bridge (1847), Lockington (1846) and, slightly altered, at Leeming Bar (1848). The old station building at Ferryhill (c 1846) also bore Andrews' touch while the aristocratic patronage of Castle Howard (1845) warranted a small *porte cochère* at the front and a balcony on massive ogee brackets overlooking the platform. The same creamy stone was used at the neighbouring station of Huttons Ambo (1845), an attractive single-storey building with low-pitched projecting roofs over end-pavilions, chamfered at the eaves, and a recessed centrepiece. Some of Andrews' single-storey crossing houses were also adapted as stations: Carnaby, Marishes Road and Leamside were examples.

Where the scenery was more dramatic, Andrews turned to a more aggressive Tudor-Gothic style. Local stone was plentiful on the Church Fenton & Harrogate and Richmond branches that reached into Dales country, and on the reconstructed Whitby & Pickering Railway. For Richmond (1846) Andrews designed a 'monastic' Gothic station like no other (Plate 18), astonishingly medieval with its arcaded and buttressed entrance, mullioned windows and tall angled chimneys in dark freestone. A remarkable two-bay trainshed in glass and iron covered the platforms and three tracks to do duty as station and carriage shed combined, and its gable ends were decorated with herringbone timbering, shell-panel openings and exquisite bargeboards.

In a much quieter key the cottage stations at Scorton and Catterick Bridge (both 1846) were in keeping; repeats were built on the Harrogate line of 1847–8 at Newton Kyme and Spofforth, the latter with a twin-arched recessed waiting shelter, as again at Moulton. Thorp Arch and the original Wetherby station were larger, had paired lancet windows, and continuous roofing reaching down over the platform as an awning. A curious end-entrance formed by buttressed pointed arches distinguished Thorp, and Tadcaster had a plain gabled trainshed with lancets in the side walls. A variation in the Whitby & Pickering stations was the addition of cusps in the mullioned windows and attractive chimney groupings at Grosmont, Sleights and Ruswarp (all c 1847). Perhaps the most dramatic station site on Hudson's lines was Durham City. Although opened by the North Eastern Railway in 1857, when Thomas Prosser was the company's architect, it was so much in the Richmond image and so unlike any of Prosser's other work that it seems a fair guess it was based on an Andrews design pigeonholed when Hudson's downfall postponed completion of this line. Perhaps the dean and chapter's hostility to the railway was the reason for choosing Tudor-Gothic. Certainly it harmonised with its surroundings, perched high above the city and looking across the Wear gorge to the cathedral and castle. Mullions, a crenellated portico on five perpendicular arches, heavy-angled buttresses and hexagonal chimney shafts formed a fitting composition at the top of the steep curving approach, with a large matching house connected by a screen wall. The broad platform awnings on elaborate box trusses and broad curved brackets—also used at the second Selby station of 1871—were probably Prosser's contribution.

John William Livock

Perhaps because it was much more restricted, Livock's work has received little notice. Yet for richness and quality his earlier work was surpassed only by Thompson's. Next to the North Midland, the Blisworth–Peterborough line of the London & Birmingham Railway displayed one of the finest series of stations to be found anywhere and marked the first attempt by that company to reflect in its country stations the splendours of Euston and Curzon Street, though in totally different form. Opened in 1845, all six major stations essayed in embryo, so to speak, the Elizabethan manorial 'E' in plan. Wellingborough London Road and Irthlingborough in brick, Thrapston Bridge Street and Oundle in stone, had straight gables. Wansford, also in stone and perhaps the most perfect of them all, was Jacobean. Lavish details such as oriels, finials and other Tudoresque decorations abounded. Thrapston had freer treatment, with bargeboarded gables and even crenellated chimney caps (Plate 19). All had flat platform awnings of simple design quite devoid of fussy valancing and forming thereby the perfect foil to the buildings behind, the one at Northampton Bridge Street sporting scrolly brackets. This station had only two gables, separated on all four faces by charming stone balustrades punctuated by ball finials, and also ran to a cluster of four Tudor chimneystacks. Oddly, with the exception of Elton, which though quieter was in the same vein, and the later Billing, the smaller stations were simple one-storey cottages notable only for their tall angled chimneys and curious cutaway corners forming waiting shelters.

Galt attributed Peterborough East, terminus of the Eastern Counties Railway, to Thompson, along with the other Eastern Counties stations, but *The Illustrated London News* said Livock was responsible, which is much more likely when one considers that it was built in 1845, two years before the Eastern Counties reached the town, in order expressly to accommodate the London & Birmingham's trains from Blisworth. Its long, loosely composed Tudor frontage in yellow-buff brick with stone trimmings was certainly more in Livock's idiom than that of Thompson, who rarely used Tudor; and the lack of embellishment could be accounted for by the ever-penurious state of the ECR who paid for it. Yet, on the other hand, the original Eastern Counties station at Ely, though smaller, had strong affinities with Peterborough, buff brick and all, but was built two years later, when Livock was busy with the Trent Valley line. So we are left with another mystery. Did Livock design Peterborough for the Eastern Counties while he was about the neighbouring Blisworth line stations, and perhaps at the same time run off a cheap edition for Ely two years in advance? Or was it merely a copy?

The Trent Valley Railway was opened from Rugby to Stafford in 1847 to avoid the detour through Birmingham. For it Livock erected another exuberant set of stations in similar style to his Blisworth–Peterborough creations, this time complete with gate lodges and other lineside dwellings to match—in fact a complete and unified series of railway buildings. Bulkington, Nuneaton, Atherstone, Polesworth and Lichfield were elaborations of his Wellingborough idiom in differing sizes, providing nicely judged asymmetrical massings of brick and stone trim crowned by a variety of slender clustered chimneys and patterned slates. Rugeley was near enough a second edition of Thrapston, while Jacobean predominated in the new Stafford station (1843–62), which replaced the earlier Grand Junction building, and Tamworth (Plate 20), resplendently proclaimed Livock's finest achievement, in a quoined brick frontage having a five-bay colonnade between unequal sized wings. A massive oriel surmounted by strapwork marked the larger wing, with uniformly fine fenestration. The roof line was enriched by a pierced stone parapet centrally emphasised, ogee gables duly finialed and hexagonal chimneystacks.

After the formation of the London & North Western Railway in 1846 Livock stayed on to do considerable work in the southern division, although the financial stringency affecting all railways in the 1850s severely limited his designs. However, Dockray recorded that the directors approved their 'businesslike look and absence of all unnecessary ornament' on the Bletchley–Banbury–Oxford branches of 1850. Nonetheless the more important stations had a quiet dignity, Buckingham and Winslow in brick, Bicester London Road and Brackley in local grey stone, while Claydon was permitted a flash of the old Livock in its ornate bargeboards, door and window detail and chimney ornament. Buckingham and Winslow, moreover, had a style mildly Italianate, with pleasant three-light main windows and a pair of pedimental projections to the frontage. The smaller buildings on the opposite platforms were in key. It seems likely that Livock worked on the main line, too; drawings of the original Pinner station (now Hatch End) show a two-storey centre block comprising an open-fronted shelter with Tuscan pillars supporting upper storey dwelling rooms, small one-storey wings and well executed Italianate windows and chimneys. St Albans Abbey station (1858) may also have been his. His last railway job appears to have been the undistinguished frontage block at Birmingham New Street (1863)—he was probably more willing to economise than Thompson—which was physically and aesthetically overshadowed by E. A. Cowper's iron trainshed, yet, where it overlooked the platforms, given interest by a long gallery guarded by a light iron railing and broken by five pilasters from which the roof ribs sprang.

Sir William Tite

The designer of London's Royal Exchange was one of the few big names in Victorian architecture to have done more than the odd prestige job for a railway. What is more, the bulk of it was done on a line not otherwise noted for its stations—the London & South Western—though his railway interests seem to have begun with the Eastern Counties Railway, for he was chairman of the first provisional committee in 1834, though so far we have no evidence that he was professionally engaged. He did work for the neighbouring London & Blackwall Railway, however, designing the Italianate terminus at

Blackwall (1840), a more modest version of his Southampton style, and the first Fenchurch Street station (1841).

From the opening of the London & Southampton Railway in 1838–40 he appears to have maintained a connection with that company for the best part of twenty-five years, leaving his mark from London to Devon. He is best known for his classical façades at Nine Elms and Southampton Terminus, those complementary termini based on the grand ideas used with less modesty at Euston and Curzon Street.

Nine Elms was the first terminus to be built on the 'U' plan, in which the frontage building was placed directly across the head of the platforms. The façade comprised a tall five-arched arcade between slightly projecting, two-storey rusticated wings, surmounted by a dentilled cornice and a buttressed parapet. Gate lodges flanked each side. A three-span wooden trainshed roof was built on iron columns, with elongated spandrel-like brackets forming arcades. Southampton Terminus was a more gracious essay in classical restraint—symmetrical, with first floor and attic set back behind a heavily rusticated ground-floor arcade, having five bays like Nine Elms but shorter, and an open balustrade of quality above. The first-floor windows had angled pediments, the attic plain ones; and a bold deep cornice with dentils almost hid the low hipped roof.

The grand manner was continued at Gosport (1841) in the hope that its size and magnificence might satisfy the demands of Portsmouth folk across the harbour for railway equality with Southampton. It comprised an immensely long fourteen-bay Tuscan colonnade in Portland stone between massive-looking pavilions, which had round-headed rusticated openings and parapets featuring tiny segmental pediments—Tite at his best. Later the station came in useful as a suitably august alighting point on Queen Victoria's journeys to Osborne in the Isle of Wight, when the matching entrance gate pillars, iron railings and even the letterbox probably were added. The overall roof, unfortunately, was well below this standard. Winchester in its original uncluttered form had a Palladian directness, with cornice and parapet.

Considering that only £75,000 was allowed in the estimates for 'stations, engines, carriages, wagons and machinery', it is a wonder that the London & Southampton stations were as good as they were. The inevitable over-spending caused no skimping: in February 1839 the chairman declared that it was 'prudent, and, ultimately, economical to construct these establishments on the requisite scale at the outset', but emphasised that there would be 'no unnecessary expense in architectural designs and decorations' consistent with 'utility and durability at the smallest possible cost'. If Tite was directly responsible, as seems probable, he did a good job on these terms. The result was a series of symmetrical, hipped-roofed, two-storey station buildings, large by contemporary standards, giving ample living and working quarters, of a plain domestic character relieved from mediocrity by segmental arched twelve-light windows and a simple, flat, all-round canopy on slender iron columns. Micheldever (Plate 21), on the main line, and the original terminus at Godalming (1849)—a larger version— were good examples. Basingstoke was given a Georgian touch in its fenestration and a one-storey projecting 'apron'. Variations and some ingenuity were introduced, probably betokening Tite's continuing interest—the smaller but exact late-Georgian proportions of Chiswick (1849) and Whitchurch North (1854), for example, the introduction of Italianate round-headed windows and restricted quoins at Kew Bridge (1849), where the sloping site dictated basement living quarters at the back, and the plainer building stretching up from the deep cutting at Weybridge (1838).

Having acquired a basic design, the South Western, ever a thrifty concern, proceeded to develop it—presumably without Tite's assistance, as the larger versions took on a barracky appearance. Corbelling and coupled chimneys relieved the earlier ones like Eastleigh (1841) and Guildford (1845), but later examples were coarsened to an unrelieved grimness at Farnham (1849) and Andover Junction (1854), the least imposing of this melancholy batch being Fordingbridge of 1866, after which further editions were eminently pleasanter. Chertsey, St Denys, Woolston and Netley set a new note in Italianate villa-type stations in 1868, each carefully varied with brick or stone quoins, stucco, different patterns of eaves corbelling (Chertsey's was delightfully ornamental), symmetry and asymmetry; all small differences showing a thoughtful interest in detail in a stock design still clearly derived from Tite's originals. Kew Gardens (1869) had round-headed openings formed by four courses of finely stepped brickwork, while stone was used to equal effect at Ash Vale (1870), only to be spoiled later by an unfeeling display of drainpipes. Aldershot, of the same year, displayed the final form, with a return to the recessed centrepiece of Chertsey and slender corniced chimneys. Tite's last essay in Italianate for the South Western at Salisbury (1859) was mainly achieved by stone-trimmed round- and square-headed openings and a low pitched roof, which, with parapet and bracketed window hoods, imparted a degree of dignity. Exeter

Queen Street (1860)—forerunner of the present Central station—was unlikely to have been by Tite. It was a remarkable two-storey wooden structure with a low pantiled roof and verandah, looking like something from a Western film set.

Although Tite was a constant advocate of classical styling, Nine Elms, Southampton and Gosport apart, his stations are chiefly remembered for his railway Tudor-Gothic, on the South Western represented at its best by his royal station at Windsor & Eton (Riverside) of 1851. It was preceded by Barnes, Putney, Mortlake and Richmond on the Richmond Railway of 1846, which *The Builder* said were 'fairly pretty country stations, of red brick with black lozenges, mullioned windows and Tudor chimney stacks, &c., all quietly and nicely designed'. Only Barnes survived the rebuilding of the 1880s.

In certain features his smaller stations were trial runs for Windsor, with its giant Tudor gable and square-headed, stone-mullioned and transomed window to the lofty booking hall, complemented by a wooden hammerbeamed ceiling and carved bosses within. Flanking it were two arcades of three narrow pointed arches (one continued round the corner to link with subsidiary gables and windows). The first-class waiting room was fitted out with Tite's marble chimneypiece and other details transferred from the old royal waiting room at Farnborough, which he had designed in 1844. The single-span trainshed gained effect from its siting on a curve. The wooden roof had twisted iron queen-posts and carved wooden corbels resting on wooden columns on one side, infilled with diagonal boarding and glass, and a long red brick wall to Datchet Lane on the other, broken by twelve large doors for the easy entrainment of cavalry. It formed a link with the royal entrance at the other end, in which the gable and window details were much richer, crowned by a bell-cote used as a lookout for warning the staff of the Queen's approach (Plate 22). The entire composition far outshone the Great Western's wooden trainshed up the hill. Where for once Brunel failed, Tite brilliantly succeeded—with one reservation. To the lozenge patterns in the long side wall was added a series of large letters in black brick commemorating the opening. A crowned 'VR' and 'PA' were followed by the monogrammed initials of the company, the chairman W. Chaplin, Tite himself, several other notables and, twice over, the year 1851. Doubtless they were thought appropriate but today, though curious, they seem almost childish.

Hampton Court (1849) was a worthy attempt at manorial treatment, with curved Jacobean-flavoured gables and, behind, a quaint little goods warehouse possessing a steep roof and a prominent line of buttresses. They looked well but were not repeated until Yeovil Town was built jointly with the Great Western in 1861, when the same red brick and creamy ashlar dressings were used in a longer Tudor façade having projecting wings and a large gable in the middle. Similar treatment at Axminster and Honiton (1860), on a smaller scale, caused them to blend well with their localities. Together with the other stations between Salisbury and Exeter, these last were designed jointly by Tite and Edward N. Clifton.

In 1859 a new station was built at Godalming on the Portsmouth Direct line, in golden-brown rubble with ashlar trim, dominated by a steeply gabled three-storey house adjoining the office portion, again in Tudor; and Petersfield, further down the line, was similarly built in stucco. Although we do not know that these two were Tite's work, they smack very strongly of his larger Exeter line stations, particularly Gillingham (1859) and Sherborne (1860), the former in brick and tile-hung, the latter in rock-faced stone. Crewkerne, as well, in golden-ashlar, was an 1860 product in the same style but spoiled by out-of-scale second-floor lintels.

The strong affinities between the South Western's small Tudor country stations, despite different origins, suggest they also were Tite's work. Those on the Exeter line of 1860 we know to be his—Broad Clyst, Whimple, Sidmouth Junction and Seaton Junction, for instance, and probably Topsham on the Exmouth branch a year later. If we cast back to the Southampton & Dorchester Railway of 1847, we find their counterparts at Totton, Holmsley, Ringwood, Poole (later Hamworthy Goods) and Wimborne. The style was the same, but the materials differed. Dorchester South broke the harmony—a wooden overall roof tacked on to a long low brick building with yellow trim bizarrely adorned by Roman-Doric pilasters of no obvious significance, an uninteresting cornice and parapet. One or two Tudor cottage stations in stucco were also found elsewhere on the South Western— Dunbridge between Eastleigh and Salisbury (1847), and Milford on the Portsmouth Direct, where it was as different from its neighbours as it could be—while the charming farmhouse-like grey stone Tudor building at the old Alton terminus of 1852, with prominent gables and mullions, suggested the same guiding hand.

We have already noted how the South Western seized the Exeter

& Crediton line from under the nose of the Great Western by gaining a majority shareholding. Its continuation, the North Devon Railway, was secured by similar means, and, when it opened in 1854, we find Tite as its chairman, probably the South Western's nominee. Hence the appearance once more of his Tudor cottage stations between Crediton and Barnstaple, the red brick and stucco very properly replaced by random stone fitting unobtrusively into the landscape. The larger building at Barnstaple Junction, like Dorchester, unfortunately failed to fit, small scattered openings in large expanses of wall giving it a somewhat gaunt aspect.

To complete this study of Tite's stations we must move north to find more Tudor cottages on the Lancaster & Carlisle Railway (1846–8), closely modelled on the Southampton & Dorchester pattern yet in their local stone entirely in keeping with the fell country. Burton & Holme, Milnthorpe, Shap and Plumpton were typical examples. Good neighbourliness was particularly striking, too, in the sedate Tudor and local sandstone of Penrith, where a prominently central eight-light mullioned and latticed window overlooked the ruins of Penrith castle.

For Carlisle itself Tite went truly Victorian-Tudor. In the lengthy, irregular two-storey frontage he placed a five-bay entrance arcade beside a clock-tower-cum-octagonal-lantern, followed by a nine-bay main section surmounted by a row of little wooden dormers peeping over the parapet. Flanking wings were gabled, one single-storeyed and the other with an oriel. There was much buttressing, with octagonal or angled crenellated shafts carried up through the parapet over the entrance, mullioned windows and sturdy chimneystacks grouped in sixes. In grey ashlar, like Conway, it kept good company with the nearby city walls and Smirke's Citadel lawcourts, from which it took its name. The interior was equally fitting, particularly the huge neo-Tudor fireplace in the high-roofed refreshment room, complete with quatrefoil decorations, Latin inscription and dog grate.

From 1846 to 1851 Tite was designing the buildings for the second Liverpool Lime Street, replacing Cunningham's Georgian end block with two Italianate side blocks (a morsel of which remains) linked by a balustraded colonnade, but retaining Foster's end screen. His railway work did not end in England, for he went on to design stations on the Caledonian and Scottish Central Railways, and in France.

David Mocatta

Forerunner of the London, Brighton & South Coast Railway was the London & Brighton, opened in 1841. David Mocatta, a pupil of Sir John Soane, produced for it what were certainly the first unit designs on a railway, based on a standard five-bay plan comprising a through entrance and booking hall flanked by two equal end blocks, either recessed or projecting, and a covered waiting area to the platform with end screens. No dwelling accommodation was provided. Each station design was given a different styling to produce harmonious variations—Horley was Tudorish, with a flattened arched platform arcade; Coulsdon had Doric columns and pilasters, though there is uncertainty about whether it was actually built; Redhill touched a more classical key, with a flat roof and wooden trainshed; Crawley was a variation of Coulsdon, with a dentilled pediment; and Haywards Heath had a low hipped roof and a verandah to front and rear. In rendered Suffolk brick with stone dressings and cornices these stations were among the foremost examples of enlightened railway building— simple attractive styles combined with true economy. Not all were to this plan: Three Bridges was mildly Italianate, and Burgess Hill, Hassocks and Balcombe had plain cottage stations, the first pair with Italianate touches. On the Shoreham branch, opened in 1840 before the main line was finished, only Hove appears to have followed the standard design: it had four sets of coupled pilasters to the frontage and dentilled eaves overhanging 5ft to form a verandah. Shoreham itself may have been Mocatta's work—a single-storey brick building with hipped roof, in three bays, with pilasters again and a flat wooden canopy on all sides.

Brighton terminus was Mocatta's first commission for the railway company. Henry-Russell Hitchcock has detected in it affinities in plan and elevation with Tite's Nine Elms, and undoubtedly it was Mocatta's masterpiece, though all *The Illustrated London News* could say about it after the opening in 1841 was that it was 'an elegant structure in the Roman style with commodious portico, &c.' The prominent nine-arched arcade overlooking the town was flanked by symmetrical columned continuations at each side and end, balustraded above to form a terrace in front of the alternately curved and triangular window pediments, rusticated quoins and deeply dentilled cornice of the upper storey. Low attics flanked a shallow parapet with a central clock. This frontage was ruined in 1882 when an ugly glass-and-iron *porte cochère* was added at the same time as the low-pitched iron trainshed, probably by J. U. Rastrick, was replaced by H. E. Wallis' dramatically curved, lofty arched roofs. Mocatta's interior comprised two sets of waiting rooms and offices, the larger for the main line and the smaller for the Shoreham branch. The booking-hall ceilings were coffered, with decorative plasterwork and iron columns beneath the boardroom and administrative offices on the first floor.

Benjamin Green

Among the paltry early stations of the north-east, so scathingly criticised by W. W. Tomlinson in his *North Eastern Railway, Its Rise and Development*, only those on the Newcastle & Carlisle Railway warranted praise. The line was opened in sections between 1835 and 1838, and the interest in its stations is historical rather than aesthetic, forming as they did the first attempt at a station style.

They were neat practical structures, at one with their surroundings, but who designed them is not certain. John Dobson, the great Newcastle architect, is credited with some of the bridges and other engineering works on the line and by Barman with London Road station, Carlisle. The smaller stations would seem less worthy of skill such as his, and as Carlisle was not markedly different from them other than in size it seems unlikely that Dobson was responsible.

A man who later designed magnificent stations on the Newcastle & Berwick Railway (1847), Benjamin Green, worked with Dobson on several railway contracts and also with his father, John, with whom he was in partnership, on the Newcastle & North Shields Railway (Chapter 5). Similarities in one or two details between the Newcastle & Carlisle and Newcastle & Berwick stations suggest that Benjamin may have been the designer of both. Admittedly there was a world of difference between the simplicity of the small early stations and the richly decorated spaciousness of the later ones, but not only had the railway climate completely changed in the intervening years but Benjamin Green had gained considerable stature in his profession. His father had built bridges at Scotswood and Bellingham and, with Benjamin as junior partner, a number of churches for the Duke of Northumberland. They had also worked with Dobson in the rebuilding of central Newcastle—which would account for Benjamin's particular discernment in siting the Newcastle & Berwick stations—so by the time the son came to work for that company he had acquired a good deal of varied experience and, moreover, found in George Hudson a railway promoter who did not spare expense when it came to stations. But at the time of the opening of the first section of the Newcastle & Carlisle Railway in 1835 he was only twenty-six years old and, apart from his current task of restoring part of St Nicholas' Church, Newcastle, had previously worked only with his father and Dobson. He could therefore have been given the Newcastle & Carlisle stations as a suitable solo job before embarking on such larger projects as the Theatre Royal and the Grey Monument.

All in ashlar with slated roofs, the most common platform buildings on this line were two-storeyed, rectangular in plan, and embellished only with a cross-gabled corbelled-out centrepiece, as at Riding Mill, Greenhead, Gilsland and Brampton Junction, with Tudorish chimneys and moulded window hoods. Only superficially different were Wylam and Stocksfield, where the centrepiece was omitted. Little single-storey station houses were built to match, detached at Stocksfield, Haydon Bridge and Hexham but forming part of the main building at Scotswood. The importance of Haltwhistle was recognised in a strong two-storey Tudor residence having large gables, Maltese-cross fashion, with smaller repeats and five clustered chimney shafts. Bardon Mill was somewhat similar but much smaller. The odd man out, Corbridge, was probably rebuilt in 1848, and was curiously like a private house with an added platform verandah on nice Tuscan columns. Wetheral also had the later addition of an iron-and-glass roof over the working area of the platform.

Whishaw, ever the perfectionist, grumbled about some of the buildings being set back too far from the rails, as they remained throughout their existence. At Hexham the light iron trainshed was detached from the station buildings, while at London Road, Carlisle, as much as 20yd separated the Tudor office building from the wooden shed, leaving passengers to stumble over intervening tracks. At others platforms were added as time went on, and some even had glass roofs built over the objectionable open space, as at Gilsland, only to be removed again in more recent times.

Turning now to the Newcastle & Berwick, we find a series of intensely individual stations, no two, from over a score, being alike. Smallest and simplest were the cottage structures like Goswick and Smeafield, yet even there the characteristic chimney shafts, eaves corbelling and hood moulds were prominently in evidence. Larger types had patterned bargeboards, as at Scremerston and Widdrington, but still no strongly definable style; then there was a gamut of finely detailed neo-Tudor, some on the 'E' plan, highlighted by the ridge-high lean-to shelter at Warkworth, the side entrance projection at Longhirst, the dormer breaking the eaves at Christon Bank, the angle-buttressed, near lancet-arched porch at Belford, perhaps Green's best frontage (Plate 13), and the manorial proportions of Beal. Throughout, the cool finely dressed buff-coloured stone was used, carefully quoined, mullioned and finialed, all precisely proportioned and sometimes extending to matching goods sheds, as at Belford and Acklington.

The best of these stations were Morpeth and Tweedmouth. Morpeth, a strong composition in rock-faced stone with ashlar quoins, occupied a hillside site with a one- and two-storey frontage. To the fine Tudor 'E'-shaped centrepiece and three-bay arcaded entrance, the oriel, finials, gables and clustered chimneys offered embellishment right in key. The platform buildings were rather cramped, though the latticed brackets were a delight. Tweedmouth was Green's *chef-d'oeuvre* between the Tyne and the Tweed. A five-bay entrance arcade with rusticated piers and Jacobean end gables was centrally disposed in a fairly long single-storey façade featuring two much larger Jacobean gables, spike-finialed. A taller twin-gabled section had an 'L'-shaped continuation of medium and small sized gables. All this was behind a station house of compelling presence. Large, irregular and imposingly placed at the head of a short approach off the Great North Road, with entrance gates to match, the entire composition was an impressive prelude to Robert Stephenson's Royal Border Bridge.

If Green was in fact responsible for the Newcastle & Carlisle stations, he may also have had a hand in part of the Great North of England Railway (1841). The main Northallerton building had a vaguely Tudor air, while the dentilled corbelling and small stone porch at Cowton strongly resembled work at Stocksfield and Haydon Bridge. An even greater similarity existed between the building at Alston, terminus of the Newcastle & Carlisle's branch of 1852, and Green's Newcastle & Berwick stations of five years earlier. Whatever the extent of his railway activities may have been, Green's work and versatility more than equalled many of his lauded contemporaries, yet he has been curiously overlooked outside his native Newcastle.

CHAPTER 4

THE FIRST PHASE CLOSES

THE sense of 'belonging' was one of the most attractive features of railway buildings up to the 1850s, achieved by the sympathetic use of local materials and styles. Then, as the railways themselves provided the means by which brickworks and iron foundries could expand into wider markets, local building traditions began to be superseded by the universal use of brick and iron. Here we shall look at the start of this decline and its accompaniment on the railways—the beginnings of a company style.

On the Brighton line the original Worthing station (1845) was built of flint with brick dressings; Glynde, Berwick and Pevensey & Westham (all 1846) were little rendered cottages; and Hailsham (1849) and Rowfant (1855) were similar, with Gothic windows and plain brick. All were well in keeping with their surroundings. The Pennine gritstone stations on the Sheffield, Ashton-under-Lyne & Manchester Railway of 1845 combined variety with their harmony with the bleak moors of their surroundings. Hadfield and Oughtibridge were in low neo-Tudor, their prominent gables accentuated by stone balls corbelled out at the apexes; Woodhead ran to a pair of low crenellated towers (one surmounted by chimneystacks) to match the gargoyled portals of the famous tunnel; Glossop Central, built at the Duke of Norfolk's expense, sported the Howard family's lion in stone on top of the parapet; and on the Hayfield branch (later joint with the Midland Railway), Hyde Central (1858) was notable for its perpendicular-style window on the stairs to the platforms.

Having changed its name to the Manchester, Sheffield & Lincolnshire, the line was continued eastward with a series of equally fitting red brick Tudor cottage stations in North Lincolnshire, such as Ulceby, Habrough, Holton-le-Moor and Goxhill (all 1848). Overall roofs accompanied the arcaded portico at Brigg, charmingly detailed stone entrance doorways at Market Rasen and New Holland Town, and a plainer frontage at Grimsby Town. New Holland's special treatment, of course, indicated its importance as the station for the ferry to Hull.

Equal regard for local traditions was apparent on the Kendal & Windermere Railway (1847) in the drystone walling at Kendal, Burneside and Windermere, while the rebuilt Lancaster Castle station (c 1855) lived up to its name and location to the extent of a fortress-like 'keep'.

One of the less remembered but extremely prolific railway engineers was Charles Liddell, who built, among others, the Newport, Abergavenny & Hereford Railway of 1854. Its stations were more solid than elegant but, in their local stone, eminently suited to the border hills, rusticated at St Devereux and Pontrilas with ornamental touches in the wooden pendants to their shallow verandahs. Abergavenny Monmouth Road was in ashlar with a whiff of Italianate. On the extension across the eastern valleys from Pontypool Road to Quaker's Yard, Pontypool Clarence Street and Crumlin High Level (1855) were quite different, in modest Tudor with deep iron-and-glass ridge-and-furrow awnings—shallow pitched with highly ornamental brackets and trefoil patterns at Pontypool, but steeper at Crumlin, where they were cross-barred and finialed on plain Gothic-style brackets.

Another of Liddell's lines was the Worcester & Hereford, which became part of the Great Western, though the two charming stations at Malvern were not his work. They were built in the dark, almost purple random stone from the hills, known as Malvern Rag, Malvern Link station (1859) being styled in quiet Tudor with matching buildings and ridge-and-furrow awnings on both platforms. In contrast Great Malvern (1862) formed a delightful extravaganza in what *The Builder* termed Gothic of Charles VI of France (Plate 23). The long, loosely composed façade displayed mini-gables, door and window treatment ranging from the square-headed through triangular to the deep-set stilted arch, quatrefoil-patterned cresting and a clock tower and spirelet of the utmost delicacy. By a local architect, E. W. Elmslie, who probably designed Malvern Link as well, the station formed part of a group that included a landscaped approach road and gardens, a bridge over the railway, and the Imperial Hotel itself, which was connected to the platforms by a curious private covered-way roofed with bell-shape sectioned corrugated iron adorned by iron cresting. Not to be outdone the Midland built an almost equally extravagant station at Malvern Wells Hanley Road on its newly opened extension from Tewkesbury in 1864, in rag again with buff ashlar trim, mullions and beautifully fretted bargeboards, including four miniature gables to mark the entrance. It completed a remarkable trio at Malvern.

Several other Great Western stations of this decade were lifted out of the ordinary by the quality of local workmanship. The finely coursed ashlar of Martock (1853) and Castle Cary (1856) were cases in point; as were Pewsey and Savernake Low Level (1862), which were given diamond-patterned brickwork and stone trim.

Three noteworthy stations in North Wales were acquired by the London & North Western when it took over several local lines. Denbigh (1858) might have been a school; large, rambling and austere, its stone frontage was broken by a buttressed tower and low spire. Llanwrst & Trefriw (1863), also stone, had tripartite arched windows and Gothic touches in the gables. Ruthin (1862), on the other hand, was in modest but competent Georgian style—late for its date—with a four-bay brick arcade, three of them blind but the fourth left open as an entrance.

Because so many of the small later stations in North Wales were notably unsuited to their surroundings, the original stations on the Bangor & Carnarvon and Carnarvonshire Railways running down the underside of the Lleyn Peninsula to Afon Wen were immediately striking for their strong native element. Griffiths Crossing (1852), Dinas, Pant Glas and Llangybi (all 1867) had tiny stone buildings offering minimal accommodation, yet, by their very Spartan ruggedness, displaying the essence of the small Welsh cottage. By contrast Caernarvon itself was prominently Jacobean in dark red brick, with the Prince of Wales' feathers on its gables above low, rustic pitched verandah roofing.

In 1857 at Lewes the London, Brighton & South Coast Railway built the second of the town's three generations of stations. *The Sussex Advertiser* called it Gothic, though in truth it was nearer a Swiss chalet, with shallow-pitched roofs, overhanging gables and elaborate bargeboards. In the next county the South Eastern continued to build numbers of wooden hipped-roof stations in the Kentish clapboard tradition throughout this period and so far beyond it that what began as fairly commendable good neighbourliness finished up as a standard economy product. Apart from the added awning there was little to choose between Pluckley of 1842 and Ore of 1888. They formed, in fact, one of the longest lived station designs. Many of them were matched by a small waiting shelter on the subsidiary platform, with a sloping roof canted upward and outward to form a short awning, usually with small well moulded wooden brackets. Those of the 1840s escaped monotony by the interspersion of other styles—for instance, on the Ashford–Canterbury line (1846), where only Chilham was in timber, Wye and Chartham being brick Tudor cottages. Strood (1847) followed the standard wooden design but was larger and ran to a gabled entrance section of some dignity (for a timber structure), with Georgian windows, moulded hoods, scrolled brackets and a recessed canopy on plain iron columns. But this was exceptional, though Earley (1863–4) must be mentioned for its two-storey building. Perched on top of the brick lower storey and forming the first floor was one of the South Eastern's standard timber structures, overhanging the platform on wooden brackets for all the world as though a second-hand building from some redundant station had been found too large to fit. Line variety slowly receded before the growing demand for economy, yet surprises were still produced on the Strood–Maidstone line of 1856, where, cheek-by-jowl with Snodland's 'four square' look, was the delightful and almost extravagant ragstone Tudor of Aylesford, echoing the much larger Wateringbury on the Maidstone branch of 1844.

In 1848 the Wakefield, Pontefract & Goole Railway was opened, including a branch to Askern Junction, later to become part of the Lancashire & Yorkshire system. The idea of a line style was apparent in its stations, which were of two distinct types with individual variations: Pontefract Monkhill, Whitley Bridge, Rawcliffe and Askern were Tudor, in brick with stone dressings; but Featherstone, Knottingley, Hensall, Womersley and Norton broke up the series with quite extraordinary manifestations of grey brick *cottage orné* with half-hipped gables and dormers. They could have been taken straight from J. C. Loudon's *Encyclopaedia*, apart from their size, and ornament was added as Loudon suggested by a close succession of shaped wooden eaves brackets repeated on a smaller scale beneath the window sills, spiky finials and pendants, elaborate porches and bay windows.

Loudon's principles were followed even more closely on the London & North Western Railway's Northampton–Market Harborough line. Pitsford & Brampton, Brixworth, Lamport and Kelmarsh were tall cottage buildings faintly disguised by Jacobean gables and partial rendering. They looked cheap, except at Pitsford, where the rendering was left off to advantage, and the hexagonal chimneys were too short. But this was the LNWR of 1859, on which one had to be thankful for the smallest aesthetic mercies.

The idea of a company style as opposed to a line style was beginning to spread. The London & South Western had been shown the way by Tite and was not slow to follow. Although not as long-lived as the South Eastern's wooden stations, a remarkable continuity in design, the more interesting for being intermittent, was to be encountered westward from Basingstoke right through to the end of the line at Padstow over more than forty-five years. As far as Salisbury the stations were plain brick houses, each with a gable overlooking the platform and a one-storey office building attached, a common enough design on many lines, as we have seen. Examples were Oakley and Overton (1854) and Porton (1857). As the line continued into Dorset, the stations were enhanced by round-headed upper windows, some coupled, an Italianate touch given greater effect by rendering at Semley and Milborne Port. Others, like Wilton South, Dinton and Tisbury, were slate-hung. All these were built in 1859–60. Beyond Yeovil was Tite's neo-Tudor, of course, but after Coleford Junction the standard pattern started again. Bow (1865) had all its main windows round-topped, which strengthened its composition against a background of squared uncoursed Dartmoor granite, with lighter dressings and edged gables. Okehampton (1871); Bridestow (1874), simply rendered again; Brentor (1890), in random with brick trim; and St Budeaux Victoria Road (1890), where the house was separate at the top of the cutting—all were from the same stable, with only material and finish varying. Nearly all the North Cornwall line stations also followed this pattern, mainly in local rock-faced granite, and Ashwater and Tower Hill (1886), Port Isaac Road (1895), and Padstow (1899) carried this mid-nineteenth century design almost into the twentieth century.

A most attractive derivative appeared on the Portsmouth Direct line of 1859, a speculative venture by the great railway contractor Thomas Brassey. The station buildings were comfortably symmetrical in red brick, with shallow hipped wings like hunched shoulders against a gabled two-storey centrepiece having symmetrical round-headed openings. Witley, Liss and Rowlands Castle were good examples. The style was also used at Stockbridge (1865), which was

Plate 9   *Cottage orné* combined with the grand manner at Kidderminster, West Midland Railway, in 1956

Page 77

Plate 10   Collegiate Gothic at Shrewsbury joint station, a view taken pre-1903 before the lowest storey was added, although the hut and scaffolding seem to indicate that work was about to start

Plate 11 Original Brunel at Culham, GWR, styled in Tudor with flat all-round awning; up platform, in 1962

Plate 12 Italianate derivative at Southam Road & Harbury, GWR, with hipped roof, in 1965

Plate 13   Benjamin Green's work on the Newcastle & Berwick Railway:
the frontage of Belford in 1967

Plate 14   Francis Thompson's original design for Ambergate, North
Midland Railway, from a lithograph by Sam Russell, 1840

Plate 15 Great Chesterford, Eastern Counties Railway, probably by
Francis Thompson, in 1955

Page 80

Plate 16 The same general style at Mostyn, Chester & Holyhead
Railway, by Thompson, in 1963. Note that small end blocks support
the flat awnings, instead of the screen walls at Great Chesterford

slate-hung, and variations in size and window groupings were introduced on the Mid-Hants line, with rendering. Similar mild Italianate
features were found at Seaton (1868), Ottery St Mary and Sidmouth
(1874).

The most emphatic Italianate stations on the South Western, and
the most faithful to their origins, were the large villas built by the
little Thames Valley Railway that formed the Shepperton branch
(1864), where something special was called for to preserve the tone
of the district. They had shallow roofs and large pedimented gables,
eaves corbelling and light rendering.

Early uniformity in the North East was not all attributable to G. T.
Andrews, for the East & West Yorkshire Junction Railway from York
to Knaresborough (1848) was at first independent, as its local brick
stations showed. Although plain, their lofty proportions had a dignified
air, a hooded stone roundel being placed in the centre of the broad
main gable. At Poppleton, Marston Moor, Cattal and Hopperton
lower two-storey wings, rusticated stone quoins and window casings
added substance. Hammerton and Hessay were smaller, and the
smallest, Goldsbrough, had outsized open-scalloped bargeboards.

Line or company styling was not otherwise so noticeable in the
North East during the 1850s and early 1860s. The Stockton & Darlington Railway, which resisted amalgamation with the North Eastern
until 1863, mainly went in for varieties of stone Tudor, with here and
there a little mild *cottage orné* half timbering, as at Piercebridge (1856),
Bowes, Kirkby Thore (both 1861) and Cockfield Fell (1863).

Two of the Midland Railway's earlier lines were outstanding for
the sympathy they showed for traditional styling, producing stations
of exceptional quality. They were the first to be constructed after the
Midland was formed by amalgamation in 1844, and were perfect
examples of strong local influences still at work despite the merging
of interests. The Nottingham–Lincoln line of 1846 began with a series
of jolly Tudor stations as far as Newark (Chapter 2), exuberant in
their embellishment. Next came Collingham, Swinderby and Hyke-
ham in descending sizes of Italianate, the first having pediment-style
gables and twin colonnades to the platform elevation, giving the
impression that the building had been placed back to front. Swinderby
had a curious three-sided projection that looked like a turnpike toll
house. The first series was in dark red brick with stone trim; the second,
further east, in buff brick. Then came Thorpe-on-the-Hill, already
mentioned in Chapter 2.

The second and even more delightful line was the Leicester–Peterborough (1846–8), which left the main line at Syston, and on which William Parsons, the Leicestershire surveyor, seems to have shared architectural responsibility with Sancton Wood. Wood probably designed the more important stations, such as Luffenham, Oakham, Ketton & Collyweston and Stamford Town. Between them the two men ran through a whole gamut of styles, with strong emphasis on the local idiom throughout. A rather austere brand of red-brick Tudor marked Rearsby and Asfordby, with, in between, a remarkably large station at Brooksby (why is not clear) having no stylistic allegiance yet oddly fascinating. Long and low, it had a deeply overhanging roof broken by three curious peaked hoods over round-topped doorways, offset by tall chimneys and concluded by a two-storey house. Melton Mowbray Town was disappointingly plain until a triple-arched brick colonnade was tacked on to compete with the London & North Western and Great Northern Joint line station opened in 1879. Restrained cottage half-timbering at Saxby, Whissendine and Ashwell was followed by more pretentious Italianate at Oakham, with a flat colonnade on over-thick square columns, and at Manton, where clean lines and simple rendering presented a clearer representation of the style.

Then, in the grey limestone country, came the surprisingly large station of Luffenham, doubtless anticipating the junction with the LNWR three years later. More surprisingly, this station was in the Francis Thompson (or Sancton Wood) style of the Eastern Counties Railway: a dominant two-storey house surrounded by a lean-to 'apron' formed verandahs at front and rear, with gabled terminal blocks on the platform side, where deep valancing gave a ponderous look. In well-quoined ashlar, it could be further evidence of the association between Thompson and Sancton Wood suggested in Chapter 3.

Ketton & Collyweston reverted to Tudor, the belfry affording an ecclesiastical touch. The full treatment, however, was accorded to the splendidly asymmetrical station at Stamford Town, where strong period touches appeared in the three-bay arcade and in the conical-topped turret bearing the original Syston & Peterborough Railway's initials on the weathervane. All told, the station was entirely worthy of the high standard of the town, and after this Uffington and Helpston were somewhat anticlimactic, though they more truly reflected the unadorned simplicity of the limestone villages they served; with their heavy stone slab roofs, they could easily have sprung from a pre-railway age.

The Midland Railway's distinctive house styles were the earliest, longest and most outstanding, extending a continuous evolutionary thread of characteristic features from 1847 into the twentieth century. The company was pushing, progressive and very proudly provincial. Based on Derby, its lines spread to Bristol, Swansea, Carlisle, Lincoln and London, and it looked after its passengers well beyond contemporary limits of commercial interest, almost to the point of benevolence, according to its rivals. It allowed third-class passengers in all trains, abolished the second class long before others did, and its rolling stock set the highest standard; so it is not surprising that the average Midland stations were solidly built and their passenger amenities distinctly good. Moreover the Midland was notable for its continuing regard for local materials, more so than any other railway, for which reason it is necessary to trespass awhile into the second phase of stations in order to follow this development to its conclusion.

After the Lincoln and Peterborough lines were built the three most characteristic and repetitive Midland features started to emerge: diamond- and lozenge-patterned iron lattice windows, elaborate openwork bargeboards and finials, and a fondness for a single-storey building in the form of a pair of gabled pavilions linked by a recessed centrepiece. The oldest to display the iron lattice seem to have been the Midland Counties Railway buildings at Spondon, Kegworth and Barrow-on-Soar of 1840, whence it spread through the system in platform shelters, warehouses and engine sheds. The openwork bargeboards appeared early on the Lincoln line's Tudor stations, to become almost as widespread as the iron lattice, in a multitude of patterns. Beeston (1847) displayed all three features, its bargeboards having entrancing intricacy.

The twin-pavilion style appeared intermittently until the 1870s, when it was used extensively in a number of guises on some of the new lines built under J. C. Crossley, engineer to the company from 1857 to 1878. As far apart as Thornbury (1872) and Shirebrook West (1875) the medium was grey stone with elaborate bargeboards and iron cresting—plain with weak Gothic door and window treatment at Dore & Totley (1870), but stronger in brick on the Walsall line (1879), with stone or brick gable copings concealing the lofty varnished roofs within, and a glass verandah between the pavilions at Streetly, Aldridge and Sutton Coldfield. In the same area, Kings Norton had

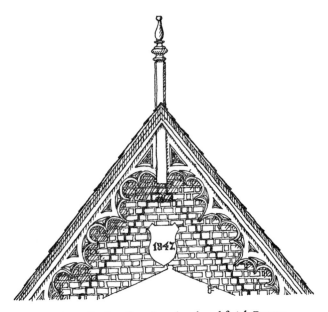

Early Midland Railway bargeboards and finial, Beeston

three pavilions to its main building. Stations in this style, apart from Garsdale and Crosby Garrett, were well suited to the Midland's engineering triumph, the Settle & Carlisle line, where they were neither too elaborate nor too plain but sufficiently varied in material and treatment to provide interest as the limestone of upper Ribblesdale gave way to the high gritstones at Dent and Garsdale, in turn succeeded by Eden Valley sandstone (p 170). Once more three pavilions were provided at the largest station, Appleby West.

Pride of place on the Midland goes to its masterly technique in iron and glass awnings. Most wayside stations in the first half of the century had no platform cover at all, and at those larger places where it was provided a flat wooden deck was employed, devoid of ornament and supported on fairly plain brackets or wooden pillars placed close to the platform edge, where they must have been a considerable inconvenience. In many instances, of course, anything more elaborate would have distracted attention from the building, and the early designers knew well how to use the simple flat verandah in their overall design as the perfect foil to a more elaborate structure behind, so well demonstrated by Livock at his Northampton–Peterborough and Trent Valley stations (Plate 19).

The Crystal Palace showed how large areas could be enclosed in iron and glass by using Sir Joseph Paxton's ridge-and-furrow technique. Paxton was a Midland director for many years, had designed Matlock and the original station at Rowsley (1849), and had sketched his first outline of the Crystal Palace on boardroom blotting paper during a meeting of a subsidiary company at Derby in 1850. So it was no coincidence that the first glass and iron ridge-and-furrow awnings appeared on the Midland's Leicester–Hitchin line at Kettering and Wellingborough in 1857. The architect was C. H. Driver, whose name has sometimes been linked with Webber, who supervised the construction. C. Biddle was responsible for the ironwork. The furrows were steeply pitched and, again for the first time, the roof of that portion of the building immediately behind was similarly profiled to give articulation with the awning. The open ends were embellished with entwined branches and capped by metal bannerettes bearing the cut-out letter 'M'. Slender iron columns offset large brackets containing more floral decoration. The whole effect was one of extraordinary lightness and grace.

The Leicester–Hitchin stations were all of a type—the usual two-storeyed house with a single-storey office building adjoining but set back from the platform and fronted by a low brick-enclosed waiting shelter, which had the ridge-and-furrow roofs of Kettering and Wellingborough but without the awning. Doors and windows were round-headed, the latter sometimes coupled, with the Midland's typical iron latticework, all matched in the goods sheds. The small stations, like Finedon, had only three ridge-and-furrow sections; Wellingborough had six, with the frontage windows in pairs set in multi-coloured brick arcading. Bedford, the busiest station, had a large brick-fronted *porte cochère* matched by a wooden lantern over the booking hall. The Midland's regard for the local product was shown by the use of white brick at Great Glen, red at Kibworth, golden ironstone at Desborough, limestone at Glendon & Rushton (Plate 24), then back to brick through the clay measures to Hitchin, and at all of them delicate wavy bargeboarding. The style was repeated in Derbyshire and Nottinghamshire—at Alfreton for example—and as far north as Ingleton (c 1861).

To follow the development of the Midland glass awning (p 133), we must again trespass beyond the immediate period. The first type undoubtedly was the best and continued to be used until the 1870s, but with embellishment usually limited to large brackets decorated with bold circles as seen south of Radlett (1867) and northward from Rowsley (1863–7), intermingled with shallower-pitched variations having hipped ends, as at Sutton-in-Ashfield General and Mangotsfield, sometimes decorated with delicate finials like the examples at Skipton. Deeper pierced principals added strength without weight and small, almost filigree brackets sprang from fluted columns at Loughborough Midland (Plate 26), Melton Mowbray Town and Cheltenham Lansdown. The final development was to shift the emphasis from decorative lightness to functionalism, and wherever possible columns were dispensed with to give unobstructed platform space. This meant that very deep brackets, usually tapered steel joists, had to be cantilevered outward from the wall—as on the outside platforms at Leicester London Road (1892)—or from central columns to form umbrella roofing over an island platform, as at Cheadle Heath. Much favourable comment was attracted by the new platforms at Sheffield Midland in 1904, where particularly broad awnings were carried on latticed cantilevers.

The Midland's glass-and-iron formula was also used in screens forming part of the platform elevation, often bearing the diamond and lozenge design, frequently in conjunction with pavilion-type buildings like those at Berkeley (1876) on the Severn & Wye Joint line, Elmton & Creswell (1875) and on the Settle & Carlisle line (1875). Lean-to awnings were little favoured, though there were good examples at Hellifield (c 1880).

The Midland was exceptional, for simultaneously another company was setting the scene for a new, low standard in station design and house styling. In the seven years up to 1853 the Great Northern had spent £11 million on 272 miles of line, yet still managed to pay a dividend. Although it ran prestige trains like The Flying Scotsman, it was a line primarily built to bring Yorkshire coal to London. Small wonder, then, that in 1850 *The Illustrated London News* said of its stations that ' . . . very little recourse has been had to any of the more costly kinds of material and workmanship'.

Of course, King's Cross was special, the functional simplicity of its façade repeating the curved grace of the twin-arched roof in a manner matched neither before nor since. It was a pity that the functionalism of the stations beyond did not equally combine the handsomeness of Lewis Cubitt's terminal. The buildings were nearly all in one mould:

a two-storey house adjoining a one-storey office building having round-headed openings beneath a shallow-pitched roof. Variations were mainly limited to the use of local brick—buff near London and Peterborough, red in Hertfordshire and Bedfordshire, grey-white north of Newark—or confined to minor detailing, like rusticated quoins at the original Biggleswade, hipped roofs at Welwyn North, Essendine and Bawtry, or gables at Sandy, Huntingdon North and Tuxford. Often the small places were crossing houses with a wooden building added, like Crow Park, Claypole and Ranskill.

Vague attempts were made to provide frontages at the larger stations: stumpy towers at Peterborough; a vast glass-and-iron awning at Grantham, which looked like a coarser edition of something from the Midland (probably a later addition); and an immense length of tediously repetitive gables at Retford. These stations were designed by Henry Goddard of Lincoln (1851). Even Doncaster, hub of the system, had a stock erection, and more surprisingly so had Hatfield, opposite the very gates of Lord Salisbury's mansion (p 163). The Lincoln line of 1848 presented a little more interest: Peakirk, Spalding, Woodhall Junction and Bardney had a squat three-storey tower apiece for the stationmaster's quarters, John Taylor being the architect. Southrey and Stixwould were low 'bijou' buildings, Langrick had a pantiled belfry, and the little building at Dogdyke was nearly all tower and nothing else. A miserable attempt at half-timbered *cottage orné* was tried at Deeping St James; Surfleet was mainly rendered, with wooden summerhouse-like verandahs. Arksey, the last Great Northern station going north, affected a weak chalet style in timber framing and cement rendering oddly offset by a low, almost Florentine, many bracketed, hipped roofed tower.

The Great Northern's most important contribution to nineteenth-century building was in distributing cheap Fletton bricks from the Peterborough brickfields to all parts of the country. More than any other company its opening marked the ending of the age of the vernacular and the beginning of universal brick. Ten years later the London, Chatham & Dover Railway copied it. Formed in 1859, the LC & D was a bid to break the near-monopoly of the South Eastern in Kent. James Staats Forbes became general manager and for nearly forty years waged a bitter personal feud with Sir Edward Watkin of the South Eastern. Both lines were impoverished in the process, and their standards of building became a byword for austere inadequacy. The Chatham's humble beginnings between Strood and Faversham

(1858) produced pinch-penny designs halfway between a small cottage and a villa, where function was all. Teynham and Rainham illustrated this, while those built two years later in the bid for London—Sole Street and Farningham Road, for instance—were even meaner. At Bekesbourne, Shepherdswell and Kearsney (1861–2) authority relented in favour of larger, better balanced buildings in the same style, with careful window glazing, but generally only where the traffic might warrant it were the purse-strings loosened a little, as at the seaside stations on the extension into Thanet. The company sometimes seemed to have a flair for the incongruous on these occasions, with a fondness for clumsy lancets at Birchington-on-Sea (1863) and Herne Bay (1861), the latter having the jarring addition of four rose windows in frames of multi-coloured brick. Margate (1864) was similar; it was designed by John Newton, who was probably responsible for the others also.

CHAPTER 5

TRAINSHEDS AND OVERALL ROOFS

THE external appearance of their stations was important to the early railway companies as a means of what today would be termed projecting an image, and for this the architect was needed. But as time went on and railways rapidly became an accepted part of civilised living, architecture became less important, except in large centres where prestige or competition called for something special. The nineteenth century was essentially the age of the engineer; art and invention moved apart as the years passed, aided on the railways by growing calls for economy. The earlier close collaboration between architect and engineer, such as that which probably took place between Francis Thompson and Robert Stephenson on the trainsheds at Derby and Chester, for instance, or between Brunel and Matthew Digby Wyatt at Paddington, rapidly faded after the 1850s. In particularly prestigious circumstances an architect would be engaged to design a frontage block to accompany a trainshed designed by the company's engineer. In other cases the engineer usually did the whole job, as we shall see in Chapter 8. Only one company, the North Eastern Railway, employed an official architect throughout the sixty-nine years of its existence, during which time there were only four appointments. The North Eastern's architects reversed the normal practice in performing both architectural and engineering functions in station design. Later in this chapter we shall examine their overall roofs, leaving their architectural work for consideration in Chapters 7 and 8.

Yet the engineers were far from being insensitive fabricators of iron, as this and the succeeding chapter will show. Joseph Paxton's Crystal Palace was the first large-scale structure to prove what could really be done with iron and glass. It was a piece of engineering daring without previous parallel, completely functional in the structural sense yet acknowledged as a magnificent piece of architecture in its own right. The railway engineers were quick to comprehend.

Before considering the development of the iron trainshed, the brief employment of the wooden roof must first be mentioned. After Liverpool Crown Street, wooden roofs of various kinds were constructed, but apart from the Brunel lines, on which they were used for many years, the wooden truss quickly gave way to light iron trusses that could span a wider area and were more resistant to smoke and steam. The second London Bridge station had a wooden trussed roof, probably by J. U. Rastrick, and so did Nine Elms, though iron columns and stiffeners were required in order to span 74ft. Thereafter the wooden trussed roof was found only occasionally, often at a small single-platform terminus where it doubled up as a carriage shed for the branch train. Burnham-on-Sea (1858) and Aldeburgh (1860) were such, and the Furness Railway had some odd specimens (see Chapter 9). Callington station had an all-wooden trainshed, surprisingly built as late as 1908, with one side open to the weather. Outside the Great Western wood was not greatly used in through stations, though the first Guildford station had wooden trusses, as did the third station at Darlington North Road. Both were in two bays, at the latter of unequal sizes with a row of iron columns down the middle. Simple wooden trusses occasionally were used over a station concourse, too, as at Lowestoft Central (1847), where they were very low on sturdy square posts and light iron brackets, reinforced later by timber diagonals, and at Littlehampton (1863), plainer, without brackets.

A little used but interesting form of construction was the laminated timber arch. Lewis Cubitt's King's Cross roof (1852) has rightly been described as the finest example, though the timber ribs had to be replaced later with iron. Each 105ft wide, the two spans sprang from arcaded side and centre walls. But King's Cross was not the only example. John Green, father of Benjamin (p 69), was building laminated timber bridges in 1839 on the Newcastle & North Shields Railway, for which a triple-arched trainshed was constructed at North Shields station, attributed to father and son, though probably by John. The central arch was 25ft wide on tapered iron columns placed close to the platform edges, and tied by two iron rods slightly inclined to meet at the base of a central strut. The two side arcades over the platforms were 12ft 9in wide, on stone rubble screen walls, tied by horizontal timber beams. In 1846 the original Preston & Wyre Railway termini at Lytham and Blackpool were provided with single laminated arched ribs springing directly from the platforms. They were 53ft wide and designed by R. B. Rampling. Unlike King's Cross, all three had pitched roofs resting tangentially on the arches.

The grandiose title of the Bolton, Blackburn, Clitheroe & West Yorkshire Railway may not have been matched by its mere 26½ miles of line, but it provided a one-sided station at Blackburn (1848) with an imposing Italianate frontage, which has been attributed to Sancton Wood, and an unusually interesting roof built on composite laminated trusses of timber and iron. The account of the opening in the *Blackburn Standard* gave a full description:

> The principals of the roof of the shed are formed by wrought iron plates and wood, revitted (sic) together and curved to the form of an arch: the rafter, formed of two plates of iron and a piece of wood between, is braced and strutted to this arch, and forms a secure and neat principal. The whole is then planked over and slated. This shed is lighted with a louvre of rough plate glass, extending the entire length of the construction.

It spanned 66ft and was 330ft long, and the platform could accommodate two trains, arriving and departing, presumably with a central crossover. The goods shed had a laminated all-timber roof truss.

As we have seen, the iron trussed wooden roof clad with slates was widely used by G. T. Andrews who favoured hipped ends. More generally the ends were vertical gables in various forms, often boarded vertically. Richmond (Yorks) had herringbone-patterned gables, Brigg and Lincoln St Marks were slatted (p 103), and Peterborough East had square-paned glazing in the upper half over a serrated lower edge. Glazed ends were common, generally over a horizontal bottom transom, though some had semi-elliptical cut-out sections over the rails, like Wolverhampton High Level. At Wakefield Kirkgate the cut-away section was so large that the gable was little more than valancing which from the inside on a dark day gave the effect of an elliptical roof.

Where the roofs had more than one span or bay, the austerity of the trusses was frequently offset by the rows of iron columns between them, with shallow brackets forming delicately curved arcades. Very light, thriftily functional single-span bar iron trussed roofs were built by the London, Chatham & Dover Railway at some of its more important stations like Sittingbourne (1858) and Canterbury East (1860). The Yarmouth Vauxhall terminus of the Norwich & Yarmouth

Railway (1844) had tapered columns and flat elliptical brackets cast in one piece. The London & South Western essayed curiously staggered twin roofs at Exeter Queen Street (1860) and Yeovil Town (1861), the end of one extending some distance beyond the other.

The early roofs were poorly lit by a few glass lights. Shoreditch (1840), for instance, appears to have had an interesting three-bay elliptical roof, the centre bay raised on arcading above elliptically bracketed cross girders, and the side bays lit by a row of circular roof lights. As the technique advanced, more glass was used, expanding from narrow strips of continuous glazing until eventually the glazed areas predominated. Continuous ventilators came to be incorporated along the ridge to let out steam and smoke, and they were sometimes large enough to form clerestories. Those at Cardiff Queen Street were disproportionately large.

The evolution of a pitched overall roof having strong company characteristics began in the light iron sheds designed by Robert Stephenson and Charles Fox for the London & Birmingham Railway at Euston. Open at the ends, they rested on plain iron columns—rather low, to be raised later—and simple brackets decorated with circles in the spandrels, a fashion copied by Tite at Nine Elms and later by the Midland Railway. Humble they must have seemed following the nobility of the vast Doric Arch and Great Hall, but nonetheless they were functionally graceful in their own right. By 1848 similar roofs adorned Edge Hill and, in three bays, Manchester Victoria. Bletchley and St Albans Abbey station roofs (1858) had the end gables filled with vertical glazing over a delicately curved transom, a feature added to the Euston sheds when they were extended (p 103).

These were the characteristics of the 'Euston Roof', which appeared at a number of London & North Western stations at intervals throughout the century, from single spans like those at Windermere, Swansea Victoria and Huddersfield (1886) to the multi-span roofs of Crewe and Preston (1880). As weight increased with width, the simple brackets gave way to heavier cross-girders, diagonally trussed at Huddersfield and Rugby, elliptically arched at Preston, losing the effect of lightness. The Crewe roofs were mainly built on side walls pierced by numerous round-headed openings. Rugby's were in three main sections (1886), the lateral spans over the bay platforms at the outer ends abutting on to a lofty ridge-and-furrow central section at right-angles over the broad island platform, and extending out over the central crossovers and the outside through lines to terminate on

brick walls and deep girders. To keep the wind off long island platforms the North Western introduced vertically glazed side screens
along the outside of the platform lines. They appeared at Rugby,
Crewe and Llandudno Junction, among other stations, though the
last did not have an overall roof.

There were other variations of the Euston Roof, too. The gable
screens at Llandudno itself each had a horizontal transom, for instance;
and the roof brackets at Buxton had vertical struts in the spandrels
instead of circles. One of the most unusual uses of the Euston Roof
was a small-scale version forming a *porte cochère* at Norton Bridge.
Complete with gable screens, it was built along the frontage, supported
in the centre by a pair of ugly cross-braced stanchions. It even survived
the rebuilding of 1964. Similar vertical end-glazing was also used to
help lighten the top-heavy effect of ridge-and-furrow platform awnings
at Long Buckby, Kings Cliffe and Wakerley & Barrowden, and the
frontage awning at Watford High Street.

Francis Thompson, probably in collaboration with Robert Stephenson, showed how light iron roofs could be used to cover large areas
in several spans, at the same time creating an atmosphere of airy
elegance. The Derby tri-junct station roof of 1840 covered 140ft in
three spans on two lines of fluted columns and decorated cross girders
substantial enough not to require brackets. The joint station at Liverpool Tithebarn Street, designed by John Hawkshaw and erected by
Fox, Henderson & Co (1850), had two sheds of unequal width, one of
which tapered; the larger shed was 136ft wide at its broadest end, and
the other 78ft wide. The roof was radical for its day in being made
entirely of iron and glass, the unglazed sections covered by galvanised
corrugated sheeting. The whole roof took only six months to erect.

Some of the earlier two-platform stations had individual overall
roofs covering each platform and the adjacent track. Mocatta's
wooden queen-post roof at Reigate on the Brighton Railway (1841)
lasted only three years, when it was replaced by the South Eastern
Railway's Redhill station, and that had separate iron sheds for the
two platforms, one a single span and the other a double span over an
island platform. It was a four-track station, with the fast lines passing
between the two sheds, an arrangement employed by the same company at Canterbury West (1846), where it included some strikingly
delicate floral ironwork in the open gables; at the third Stafford
station by the London & North Western (1861), which survived until
electrification in 1964 (Plate 28); and on the East Lincolnshire Railway

(later part of the Great Northern) at Boston in 1848. The neighbouring stations at Alford, Firsby and Louth, though only two-tracked, had twin spans supported on a row of iron columns and brackets down the middle between the lines, Firsby's being of considerable decorative merit (Plate 27).

A pair of pitched roofs covered the island platform and adjacent rails at Kirkby Stephen East (1861), with the station building between them and a screen wall at each side. A similar plan at Mirfield on the Lancashire & Yorkshire (1866) was covered by a low cavernous roof in one single span. The high-level island platform at Portsmouth & Southsea (1876) had a pretty little overall roof on a central row of paired columns from which tapering iron principals were bracketed out in hammerbeam fashion. The gables were nicely curved, pierced and serrated, and at one end articulated with an umbrella awning over the platform extension. The roof's location on a gentle reverse curve added to its effect.

The great achievement in station engineering was the arched iron roof. Its development allowed wider and higher spaces to be covered; more, it made a dramatic visual impact and soon extended itself to market halls, shopping arcades and seaside piers. Like the pitched roof, general development in various forms was overlapped by individual development on one particular railway. As the Euston Roof typified the London & North Western, so Dobson's Newcastle Central started a family of arched roofs on the North Eastern.

To complement his classical façade, Dobson designed three 60ft wide semi-elliptical sheds that were completed first, in 1849. Built on a sharp curve, to fit which the rear wall of the frontage block was also curved, they created a spectacular vista. The central span was higher than the others, resting on wide-spaced plain tapered columns with shallow-bracketed two-tier cross girders matching the curves of the roof ribs, only every third of which rested directly over a column. The bracing of the two tiers was said to be in the Gothic style, but Dobson covered them with rectangular panelled boarding to tone with the classical frontage. Dobson had precedents in Paxton's Chatsworth greenhouse of 1836–40 and Decimus Burton's Kew Palm House (1844–8), of course, but what made Newcastle so decisive a turning point was the curve.

Continuing now with the work of the North Eastern Railway's architects, the first years of Thomas Prosser, who held the post from 1854 to 1874, tended to be unimaginative, perhaps due to his preoccupation with modifying and completing Dobson's block at Newcastle. He followed G. T. Andrews' methods in the roof at Bishop Auckland and probably at Redcar and Saltburn, too, after the acquisition of the Stockton & Darlington in 1863. Hornsea Town, with its pedimented five-bay *porte cochère*, although built by a nominally independent company in 1864, may have been influenced by Prosser if not his actual work, again in the spirit of Andrews. In fact, Prosser's first major departure from the Andrews tradition did not appear until the New station at Leeds was completed in 1869. W. W. Tomlinson's tart comment (*The North Eastern Railway, Its Rise and Development*, 1914) that it added nothing to the architectural embellishment of Leeds was justified by the almost complete lack of any kind of frontage, the offices being inside the wall, an omission that could perhaps be explained by the joint interest of the London & North Western. The roof, however, was almost unique. The pointed iron-and-glass spans were Mansard-shaped on very light trusses, brick screen walls and foliated columns. In outline it echoed the little overall roof at Alston, on the Newcastle & Carlisle's branch, which may have been added about this time. The irregular plan of Leeds New, and the use of a straight-pitched roof over the eastern bay platforms, gave it an untidy look, while below another noteworthy feature was largely unseen. The station was built on brick arches, the criss-crossing of which produced brick vaulting of the highest workmanship.

Prosser's other major work was the new through station at York, completed in 1877, for the roof of which he fell back on Dobson's basic Newcastle design. The York site, too, was sharply curved, lending itself to the creation of an even more satisfying exercise in perspectives. Prosser characteristically produced a strikingly mediocre frontage block but allowed himself no restraint in the trainshed. Compared with Newcastle, it was elaborately massive. The spans comprised five-centred arches, almost imperceptibly tied with slender iron rods, the tapering ribs being pierced with quatrefoil holes and projecting down below deep open-patterned cross girders like pendulous lobes, originally adorned with heavy pendant finials. The columns, thick, foliated and Corinthian, supported every third rib as at Newcastle, though the 'clasping' action of the intermediate ones on the cross girders was copied from Paddington. The bracket spandrels were solid castings decorated with the rose of York and the company's arms. The final touch was given by the curved transoms forming three crescent-shaped areas of glazing in the gable-end screens (p 103), perfectly complementary to the curves of the roof and of far greater effect than the flat-bottomed gables at Newcastle. Just as Prosser altered Dobson's frontage, so his own York work was altered by his successors, who were called on to complete it, although not so drastically. Despite this, Dobson and Prosser can be said to have set the pattern for the North Eastern's overall roof design, after a short interlude, for the next thirty years.

That interlude was provided by William Peachey. In quick succession two appointments followed Prosser's—Benjamin Burleigh (1874–6) and William Peachey (1876–7). The former seems to have done little beyond his modifications at York, but Peachey crammed at least one remarkable achievement into his short period of office—the new station at Middlesbrough. Opened in 1877, the High Victorian Gothic frontage (Chapter 6) was fully complemented by the lofty lattice-arched pointed roof. The larger of the two very unequal spans was 74ft wide and 60ft high, the greatest height in proportion to width ever used in a trainshed. Meeks attributes the engineering to W. J. Cudworth, later a divisional engineer on the NER, and calls it 'the Sainte-Chapelle of trainsheds'. South Shields (1879) was probably to Peachey's design, too, this time a light pitched roof in one broad span, again removed from the ordinary by a curve.

Thereafter the semicircular arched roof became characteristic of the North Eastern Railway's principal stations. William Bell followed Peachey and stayed with the company until the end. Although much of his work on smaller stations was of repetitive mediocrity—in which he was not alone at this period—his high arched roofs were superbly majestic. They began at Sunderland in 1879, a single span built on the retaining walls of a cutting, followed by twin spans at Darlington Bank Top in 1887, where the progress in structural ironwork was demonstrated by dispensing with intermediate ribs between the columns in favour of heavier purlins and deeper brackets to the cross girders. The spandrels enclosed coats of arms and floral work like those at York, and a small central arcade added an attractive touch.

The same year Alnwick received a new station that in many ways was a smaller edition of Darlington, though lighter and less elaborate. Bell reverted to deep diamond-patterned cross girders at Stockton in 1893 to permit even wider spacing between his columns, which were very broad and fluted at the bases. The last phase was marked by the enlargement of Hull Paragon in 1905, where much lighter roof spans on latticed steel cross girders were lifted on extensions of the columns above the capitals. By raising the point of springing, the ribs were reduced to shallow segments, necessitating very deep gable-end screens, which, as at Bell's other stations, had flat transoms and rectangular glazing. A feature of Bell's roofs was the tangential centre light-cum-ventilator lifted above the top of the ribs on iron hoops of varying size and number. On a smaller scale, this type of roof was used in 1915 for the expansive covered portion of Monkseaton station, where arched cross girders with quatrefoil decoration sprang from square Ionic columns—unusual for this late date—while the hoop motif was used in the double-pitched glass-and-steel awnings at Goole in 1912.

Some of Bell's smaller stations had overall roofs that in effect were repeats of his double-pitched style of awning, spanning the tracks between on light horizontals pierced with the favourite quatrefoils. Starbeck and Jarrow had them, the latter above earlier lean-to shelters that were left intact beneath. West Hartlepool (1880) relied on latticed girders and Whitley Bay (1910) on thicker solid girders with circular holes, and all had profusely decorated brackets, excellent examples of fine cast-iron work. Tynemouth (1882), in particular, was a riot of fancy slender columns, brackets and girders; but for grace and restrained artistry in iron the hammerbeam-type roof over the approach drive at Thornaby was probably the best example on the system.

To follow the general application of arched roof design we must return to 1854, the year in which Paddington was completed by Brunel and Matthew Digby Wyatt. Dobson's principles were followed in the main framework, with the innovation of bringing the intermediate ribs down below the cross girders in a 'clasp', which, as we have seen, Peachey copied at York. The columns were octagonal, and—a Crystal Palace touch repeated again only at Liverpool Street—two great transepts broke up the main arcades in an intricate geometrical pattern which was unique. The Crystal Palace contractors, Fox, Henderson & Co, erected the station, using ridge-and-furrow glazing on Paxton's principle. Wyatt's restrained decorative touches were highlighted by the graceful wrought iron end-screens (later replaced by conventional glazing), and the iron balcony to the office once used by Brunel, from which he could look down on his great station.

The collaboration between Brunel and Wyatt marked the beginning of the end; henceforth the two disciplines started to diverge on different, and not always harmonious, lines. Trainshed and frontage buildings were frequently designed separately with little regard for each other; when one man was responsible for both, invariably he was the engineer. In 1854 two new stations were completed with iron roofs quite different from any previously constructed. One was the segmental arched roof at Fenchurch Street by George Berkeley, the Great Eastern's engineer, which was rather short and was carried forward over the frontage block to form a giant curved pediment, replacing Tite's earlier station. It was 101ft wide and tied by prominent rods and struts. The other was a station roof of dramatic quality—E. A. Cowper's great 211ft wide crescent truss at Birmingham New Street, another Fox, Henderson job and at that time the widest single span attempted, unsurpassed until the building of St Pancras twenty years later. The trusses were extremely light and on the frontage side sprang from elegant pilasters below which ran an elegant iron balcony overlooking the platform. They formed the main noteworthy feature of Livock's building, which otherwise was considerably less impressive.

In 1855 the Leeds, Bradford & Halifax Junction Railway's Adolphus Street terminus was opened at Bradford. Like Leeds New fourteen years later, it had a Mansard-shaped roof, 100ft wide and rather flattened, behind a four-storey weak Italianate façade with a small central pediment. In 1867 it became a goods station. Experimentation continued as engineers sought to cover larger areas with their spans. In 1860 Victoria station was opened for the Victoria Station & Pimlico Railway, the sole example in this country of the 'terminal company' familiar in the United States, and the London, Brighton & South Coast Railway used it first, their portion having a new kind of shed, whose spans formed a series of transverse 50ft wide pitched roofs, hipped at the sides, on deep triangular-trussed girders. Two years later the London, Chatham & Dover arrived, and for them a separate station was built alongside, though there was no communication through the dividing wall; it was left to the Southern Railway to make this in 1924. The Chatham's roof, by Sir John Fowler, comprised a pair of handsome segmental arches of latticed ribs tied by radial struts to tie rods formed in a shallow arc. The old Brighton side roof was renewed in 1904-8 by four conventional laterally pitched sheds, ugly and heavy on deep latticed girders, but the Chatham's roof remained, to be repeated on a smaller scale in one span at Ramsgate Harbour station in 1863. These roofs were two of the few impressive architectural features on a line not noted for its stations.

In the thirty years from 1860 to 1890 the potential of the arched roof for covering great widths was exploited fully. Sir John Hawkshaw built spectacular lofty crescent trussed roofs at Charing Cross and Cannon Street for the South Eastern Railway in 1864 and 1866 respectively, the latter's skyline punctuated at the outer end by the well known pair of Baroque towers overlooking the river. At this period the Great Western constructed a low, very shallow crescent roof for its new station at Worcester Shrub Hill (1865), and probably about the same time at Penzance (p 103), in replacement of Brunel's wooden sheds. Elliptical roofs without ties characterised the Metropolitan Railway's stations on its 'cut-and-cover' line (1863–8), where the retaining walls formed ideal supports; examples were Faringdon, King's Cross, Notting Hill Gate and Kensington High Street, with attractive fan-like glazing bars in the gable screens. Elliptical roofs were attractive in their own right, particularly when built on a gentle curve like William Baker's pair at the third Liverpool Lime Street (1867). Each was 200ft wide and on a bright day made a splendidly contrasting vista against the gloom of the deep rock cutting beyond.

Arched roofs without ties were essentially functional and, on rare occasions when the designers could bring themselves to eschew needless decoration—in the King's Cross idiom—effectively produced an impression of spacious lightness. The ribs of the Midland's Bath station at Green Park (1870) in fact carried a pitched roof with balancing arches to the side arcades and the cross platform behind the buffers, completely devoid of decoration. Its complete contrast to the frontage was in a way a prelude to St Pancras (1874), where W. H. Barlow and R. M. Ordish designed vast, latticed, pointed arches, 243ft wide. They have, of course, been frequently described elsewhere and need no further praise here. In 1878 the new Great Western and Midland joint station was completed at Bristol (Chapter 6), the pointed arch roof overshadowing Brunel's original Temple Meads station; the new station lacked the sweep of St Pancras but its sharply curved site created its own emphasis.

As Curzon Street was the counterpart of Euston on the London & Birmingham Railway, so Manchester Central (1880) was complementary to St Pancras on the Midland, although it was only partly owned by the latter company, being the property of the joint Cheshire Lines Committee, in which the Great Northern and the Manchester, Sheffield & Lincolnshire were the Midland's partners. The station proper was very similar to St Pancras, having a very slightly pointed arched roof springing directly from the platforms, only 30ft narrower

(210ft) than St Pancras's, and also built on brick arches with goods sidings beneath. Even the gable screens were similar, but decorated with a frilly valance along the curved edges and, at the outer end of the station, with a bottom transom broken by three shallow arcs where the tracks entered (p 103). The similarity ended with the frontage, however, for Manchester Central was permanently endowed with a 'temporary' wooden one. Liverpool Central, at the other end of the Cheshire Lines system, dated from 1874, and had a five-centred arch with lighter latticed ribs, tied like the Chatham's roof at Victoria by arc-shaped rods and radial struts that were reflected in the gable glazing. Sir John Fowler designed them both.

In the 1880s the London & North Western built three very similar arched station roofs, two of them in Manchester. The first was erected in four spans when the joint London Road station (now Piccadilly) was enlarged in 1881–2; heavy latticed cross girders and prominent trusses obscured the shape of the curves with conflicting lines and angles. The second was at the new Exchange station in 1884, in three spans with the centre one wider than the other two. A year later the third was built as an extension of Birmingham New Street to accommodate the Midland company's trains, virtually a separate station with a carriage drive between it and Cowper's older part, which was mainly used for the North Western services thereafter. The new roof was in two spans, and once again the sharp curvature of the platforms added a stimulating dimension its Manchester counterparts lacked.

The same dramatic combination of curves was produced at Brighton when a new lofty roof was built over J. U. Rastrick's original low shed, which was then demolished. Like Bath, the ribs carried a pitched roof that gave the impression both of an arched interior and a triangular section outside. Brighton was somewhat lop-sided, two broad bays overshadowing a much narrower one. The iron column brackets carried the London, Brighton & South Coast Railway's arms, and a striking feature was the large clock suspended over the concourse, Baroque-like in its intricate wrought-iron work. The new roof, completed in 1883, was the work of H. E. Wallis. In 1887–8 the Lancashire & Yorkshire Railway rebuilt Bradford Exchange station with a short, straight double arched roof, notable for its striking fan-like glazing bars in the gables and delicate iron whorls and curves in the brackets (Plate 29). One of the oddest arched roofs was the Stockton & Darlington's at Barnard Castle (1861), a series of pointed iron ribs corbelled from the walls nearly at platform level and quaintly cruck-like in appearance.

The third roof type to be used to any extent was derived directly from Paxton's ridge-and-furrow technique but applied horizontally. The degree of prefabrication that enabled the Crystal Palace to be erected so quickly was used by the same contractors, Fox, Henderson & Co, at Oxford Rewley Road (1851–2). At first sight its wooden frontage and side cladding would occasion little favourable comment, but the transverse ridge-and-furrow roof on braced horizontal girders and side columns was an important step forward in iron-roof design. In the reconstruction of the Brighton's station at London Bridge begun in 1853, the most outstanding features were the strong clean lines of the shed, which consisted of a lofty arched crescent-trussed hall in the centre flanked on each side by transverse ridge-and-furrow roofing with hipped ends on broad latticed main girders, and slender elliptical cross-girders with fragile ironwork in the bracket spandrels. The Furness Railway platforms at Carnforth (probably 1867), Carlisle Citadel (1881)—by Blythe & Cunningham and 'glazed on Rendel's Patent Indestructible System'—and the third roof at Stoke-on-Trent (1893) followed the Oxford pattern on a larger scale. They were low and unimpressive, quickly darkened by smoke. Carlisle had a set of remarkable end screens, deep with Gothic-shaped glazing bars to tone with Tite's frontage building. Rather unusually the Great Western adopted the same roof style at Plymouth Millbay, probably when it was reconstructed in 1902. After Hawkshaw's arched roof at Charing Cross collapsed in 1905 it was replaced by the same dull pattern of ridge-and-furrow on steel girders, and at the rebuilding of Waterloo between 1909 and 1922 a good many uninspiring acres of ridge-and-furrow were put up. Such roofing was useful for covering small or irregular areas outside a main roof—concourses, *porte cochères* and cab drives—and it was used in these ways at Leeds Wellington and Birmingham New Street.

The Great Eastern Railway's Bishopsgate terminus (formerly Shoreditch) had become outgrown by the mid-1860s, and to replace it a large—at the time considered by some too large—new station was built at Liverpool Street. It was finished in 1874–5. The company's engineer, Edward Wilson, was responsible for the whole design and for his trainshed he produced a series of vast, immensely high pitched roofs, in which much broader than usual spans were achieved by using very light trusses with curved ties, producing an elliptical effect in the interior which was heightened by shaped spiky-frilled valancing at the open outer ends in place of the more usual gable screens. The thrust of the main spans was taken by double rows of slender columns, with arcades of deep brackets containing filigree ironwork in their spandrels. The entire effect of tall columns, ridge-and-furrow arcades and airy steep-pointed aisles and transepts terminating in pointed-arched side walls was wholly Gothic, but Gothic of a special kind. With most of the roof glazed, when clean it gave the impression of something between an iron cathedral and a vast Victorian greenhouse. Nothing quite like it had ever been attempted before and it remained unique, transcending even Paddington.

High pitched roofs of lesser aesthetic quality were built by the Lancashire & Yorkshire company at Liverpool Exchange (1886-8), with a transverse shed over the cab drive, and at Blackburn (1888), but they were utilitarian structures, like the Great Central's roof at Marylebone on the last main line into London (1899). The only station to approach the airy spaciousness of Liverpool Street was the same company's Nottingham Victoria, owned jointly with the Great Northern and opened in 1900. A broad central span was flanked by two narrower ones, the light steel curved ties and diagonal struts giving emphasis to the robust lattice work in the elliptical cross girders. It was almost the last great station roof in the United Kingdom, and made a fitting conclusion to nineteenth-century structural engineering.

Designers went on experimenting until large overall roofs began to fall into disfavour in place of cheaper, more easily maintained awnings at the beginning of the new century. A remarkably light roof was used by the Midland for their joint station with the North Eastern Railway at Ilkley in 1887, comprising four pitched bays carried on light horizontal girders and columns, fairly low but glazed all over to give ample light. The design was used again at Bradford Forster Square (1889-90), there being two bays to each span between side walls and a central row of columns. Then when a new station was built at Leicester London Road in 1892, a loftier example covered two broad platforms and three tracks in one span of three bays, a tribute to its lightness and the use of steel.

When the high-level through platforms at Manchester Victoria were reconstructed in 1881, massive transverse roof bays were built right across the broad island platforms and the intervening through lines later used by the North Western trains to and from Exchange. The deep girders were perforated in floral patterns, from which sprang

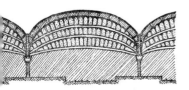
(a) Prosser's York, NER

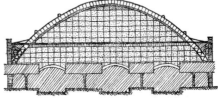
(b) Fowler's Manchester Central, CLC

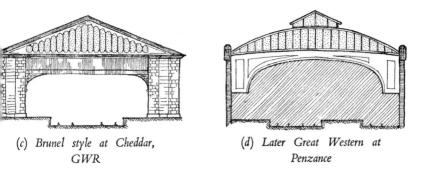

(c) Brunel style at Cheddar, GWR

(d) Later Great Western at Penzance

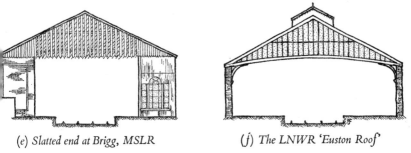

(e) Slatted end at Brigg, MSLR

(f) The LNWR 'Euston Roof'

Six overall roof screens

curved ribs with straight-pitched glazing laid on them tangentially, rising to a flat top closed by narrow ridge-and-furrow work running at right-angles. It was an extraordinary combination of structural styles and principles, and exceedingly cumbersome. By contrast there were two bays of more conventional curved pointed-arch roofing over the low-level terminal platforms, to which in 1904 two more were added, wider, longer and straight pitched but unusually curved at the apex to complement the arc of the ties.

The London & South Western, of all companies, built one of the most compellingly original overall roofs in these later years, at Bournemouth Central (1885). It was monumental, its massive skyline on deep latticed girders tied to high screen walls by unusual horizontally diagonal braces, curving down on huge elaborate brackets to supporting buttresses (Plate 30). The buttresses were repeated on the outside of the walls, which formed the only façades, capped by stone pediments with narrow lancet windows between. The roofing itself comprised a series of lateral, shallow ridge-and-furrow clerestories, and the great height compelled the addition of deep, prominent, glazed end screens, each in three sections.

Reconstruction of Shrewsbury joint station in 1903–4 produced an even more massive transverse roof than Manchester Victoria, without the advantage of height to reduce the cumbersome effect. Giant latticed girders spanned the whole width of the station, roughly equalling in depth the distance between the platform and the lowest horizontal. They carried pitched glazing on lighter arched lateral spans, forming a complex of steelwork akin more to the art of the bridgebuilder.

The last large through station rebuilt was Birmingham Snow Hill, 1909–14, by the Great Western. Like Leicester London Road and the two Nottingham stations that preceded it, the plan was based on a pair of wide island platforms with one set of rails along each outer face and four in the middle, the centre pair for goods trains passing through the station. Transverse shallow-pitched bays, covering only the platforms and side tracks, were carried on latticed girders and square iron columns with Ionic capitals; the centre section was left open to the air, where the glazing was terminated by elliptical frilly valancing, corresponding with the ends of the bays over the side walls and the general style of the platform buildings.

Plate 17   G. T. Andrews' original frontage block at Hull Paragon,
York & North Midland Railway, in 1966

Page 105

Plate 18   Contrast at Richmond (Yorks), where Andrews chose
medieval Gothic: the entrance arcade in 1966

Plate 19 Subdued Tudor by J. W. Livock at Thrapston Bridge Street,
London & Birmingham Railway, in 1954. Note the tastefully discreet
platform canopy

Page 106

Plate 20 Livock's ebullient Jacobean frontage at Tamworth, Trent
Valley Railway, in 1958, but spoiled by the mutilated arcade

CHAPTER 6

PLANS AND LAYOUTS

AFTER the first years of success the external aspect of many of its stations became a secondary consideration to a railway company, and after more years to some it became barely a consideration at all. But a good deal of attention was given to the arrangement of platforms and, in the majority of cases, the accommodation for passengers. It has been observed that the first important terminals, Liverpool Crown Street and Manchester Liverpool Road, had only one platform, adjoining the station building, the most obviously simple arrangement for dealing with a relatively small number of trains terminating and starting their journeys. We have also seen how Brunel adapted the same plan at his through stations, such as Reading and Taunton, a more difficult operation as most trains continued elsewhere and the long single platform had to be able to accommodate two trains travelling in opposite directions; and how he solved it by building separate 'up' and 'down' buildings, each with its own set of offices and appointments, central crossover roads being provided to allow trains to use each end of the platform more or less independently. Francis Thompson used the same plan at Derby and Cambridge but instead of two buildings he provided one long one, copied at Huddersfield, Ipswich and other centres. As traffic increased, the conflicting train movements at the central crossover created bottlenecks and soon separate 'up' and 'down' platforms were found to be essential. Gradually the single-sided stations had extra platforms added or were completely rebuilt, although some lasted a surprisingly long time, and Cambridge is with us still.

Separate entrance and exit ways to the platforms were generally provided at the important stations and, once inside, separate accommodation for the classes. This rigid demarcation meant that waiting rooms for each sex had to be doubled or tripled. First-, second- and third-class rooms were quite usual, and at the most important places first- and third-class refreshment rooms, too—the second class generally paid first-class prices—so that the reason for vast ranges of buildings at the large stations can be understood.

The one-sided terminus was quickly found to have disadvantages when more platforms were needed. Either the arriving or the departing passenger had to walk some distance from the entrance to his train, or, worse, walk across the lines. The 'head' station was seen to offer greater convenience, and early examples like Curzon Street at Birmingham, Nine Elms and Brighton were contemporary with side terminals like Hull and Scarborough. Paddington was really a combination, as its buildings were built alongside the main departure platform and the other one had to be reached by a retractable drawbridge across the lines. There was no direct connection with the arrival platform at all, which in effect was like a separate station. It is doubtful if this arrangement was ever really convenient, though it was not changed for very many years.

The 'head' station, which has become so familiar, had the building erected across the head of the platforms behind the buffer stops, with a cross-platform between. At his York terminus G. T. Andrews enlarged on the idea by extending his building partly down each side in a squared 'U' plan. A few side termini became through stations when lines were extended: the end was removed from the Midland station at Lincoln St Marks in 1849 when the Manchester, Sheffield & Lincolnshire Railway connected with it; and when the London & South Western finally reached Plymouth in 1891 they did so from the former terminus at Devonport Kings Road.

In a way, Euston and King's Cross were hybrids. They were basically side terminals with a large screen across the head of the platforms to form a frontage—at King's Cross the end wall with the famous curved roof sections and clock turret. At Euston the frontage was formed by the great arch, quite separate from the platforms, through which cabs entered for the departure platform. The entrance for the arrival platform was between the easterly pair of flanking lodges, the western pair giving on to open land reserved for future expansion, soon to be needed. Euston grew indiscriminately, like so many others but rather worse, culminating in a hotchpotch of sheds on three sides of P. C. Hardwick's Great Hall, though separate arrival and departure sides were maintained until the reconstruction of the 1960s. The first

Liverpool Lime Street also had a detached screen wall and arches forming its frontage, but with buildings built along both platforms to form in plan a balanced layout.

Most early large stations, the termini in particular, had carriage sidings between the two platform roads. Derby, King's Cross and Manchester London Road were like this—even St Pancras, as late as 1868, had them—but as more platforms were needed they were removed and separate carriage sheds built further out.

Of all the great stations, the greatest maze was presented by Waterloo before the twenty years of rebuilding was started in 1902. The butt of music-hall comedians, it was notorious for the ease with which passengers could lose themselves. They were not helped by another station of the same name across the road belonging to the South Eastern and connected by a footbridge, not to mention the three, at one time separate, underground stations and the London Necropolis Company's private establishment nearby (Chapter 11), all called Waterloo. The South Western and South Eastern stations were also connected by a single line running right across the concourse of the main station as a sort of continuous level crossing and out through a hole in the wall on to a bridge over Waterloo Road. Mercifully it was little used and was removed when the new station was built.

The Bristol stations of the Great Western and Bristol & Exeter companies were built at right-angles to each other, quite separate until new platforms were built on the curved connecting line. Brunel's elevated Great Western terminus was entered at one side through booking offices beneath the departure platforms, and there was a corresponding way out on the arrival side. The company's general offices were at the outer end behind the Tudor façade, on four floors extending over the buffer stops. The Bristol & Exeter's terminus was the poor relation—one of Brunel's wooden sheds—though the imbalance was somewhat redressed when S. C. Fripp built a detached Jacobean block of offices in 1852. The shed was done away with during the enlargement of the station, completed in 1878, when additional platforms were built on the curve beneath an overall roof (Chapter 5). The Great Western terminal platforms were retained and the station thus had distinct but connected terminal and through sections. A similar feature, though very different in layout, marked the Victoria and Exchange stations at Manchester.

As side stations grew in size, problems arose in getting cabs in and out. At the departure side they could drop their passengers outside the booking office, but ingress and egress on the arrival side created congestion as traffic increased, a problem which was solved at Paddington and Euston by constructing bridges over the arrival lines at the other ends of the stations, and at Charing Cross and Manchester Exchange by a subway, so leaving the main entrances clear. Meanwhile, at the 'head' stations, the early notion of distinct entrances and exits to the platforms was gradually abandoned, a trend accelerated by the growing use of the same platforms for arrivals and departures, particularly where there was heavy suburban or short-distance traffic. The cross-platform was enlarged to become a concourse or circulating area, where, as the name implies, incoming and outgoing passengers mingled. Booking offices, waiting and refreshment rooms and staff accommodation were arranged around the perimeter, and the flow of passengers was regulated by a barrier at the end of each platform.

The first stations to have island platforms were some of the early junctions, where they were found to be space-saving and simple for cross-platform interchange. Normanton (1840) and Swindon (1841) were built to this plan, with a large block of buildings on each platform housing identical accommodation. A subway and footbridge connected the Swindon platforms and a footbridge at Normanton, both extended to street entrances at one side. Adaptations at other stations, not originally junctions, often led to cramped conditions. At Eastleigh and Doncaster outer faces were added to the platforms, thus severing frontage buildings from the street and, at Eastleigh, necessitating the construction of an awkward swivel bridge for luggage. The rebuilding of many large provincial stations in the closing quarter of the century saw a revival of the island platform plan when both through and terminating traffic had to be provided for. Darlington Bank Top, Rugby Midland and Leicester Central each comprised one very wide island platform with bay platforms let into each end, lines for non-stopping trains passing along the sides clear of the station altogether. Leicester London Road, Nottingham Midland and Victoria, and Birmingham Snow Hill all had two broad spacious island platforms with bays at one or both ends. The tunnel at the London end of Snow Hill necessitated a separate terminal station at Moor Street (1909) to serve in effect as the southern bay platforms.

Full advantage was taken of rebuilding to ease the flow of passengers as well as trains. Large entrance buildings with amply covered cab drives were built on road bridges at one end of the stations, where spacious, lofty booking halls gave on to broad staircases leading down to platforms long enough for two trains apiece. Through trains and goods trains used separate tracks outside or down the middle, clear of the platforms. Crewe in its final form in essence comprised three great island platforms, and all the stations on the London Extension of the Great Central, large and small, were built on the same principle, Carrington and Arkwright Street in Nottingham being the only exceptions.

Because there were so many smaller stations, the variety in their layout was enormous, and a short selection of typical types and oddities will have to suffice. Many factors, of which geography and traffic were only two, entered into the layout: relationship between the railway route and the place served, convenience of road approaches, engineering works to avoid or perhaps a junction to consider—all influenced the final form, not to mention accidents of history and the money available at the time. The standard concept of a station is a platform with a building containing the necessary rooms and offices adjoining it in the middle. Less usual is one with the building separated from the platform by an open perambulating space, such as existed at some of the Newcastle & Carlisle Railway's stations (Chapter 3). This plan was usually the result of adding platforms where none originally existed, and often the building remained at ground level beyond the platform end, connected to it by a short path sometimes but not always fenced off from the rails. Topcliffe, Pipe Gate and Foleshill were three widely scattered examples, the last actually rebuilt in this fashion. Stogumber, Wickham Bishops, Worthington and Neen Sollars were among a number of single platform stations where the main station building was across the line, and reached by a footway. Staggered platforms were not uncommon on double lines, usually on opposite sides of a level crossing or sometimes a bridge. The South Eastern Railway was especially partial to them.

At first the railways tried to locate stations where the line was level with the surrounding land, so that they could be built with little difficulty, but engineers soon realised that a cutting or embankment could be used to advantage by placing the entrance building on a road overbridge or adjacent to an underbridge with stairs to the platforms. A station in a cutting could on occasion result in a building reaching up, so to speak, from the platform, two or more storeys high, with the entrance on the top floor, as found at Roade, Gravelly Hill and North Rode. The reverse applied at Ash Vale, Mansfield Central and Shifnal, which all had buildings three or more storeys high, with ground-level entrances and several flights of stairs to the platforms above. As the century progressed some companies built long sloping ramps instead of stairs, an economical measure that saved the cost of a separate luggage lift or the inconvenience of a crossing. The Lancashire & Yorkshire Railway's subway ramps and those from overbridges down to island platforms on the North Eastern between Copmanthorpe and Church Fenton were good examples.

Most two-platform wayside stations had one thing in common—the dominance of the main building on one side over the subsidiary building on the other, which was often little more than an open-fronted shelter. This contrast in sizes was extreme at Betws-y-Coed, where a rambling two-storey stone building complete with refreshment room (for the tourist traffic) faced a London & North Western standard wooden shelter. It was in fact exceptional to find opposing buildings which balanced—though some of the same company's better wooden buildings did—and very often equal-length awnings at a suburban station tended to mask the unequal sizes of the structures beneath. But when a station was designed all of a piece, careful matching could be done despite differences in size. The London & South Western's Frimley and Bagshot stations were excellent examples, as were the stations on the Maidstone–Ashford line of the London, Chatham & Dover, and on the Settle & Carlisle line of the Midland.

Subsidiary buildings and awnings, even the main building, were sometimes built against an adjoining goods shed. At Blythe Bridge the North Staffordshire company extended the goods-shed roof down over the adjoining wooden waiting-room to form a lean-to roof; a waiting room formed an integral part of the wooden goods shed at Newton Kyme on the North Eastern; and at Midge Hall and Rishton on the Lancashire & Yorkshire the main station buildings were built back-to-back with the goods shed, the combined buildings at the latter even including the stationmaster's house.

The earlier chapters in this book have shown that most of the smaller station buildings of the first half of the nineteenth century combined offices with domestic quarters for the stationmaster on the upper floor. When the line was on an embankment, the order could be reversed. Upside-down buildings could be seen at Penkridge and Launton on the London & North Western system, Summerseat on the Lancashire & Yorkshire, Kew Bridge and Portchester on the South Western and Walcot on the Shrewsbury & Wellington Joint line. Even odder, the three-storey platform building at Hornsea Bridge on

the North Eastern Railway was built over the coal drops, the rail
wagons running in under the waiting room. The booking office was
in a separate building across the yard. The booking office was similarly
detached at Crowle Central, where it was across a bridge spanning a
Lincolnshire dyke alongside the railway; at Wilpshire, where it was
placed on the end of the footbridge halfway down a footpath from
the road; and at Sandhills, where it sat on a landing halfway up a
wooden staircase built on the side of the viaduct supporting the
platforms.

More often a draughty passageway had to suffice for the purchase
of tickets—in cold glazed tiles at Dinsdale or behind an open stone
Gothic screen at Thorp Arch. On occasions booking offices served
other purposes, too. The booking clerk at Penmaenpool issued tickets
for the Cambrian Railways' toll bridge across the Mawddach, while
Redbridge station accommodated the pay office for the London &
South Western wagon works next door. But economy in booking
offices was not always important and it is surprising how often a
relatively small station would have two. The London & North Western
in particular was generous in this respect. Cannock was one example,
probably because there was no way of crossing the line except by
going round by road under the bridge. They were also indicative of
the traffic this station once handled, which was the reason for Wilmslow
having as many as three booking offices.

One or two examples have already been given of existing buildings
taken over for a station when the railway arrived. The observant
passenger entering the Great Western's station at Staines West might
have remarked on the similarity between the booking hall and the
entrance hall of a villa of, say, the late 1840s. The station was opened
in 1855 and the convenient house of the manager of a mustard mill
was acquired for a station building. Similarly, at Mitcham, probably
one of the oldest buildings on a railway was used: its unassuming
Georgian aspect suggested the house of a small town merchant in a
middling way of business, with his dwelling rooms on the upper
floors and offices flanking the covered cartway below leading to a yard
at the rear. The Surrey Iron Railway (1803) passed its door and
possibly used it, but it was not taken over by the Wimbledon &
Croydon Railway—later part of the Brighton company—until
1855.

Always thrifty, the Eastern Counties Railway used a fine old
Georgian mansion at Enfield for a station when it opened a branch to

the town in 1849. Likewise, for its Newcastle terminus, the Blyth & Tyne Railway (1864) adapted Picton House in New Bridge Street— a dignified commodious house built by John Dobson in the early 1820s. By far the oldest building in railway use, and the best known, was The Red House at Bourne, which dated to the early seventeenth century and reputed to have been the home of Sir Everard Digby of Gunpowder Plot fame. The Great Northern built its station alongside in 1860, taking over the house for a booking office and surely the grandest of all stationmasters' residences. Likewise the Court House at Barnsley, built by Reeves in 1861, served for judicial purposes for only nine years. It was taken over by the Midland Railway and named Court House station in 1870, though its Italian Renaissance frontage and Royal Arms were left undisturbed, and a wooden trainshed was built alongside at first-floor level.

Stations at branch-line junctions would normally be provided with one or two short bay platforms for branch trains; otherwise it was necessary to shunt the branch trains on to sidings until one of the main-line platforms was clear. Sometimes the branch platform would have an overall roof—even though the main platforms had not—that would form a carriage shed for the train. Tebay, Oxenholme, Three Bridges and the Northampton platform at Blisworth had them.

A good number of junction stations were built in the fork of the lines, 'V'-shaped in plan, but Ashchurch was triple-forked with single branch platforms curving away on both sides of the main line. Differences in levels led to awkward layouts, too: at Colbren Junction on the Neath & Brecon Railway and Buildwas on the Great Western, for instance, one platform was higher than the other. At some stations the main and branch platforms might be some distance apart. A covered way joined them at Stonehouse Bristol Road, but at Ashby-de-la-Zouch passengers changing for the Melbourne line were faced with a walk across the goods yard and along a footpath. Really rare were stations with continuous platforms on three sides of a triangular junction. There were only two, Ambergate and Queensbury, the more remarkable in that both were built on viaducts. Ambergate, the Midland's third and final station there, had wooden platforms and buildings. Queensbury, over 750ft above sea level, was the junction between the Great Northern's alpine lines between Bradford, Halifax and Keighley and was unique in having its platforms connected by a footbridge, a subway and a footcrossing. Earlestown, though having platforms on all three sides of a triangular junction, could not truly be called a triangular station, since the platforms for the Manchester–Warrington trains were quite separate and joined to the others by a footpath. Just to add to the complications, the triangle was neatly bisected by a single line branch to Haydock Colliery that crossed the main Liverpool–Manchester line on the level.

The prospect of mutually advantageous business where two companies' lines crossed often led to stations being built close together for the exchange of passengers. The London & North Western and Great Central crossed at Shotton and at Hope Exchange, at both of which high- and low-level stations were built, connected by footpath and stairs; Builth Road had similar LNW and Cambrian stations, as had Minffordd on the Cambrian and the narrow gauge Festiniog Railway. Some were actually built at right-angles, one above the other, with the high-level station on the bridge, like Hengoed (Brecon & Merthyr and Great Western), Tamworth (LNW and Midland), Middlewood (LNW and Great Central & North Staffordshire Joint) and Dukeries Junction. Most of them, even if they did not actually serve a town or village, had access for whatever local population there might be, but Dukeries Junction was built purely for exchange traffic and simply comprised platforms on the bridge carrying the Lancashire, Derbyshire & East Coast Railway over the platforms on the Great Northern main line below (Plate 31). The public were catered for by the companies' respective stations at Tuxford not far away.

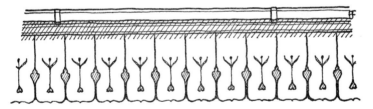

LBSCR valancing, with floral design, East Grinstead

High- and low-level stations were also found under the ownership of the same railway. When the Brighton built its Oxted–Haywards Heath line in 1882, it ran under its earlier line from Three Bridges to Tunbridge Wells at East Grinstead where a 'T'-shaped station was opened, an existing station on the high-level line being closed a year later. The London & North Western had several stations of this kind: Dudley Port, Lichfield Trent Valley and Warrington Bank Quay, although there were also 'town' stations at Dudley, Lichfield City and Arpley. Willesden Junction developed into what was really three stations in one, the Low Level main line station, the High Level for the North London trains and the so-called 'New' station used by the Watford electrics and the Bakerloo line.

Railways crossed on the level at a number of places, but adjoining stations were only built at one—Highbridge, where the Somerset & Dorset Joint Railway intersected the Great Western. Dorchester South suffered from a most peculiar arrangement, purely historical. The up platform was built on a short terminal spur to the goods yard, and dated from 1847, when it had been regarded as a temporary terminus by the original Southampton & Dorchester Railway and as the jumping-off point for Exeter. When two years later a connecting line was opened from a point just short of the station to the nearby Wilts, Somerset & Weymouth Railway, in order to allow through running to Weymouth, a separate down platform was built on the sharp curve almost at right-angles to the older platform to which up trains had to reverse. The company by this time had passed into the ownership of the London & South Western, which eventually reached Exeter by a more direct route through Salisbury and Yeovil. Neither the South Western nor the Southern Railway improved the layout at Dorchester, and it was left to British Railways to build a new up platform on the curve opposite the down in 1970.

The often decisive influence of geography on a railway received very little attention until 1962, when Professor J. H. Appleton in his *Geography of Communications in Great Britain* observed that 'railways often have to be content with what is left over after the requirements of other land users have been met'. This restriction was particularly apparent in the string of curious stations on the Lancashire & Yorkshire Railway's main line as it descended the twisting narrow gorge of the Yorkshire Calder from Summit Tunnel to Sowerby Bridge. By 1841, when the railway came, precious little space had been left in the upper reaches by the river, road, the Rochdale Canal and industry. The first station was Walsden, where the main building in effect formed the end house of a dark stone-built terrace, typical of the district, backing on to the up platform and fronting the parallel main road. Because Todmorden, $1\frac{1}{4}$ miles further down, was a junction, a refreshment room was deemed necessary when the station was rebuilt in 1865, but, as space was limited, the landlord of the Queen Hotel opposite contracted to open a refreshment room on his first floor, level with the platforms, to which it was connected by a footbridge across the intervening road (Plate 32).

The next station, Eastwood (1841), was built on a shelf above the valley. The platforms were low, barely above rail level, narrow in the extreme, and staggered on either side of a level crossing reached by a steep road. There was no space for platform structures, so the station offices were built into the hillside on the opposite side of the road which, after crossing the line, turned sharply parallel to it. The station existed in this primitive form for over a century, until closure in 1951.

Hebden Bridge originally was fairly normal, but was rebuilt c 1906 with staggered platforms connected by a subway oddly reached by stairs on one side and a ramp on the other. Mytholmroyd was partly built on a viaduct with a three-storey building alongside, taller than it was long, containing five flights of stairs. The platforms were connected by a wooden subway slung beneath one of the arches. At Luddendenfoot the station offices were set at right-angles to the platform along the approach road.

The valley widens at Sowerby Bridge, junction for the Leeds and Bradford lines, affording the LYR a chance to spread itself when it replaced the original station with a new one on a larger site in 1876-9. An imposing range of two-storey stone buildings, 'L'-shaped in plan, faced the broad approach. After traversing the booking hall, the passenger entered a spacious glass-roofed concourse, but facing him was not the expected array of platforms—simply a garden. The four main platforms were to the left along the foot of the 'L', while on his right hand, out in the open, a miserable bank of cinders edged with sleepers, one coach long, did duty as the platform for the Rishworth push-and-pull trains. It was added in 1907, before which these trains had to back out of the main station and reverse on to the branch.

CHAPTER 7

HIGH VICTORIAN

CHRONOLOGICALLY this record may appear to move back and forth too often, but the styling of Victorian architecture was like that. Neither before nor even in our own time have such comprehensive changes affecting the whole of a society's activities taken place in so short a period. As a result, artistic and aesthetic values were confused by the sheer speed of technological progress. The development and decline of what we call Victorian architecture happened in a mere seventy odd years; inevitably such stages in this process as can be defined overlapped and intermingled. It has been suggested that the Gothic of the Houses of Parliament was thirty years before its time. Equally the classicism of a building like the Harris Library at Preston (1882–93), described by Pevsner as 'almost unbelievably late for its style', can be thought of as forty years behind. Wide variety of this kind was part of the essence of Victorian building and gives it fascination today.

Another part was the belief in stylistic eclecticism—'the peaceful co-existence of styles'*—which was the direct opposite of classical and Gothic purism. In it, all styles could mingle provided that in the eye of the designer they did not clash. Eclecticism was the principal feature of what has become known as High Victorian, with its free rendering of Italian, French, Gothic and classical, followed by the Domestic Revival of the last decades of the nineteenth century, merging into the pomp and circumstance of the so-called Edwardian. High Victorian is a quality which eludes definition, though Robert Furneaux Jordan in *Victorian Architecture* (1966) categorised its negative aspects: it was neither pure engineering in iron and glass (although this was strongly

* Sir John Summerson. *Victorian Architecture: Four Studies in Evaluation* (1970)

associated with it in stations, of course), strivings to imitate 'authentic' Gothic or classical forms, nor the Arts and Crafts movement of the final years. It began about 1850 and flourished around 1860 to 1890. For the purposes of this chapter the term is taken out of its strict architectural context and used to include its direct derivatives up to about 1910 and some of the activities generated in the period, such as the development of seaside resorts.

Whatever other reactions it may have induced, High Victorian architecture demanded attention by its richness, brashness, ostentation and, where all else failed, sheer bulk. It was the natural product of an era of unprecedented technical and commercial self-confidence, a time when the railways were a power in the land, monopolising transport and collectively the largest employer of labour. Amalgamations and absorptions ('take-overs') were forming large multi-million pound organisations and although profits at best were generally moderate, often distinctly low, intense competition in the second half of the century demanded high capital expenditure. The need for impressive stations was not now so much a symbol of achievement, though this was to a degree still present, but more a means of out-doing a competing line or the result of civic and commercial pressures to complement a new town hall or other public building. Simultaneously the growth of the railways' own business was an important factor. Greater emphasis was placed on comfort and speed, third-class passengers were carried in all trains, the abolition of second class was initiated; all these encouraged an increase in traffic that led to more and larger trains needing bigger stations to accommodate them.

Many of these new or reconstructed stations were recognised as reflecting the true spirit of the time. Meeks quotes the *Building News* of 1875:

> Railway termini and hotels are to the nineteenth century what monasteries and cathedrals were to the thirteenth century. They are truly the only representative buildings we possess. . . . Our metropolitan termini have been leaders of the art spirit of our time.

We have already looked at the development of the trainshed. Now we must turn to the large frontage building of the High Victorian era, its immediate forerunner, and those which came directly after.

Classical stations were dying out in the early 1850s, but not without a flourish. The two Wolverhampton stations were studies in quiet effective classicism, built as a result of direct competition. The High Level station of the London & North Western (1853) was the more elaborate, with a prominent five-bay centrepiece featuring Corinthian pilasters and a dentilled pediment containing the town's coat of arms. The Great Western and the Oxford, Worcester & Wolverhampton, not to be outdone, jointly opened their Low Level station a year later; it was more restrained, with a plain central pediment, matching miniatures over the upper windows, and projecting end blocks. It was the more remarkable for being in blue engineering brick with stone dressings, and so in the spirit of the times, and the lofty booking hall with double-tiered pilasters, cornices and decorated domed ceiling, despite being on the heavy side, made up for external simplicity. In 1854 the reconstruction of Wakefield Kirkgate station by the Lancashire & Yorkshire and Great Northern Railways produced a quietly symmetrical frontage, with a short broken parapet at each end and a low centrepiece containing a clock beneath a plain pediment. It wore a Palladian severity, but did not lack dignity. Yarmouth South Town (1859), on the East Suffolk Railway, pleased at once by its restraint and purity of line, again with central pediment, clock and, around the interior of the concourse, three tiers of handsome blind arcading.

G. T. Andrews' classical-Italianate frontage block to the original York station of 1838 (Chapter 3) contained in part the first hotel to be incorporated in a station, followed in 1851 by the Royal Station Hotel at Hull, which was built across the head of his 1848 station, similar to but grander in manner than the entrance buildings at the side. Meanwhile the great classical centre block at Huddersfield (1849) was fitted out as a hotel, one of the most handsome built by a railway. In 1854 P. C. Hardwick used the same idea at Paddington for his Great Western Hotel, in which he introduced into England a combination of French Renaissance and Baroque styling, probably its first appearance. Curved and straight Mansard roofs, a multitude of dormers, balconies and ornate brackets were set off by elaborately massive corner towers and a centre pediment sculptured by John Thomas illustrating the great Victorian beliefs in Peace, Plenty, Industry and Science. It was the largest and most luxurious hotel yet built in the country, and, although it seemed inappropriate in front of Brunel's iron trainshed, it was the first railway building that can truly be identified as High Victorian.

That same year J. W. Livock completed the four-storey office and hotel block at Birmingham New Street, in plain Italianate with an arcaded ground floor in Derbyshire stone and white brick above, two turrets providing a flourish to the roof line. Additions to the Queens

Hotel in 1911 and 1917 detracted from the original and once again it played second fiddle to the great arched roof. By 1860, French Renaissance styling had caught on when the Grosvenor Hotel was built (1860-1) as an important adjunct to the new Victoria station; but J. T. Knowles' handling, with bulging curved roofs and tremendous bulk, was coarse compared with Paddington. It was built on a corner of the Brighton company's station instead of across the head, which was occupied by a miserable wooden structure mercifully all but hidden by a large iron *porte cochère*; immediately adjoining was the Chatham company's station frontage, equally uninspiring.

The middle and late Victorian years were uncertain architecturally. Individuals might stoutly defend their preferences but collectively there were none of the fundamental concepts of earlier periods. The copying and adaptation of historic styles, the only underlying theme, led to endless argument, which still echoes today. So far as railway stations were concerned the engineers knew what they needed—bigger and better trainsheds—but no one was really sure what a station should look like from the outside. The accent was now on the vertical lines and towers started by the Paddington hotel, though it took time for London ideas to spread through the provinces. The rebuilding of Exeter St Davids in 1864, for instance, by Henry Lloyd of Bristol and Francis Fox, the Bristol & Exeter Railway's engineer, saw the replacement of Brunel's one-sided station by a single-span ridged iron and glass roof on stone side walls pierced by round-headed openings between Doric pilasters. The predominating feature of the façade was a long broken balustrade screening the roof, and punctuated by twenty-six massive stone classical urns. Stockport Tiviot Dale (1865) was built with a continuously arcaded frontage of over thirty bays, with a Dutch gabled centrepiece and projecting seven-bay arcade. The strange mixtures at Nottingham London Road (Low Level), completed in the same year, typified the trait. Large, asymmetrical and partly curved, it combined a Frenchified gable and turret; square, round-headed and Venetian windows; a highly original 'T'-shaped *porte cochère*; and Tudor-inspired diamond-patterned parapets interspersed with stone balustrading. It was even stranger that such a pile should fall into the ownership of the Great Northern, of all companies.

Amid the growing competition, a uniquely co-operative venture by fierce rivals took place at Buxton, where in 1863 the Midland and London & North Western Railways opened separate stations side by side. Each occupied an iron shed which, though strongly displaying their respective owners' characteristics within, presented to the outside world and the town of Buxton in particular a remarkable unanimity in their identical gabled end screen walls. In freestone, each contained a giant fan window, the only difference being the name of the company inscribed in gilt lettering around the circumference. The companies were doubtless coerced into collaboration. There is a strong possibility that Sir Joseph Paxton was associated with the design, if not responsible for it, not only as agent for the Duke of Devonshire, who had a financial stake in both companies and owned most of Buxton, but also as a director of the Midland. So he and the Duke were in a strong position to exert pressure.

Meanwhile the first large hotel frontages on head stations in London were being built for the South Eastern Railway at Charing Cross, opened in 1865, and Cannon Street, 1866. Both were by E. M. Barry, son of Sir Charles Barry, in the French Renaissance style now thoroughly in vogue—immensely tall, with strong horizontal lines offsetting projecting verticals and topped by lines of dormers, beneath pavilion roofs, turrets and spirelets. French influence was also marked above the cornice of the North London Railway's terminus at Broad Street (1865), a composition of elaborately crested convex and straight Mansard roofs, a recessed centrepiece and a fairly restrained Italianate façade in polychrome brick and terra-cotta. An unusual low screen wall separated the driveway from the street, spanned later by an ugly wooden footbridge.

Mills & Murgatroyd used Italianate of a somewhat cumbersome kind in 1866 for the new three-storey office frontage block at Manchester London Road, with separate iron *porte cochères* over each of the joint companies' entrances. Its commanding position at the head of a broad inclined approach gave the station an imposing appearance. In 1866 also, a remarkable series of medium-sized stations was begun by the London, Brighton & South Coast Railway, which continued for the next twenty-odd years. Denmark Hill was the first, again strongly Italianate below the cornice but with French convex roofs, built on a road bridge with distinctive round-headed glazed arcading overlooking the platforms and enclosing the stairs. Later in the same year came the completion of Groombridge and Tunbridge Wells West, in which round and square-headed openings set in variegated brick started a company fashion. Tunbridge Wells was sufficiently important to warrant a clock tower crowned by a pyramidal roof and lantern; Groombridge had only a modest turret. A smaller but more

Plate 21 William Tite's severe, practical yet dignified building at
Micheldever, London & Southampton Railway, in 1962

Page 123

Plate 22 Tite's royal entrance at Windsor & Eton Riverside in 1957,
showing the royal cipher and crown in the brickwork

Plate 23 The delicate individuality of Great Malvern, by E. W. Elmslie, for the Worcester & Hereford Railway, in 1952

Page 124

Plate 24 The beginning of Midland Railway standardisation on the Leicester–Hitchin line: Glendon & Rushton in 1961. Note the typical bargeboard and lozenge-paned windows

elaborate version was opened at Leatherhead in 1867, the turret colourfully embellished with a herringbone frieze. A gaily scalloped canopy on foliated brackets sheltered the frontage and the platforms. The ironwork and decorative touches here, at Dorking North and at Box Hill & Westhumble (both also 1867) were the work of Charles H. Driver, who built the Leicester & Hitchin stations (Chapter 4); W. Jacomb Hood was responsible for the overall design. Box Hill was charmingly French, the turret dominating tall steep roofs with patterned tiles, exposed gable timbers and a cosily arched porch on short decorated columns. All three stations were exceptionally decorative as a condition under which the Mickleham Valley landowner agreed to sell to the railway.

Another Brighton feature, a large pagoda-like wooden lantern set on top of a hipped roof and surrounded by a trellis of ornamental ironwork, appeared at Eastbourne, a station that represented the full panoply of Brighton Italianate in the Denmark Hill style with French Renaissance roofs (Plate 35). A mightily muddled composition it was, too, the lantern, which lit a spacious concourse below, having to compete with a more sophisticated edition of the Leatherhead turret complete with dentilled cornices and clock. A new building on the down side at Forest Hill in 1883 combined the lantern with the pyramidal top, and a larger lantern at the third Lewes station (1889) sat over the booking hall, Eastbourne fashion, behind a low parapet pierced with circular holes and punctuated by huge 'acorn and spike' urns. The up side of Forest Hill, incidentally, was rebuilt in 1881 by F. Dale Banister in a quite different manner, flaunting a tall Romanesque tower over an arched porch. It replaced part of the old London & Croydon station and was probably intended for the benefit of some of the top railway officials who lived in the district.

To return to the late 1860s, another Brighton product of note was Battersea Park, three storeys high and sandwiched between two bridges. It had rare sophistication, seen in the interplay between deep-set polychrome brick ground and top floor openings, plain broad string courses and shallow French-like stone-set windows on the middle floor. The keystones were decorated with flower motifs seen on the company's later lines in Sussex and at the Great Eastern's Chingford station. The lofty lantern-lit entrance hall had blind arcading and a row of pencil-thin arcaded columns down the middle, the spandrels decorated in the most extraordinary manner with classically moulded female heads in roundels (Plate 34).

The short-lived Croydon Central (1868–90) smacked of Groom-bridge, but the full development of French-Italianate as the Brighton saw it appeared at Portsmouth & Southsea, jointly owned with the London & South Western. Completed in 1876, it was a case of rags to riches. Sir Sam Fay's short history of the South Western (*A Royal Road*, 1883) described the original 1848 station as 'a miserable structure . . . the booking office and waiting room were constructed of deal boards lined with canvas; and every part of the station was of like character'. The new station could hardly have contrasted more, its two-storey centrepiece, with decorated parapet and clock, coupled pilasters between round-headed openings, and prominent cornice being matched by end projections scaled down to exact proportion. An iron *porte cochère* formed a balcony resplendent with iron balus-trading on the Denmark Hill pattern, and the lofty booking hall was lined with blind arcading above the cornice at mid-height.

In April 1873 *The Illustrated London News* commented favourably on the North London Railway's rebuilding of Camden Road, Caledonian Road & Barnsbury, Highbury & Islington, Canonbury, Hackney and Bow stations, 'substituting buildings of a handsome and commodious character in place of old wooden buildings' dating from 1850. By E. H. Horne, they were designed in a distinctive Venetian Gothic style not repeated elsewhere on the railways in England but owing something to the great *palazzo*-styled warehouses of Edward Walters in Manchester. In white Suffolk brick, Portland stone and terra-cotta, their vast barn-like interiors were enclosed by high Mansard roofs and a riot of iron cresting. A much subdued edition at Acton Central on the North & South Western Junction Railway probably indicated the North London's interest in that line. The same general fashion, far larger but much less elaborate, was somewhat surprisingly assumed by the Great Western for its second station at Birmingham Snow Hill in 1871. A company given neither to Italianate nor to overmuch elaboration, it developed instead its own type of French-styled stations (see Chapter 8). A year earlier the French-inspired Great Western Hotel, by Chatwin, had been opened in Colmore Row adjoining the station. Its strong classical overtones and the ingenious arresting zig-zag of pointed window hoods on the second floor were its distinctive features. It was not built by the railway but was acquired later by the Great Western for offices, and its symmetry was broken in 1908 when an entrance to the third Snow Hill station was driven through the ground floor.

Towers continued to be a mark of importance. Even the much maligned London, Chatham & Dover aspired to one at Herne Hill (1862), in an Italianate Gothic style that was used again at a number of its smaller stations. The rich Italianate station frontage of the West Riding & Grimsby Joint Railway (Great Northern and Manchester, Sheffield & Lincolnshire) at Wakefield Westgate (1867), designed by J. B. Fraser of Leeds, included one of the most imposing railway clock towers, 77ft high from the elevated forecourt and 97ft from the street (Plate 37). For a century it was a prominent visual and audible landmark in the city. *The Builder* tells us that the lantern on the brick tower was of cast-iron ribs surmounted by a gilded weathervane, the space between the ribs being partly filled with ornamental cast-iron plates from which hung the bell. The booking hall was graced by a wooden coffered ceiling.

Although it was bankrupt, the Chatham managed to build a second London terminus, this time with a hotel, opened in 1877. A separate company was floated to construct Holborn Viaduct station, for which Lewis H. Isaacs designed an arcaded French-Italianate front with good classical touches, imparting considerable dignity. The company made a less successful effort, architecturally and commercially, at Blackfriars (1886), by J. Wolfe Barry, the company's engineer, jointly with H. M. Brunel and W. Mills. Along with Euston and Manchester Victoria, the frontage was adorned with a list of possible destinations —here cut in the stone—which in some cases demanded the most circuitous of routes, including Baden-Baden, Constantinople and Nice, reminders of Blackfriars' unfulfilled aspirations as a station for the Continent.

Classicism was not entirely dead, as the Midland demonstrated at Bath Green Park in 1870 with a Georgian frontage building of quite outstanding merit, the complete complement to the arched iron trainshed behind (Chapter 5). Slender Ionic columns above the rusticated ground floor, balustraded parapet and excellently proportioned fenestration were well balanced by the delicate iron *porte cochère*, in all reflecting well the Georgian of Queens Square. Among stations it had no peer.

A very different hotel block was erected in 1871 by Alfred Waterhouse in front of William Baker's trainshed at Liverpool Lime Street for the London & North Western Railway. The strong vertical emphasis seen at Cannon Street and Charing Cross was apparent here, the six storeys being, as Meeks comments, quite decorous as far as the cornice. Immediately above the central entrance arch, tapered columns and balconies enlivened the window openings on the first two floors, with rather whimsical figures of a king and queen too high to distinguish. Above the cornice, however, the attic and roof erupted with rows of dormers and chimneys punctuated by four pyramidal corner towers with a slender spirelet apiece. A fragment of Tite's earlier side building remained in Lord Nelson Street.

From 1868 to 1873 a Gothic building unequalled in scale and exuberance arose in London: Gilbert Scott's Midland Grand Hotel at St Pancras. The Midland had arrived; a provincial railway newly in the capital which had not only to be known but to be seen. St Pancras was the status symbol of the Midland's achievement. The great roof has already been briefly mentioned in Chapter 5; the hotel itself may be considered magnificent, revolting or simply vulgar (I am unashamedly among those in the first category), but it cannot fail to fascinate as a whole and in its innumerable parts. There is always something new for the observant eye to see: the mosaic-like blue, orange and yellow tiles in the diamond-patterned frieze beneath the iron crenellations along the base of the roof in the train hall ('shed' cannot be justified for such a place); the lion rainwater heads in the inward cab drive, their mouths stoppered, dragons entwined around their feet; coats of arms and heads on the capitals and corbels beneath the great striped brick vault of the western tower; the delightful corbel figures of railwaymen in the booking hall, contrasting with the empty niches on the exterior which Scott was never allowed to fill; and the great 'west window' on the main staircase; these are just a few of the countless features which make the station so continuously fantastic, the highwater mark of eclecticism. There was even a sly dig at Euston in the figure of Britannia (self-assumed emblem of the London & North Western) perched on an eastern gable beneath the clock tower, her back significantly turned towards the rival company's establishment further up the road.

High Victorian Gothic—commercial Gothic—really got under way on the railways with St Pancras, closely followed by the building of the Great Eastern's new London terminus at Liverpool Street in 1875 by the company's engineer, Edward Wilson. His Gothic was uncompromising, in red brick with a bare modicum of stone dressings; and the building's unwieldly bulk was emphasised rather than relieved by the squat pointed top tower. On an awkward site, its main claim to fame was the ingenious way in which Wilson used the downward ramp to disguise the ground level below the street. When C. E. Barry added the Great Eastern Hotel in 1884, he chose pseudo Dutch Renaissance instead.

St Pancras influenced at least two major provincial stations, both built by William Peachey for the North Eastern Railway. His Middlesbrough station of 1877, in dark grey stone with free Gothic styling, was much subdued but nonetheless displayed boldness and originality. The sloping carriageway and terrace fronting it were carried on a series of low pointed arches with a pierced parapet based on Scott's arrangement, while the pointed arched roof (Chapter 5) strongly echoed Barlow's. At Sunderland (1879) a similar parapet enclosed the top of the brick *porte cochère* on the sturdily uncompromising Venetian Gothic façade, and the turreted clock tower in essence was a simplified scaled-down version of St Pancras (Plate 33).

Red brick Venetian Gothic of a much feebler stamp characterised Birkenhead Woodside (1878), probably by R. E. Johnston, the steep roof echoed by the high pointed arch of the iron *porte cochère*. The entrance building was never used for its purpose, a side entrance direct from the street to the concourse forming the inconspicuous main entrance instead. The rear screen wall inside was decorated in a garish red and cream brick, lacking the finesse of St Pancras, and the twin-arched trainshed had a skimpy look. The best feature was the well detailed woodwork in the lofty, pointed arched booking hall. The wide differences in architectural opinion as to what was a suitable railway-station style are well illustrated by comparing Woodside with another frontage built in the same year—Bristol Temple Meads. Both were Gothic in the broad sense, yet vastly different. No doubt the designer of the Temple Meads extensions was trying to identify his building with Brunel's adjacent Tudor façade, or indeed with Bristol itself; he wisely chose rock-faced local stone for his material but then indulged in such a riot of crocketed spires, turrets and ornamental cresting that *The Builder* belittled its 'Pseudo-Gothic of the commonest and most vulgar kind, utterly wanting in refinement and knowledge'. 'Who is the architect?' demanded the editor; 'The shareholders ought to know who is wasting their money.' It seems likely from the tone of this comment that he knew full well the designer was Sir Matthew Digby Wyatt, but did not care to risk a libel action.

The 1880s and 1890s saw railway architecture reach its lowest ebb in unattractive buildings like the dreary North Western Hotel at Holyhead (1880); the heavy 'Free Renaissance' of Liverpool's Exchange Hotel (1884), relieved only by columns to the windows; and the unoriginal, almost old fashioned Italianate of Manchester Exchange (1884) and Blackburn (1888), unremarkable except for their size. The well proportioned brick *porte cochère* of Stockton (1893) was dwarfed against the twin-arched trainshed to which it acted as frontage. A late classical composition at Halifax Town, with balustraded roofline, was essayed by the Lancashire & Yorkshire in 1885, who then proceeded to hide it behind platform awnings and a massive wooden entrance canopy.

Odd spots of Tudor-Gothic continued to appear, Cardiff Queen Street (1887), headquarters of the Taff Vale Railway, in particular presenting a remarkable exercise in skyline technique and eclecticism. Above a line of mullioned windows a large false gable reared up, flanked by two smaller ones, pierced by a large quatrefoil opening and interspersed with conical turrets, all capped with pinnacles and exceedingly freely decorated. At one end of this long freestone block the company's offices projected from the corner in brick Italianate with a mildly Baroque clock tower. As late as 1891 weak Tudor-Gothic was the main feature of the London & South Western's new terminus at Plymouth Friary, in rock-faced stone with pointed blind arcading to the end screen wall. With the rambling turreted Italianate of Devonport Kings Road, it symbolised Waterloo's defiant counterblast to the Paddingtonian monopoly at Plymouth.

Turrets and towers went on sprouting in profusion as the main points of relief, in many cases as though last resorts to give distinctive character. The Great Eastern's new port at Parkeston Quay (1882) demanded a grandiose station, which H. H. Poswell's building was, though unfortunately little else. As at Southport Lord Street (1884) and William Bell's Darlington Bank Top (1887), the main feature was a pyramid-topped Italianate clock tower, though at Bank Top it was set in a well proportioned arcaded frontage with Dutch gables. The classical sobriety of G. T. Andrews' Scarborough façade (Chapter 3) was shattered by the addition in 1884 of an overpoweringly tall Baroque clock tower that was a confusion of shapes and misapplied motifs. G. E. Grayson designed two of the tallest of railway station towers for the Mersey Railway at Liverpool James Street and Birkenhead Hamilton Square in crenellated Italianate with corner turrets, so large as to completely dwarf the small entrance buildings. But they were functional, housing the elevated tanks for the hydraulic lifts to the underground platforms (Plate 38). Possibly the smallest tower was at Bradford Forster Square, which the Midland rebuilt in undistinguished fashion in 1890, with an arcaded screen to the street and a low balustraded building behind punctuated by tall chimneys, taller even than the stumpy octagonal tower at the end with its minaret-style cap. The station was much overshadowed by the even less distinguished Midland Hotel. Perhaps the most fantastic clock turret of all was the pointed wooden French affair that perched so incongruously on top of the frontage awning (of all places) at Bury Bolton Street on the Lancashire & Yorkshire.

The best large railway examples of the so-called 'Free Renaissance' style were on the Great Eastern. John Wilson, son of Edward, assisted by W. N. Ashbee, rebuilt Norwich Thorpe in 1886, a textbook example of the style at its most lavish and colourful yet dignified withal. The convex pavilion roof, French centrepiece, elaborately moulded urns and pedimental clock were well displayed in deep red brick and contrasting Bath stone dressings, with classical motifs. Pilasters and a decorated coffered ceiling gave an Adamesque touch to the booking hall, which led to a spacious, well lit concourse (Plate 36). The same handsome brick *porte cochère* with four-centred arches was used to equally good effect but in a smaller, more subdued manner at Hertford East (1888), where the main building was in the very 'free' Tudor styling also adopted in the 1894 extension of Liverpool Street.

'Free Renaissance' was contemporary with, and in some cases similar to, the Domestic Revival styling which was the work of individualistic reformers like Eden Nesfield and Norman Shaw. They endeavoured to introduce the simple lines of the English vernacular into High Victorian building, the result being a strong emphasis on restraint which, however, eventually gave way to the ritzy Edwardian-Baroque of the early 1900s. Restraint certainly characterised Southampton Central, rebuilt in 1892; its banded brick gables, door and window treatment were very much in the popular new style, and it was notable for its 100ft high clock tower with ogee-shaped cupola top.

Terra-cotta and swag were favourite forms of decoration at this time, particularly with the Midland among the railways. Charles Trubshaw chose dark orange-brown terra-cotta for much of the facings at Leicester London Road (1892), a bulbous unwieldly structure featuring an immensely long *porte cochère* massively arcaded—actually in two sections on split levels, one for arrivals and one for departures —and an angled hexagonal clock tower. He used the same arcaded feature at Sheffield Midland (1904) in stone, but without a tower it looked flat and uninspiring, and the *Sheffield Telegraph* called it a splendid opportunity lost. That same year A. E. Lambert completed the rebuilding of the opulently Edwardian Nottingham Midland in dark maroon terra-cotta with heavy chunky rustication and a central turret on another large arched *porte cochère*. These three stations demonstrated well the gradual transition from Victorian to Edwardian, displaying an ostentation typical of these prosperous years yet quite foreign to the Midland Railway (St Pancras excepted). The reason behind it, of course, was competition from the Great Central Railway (formerly the Manchester, Sheffield & Lincolnshire) whose main line to London, opened in 1899, was a direct rival.

Great Central terra-cotta work, Leicester Central

The entrance to this new company's station at Leicester Central (1899) was designed on a similar plan to London Road, though smaller and quieter in scale. A brick and terra-cotta screen wall had blind arcading and a parapet carrying a rich succession of niches, urns, elliptical pediments and, seemingly perilously perched in the middle, a rather absurd looking Baroque clock turret. On the same line, Nottingham Victoria (1900), jointly owned with the Great Northern, was an imposing two-storey building in local red brick with Darley Dale stone facings; it had an elaborate, somewhat spiky French Renaissance style with Baroque touches and an asymmetrically placed Goliath among clock towers. Having exhausted its capital on the London extension, the Great Central was reduced to building a very

Plate 25   The early, simple style of Midland Railway glass-and-iron awning on one of Edward Walters' later buildings at Bakewell, the end glazing having been removed. Photographed in 1962

Page 133

Plate 26   Its more elaborate successor at Loughborough Midland in 1953, with shallow pitches and hipped ends

Plate 27 Twin-span pitched overall roof at Firsby, East Lincolnshire Railway, in 1965. The centre columns form decorative iron arcading, but the cladding above the rails has been removed and valancing fitted

Page 134

Plate 28 Separate pitched roofs over each platform at Stafford, LNWR, in 1957, modified similarly to Firsby

Plate 29   The fine arched roof at Bradford Exchange, LYR, in 1957,
with radial 'fan' glazing in the end screens

Page 135

Plate 30   Bournemouth Central's massive roof in 1962, with centre
sections removed, LSWR

Plate 31   Dukeries Junction, GNR, looking north, showing goods train passing through the high level platforms of the Lancashire, Derbyshire & East Coast Railway

Page 136

Plate 32   The curious footbridge connecting the up platform at Todmorden, LYR, to the refreshment room in the Queen Hotel opposite, in 1955

pallid insignificant new frontage at Sheffield Victoria (1908). It was a pity, for the site, at the head of a long broad approach slope, was worthy of something better. Even the low tower with its Queen Anne parapet seemed half-hearted. As it was, it was largely left to the uncompromising bulk of the Royal Victoria Hotel to proclaim the Great Central's presence.

Although completed in 1897, the Lancashire, Derbyshire & East Coast Railway's headquarters and terminus at Chesterfield Market Place was decidedly Edwardian in aspect; but Edwardian of a sober kind, with a two-storey restrained 'Free Renaissance' front and Mansard roof. This comparatively large station had a rather sad atmosphere, perhaps because its over-ambitious builders reached neither Lancashire nor the East Coast. Marylebone (1899) was the most subdued of the London termini, operationally as well as structurally, a loose assemblage of gabled bays with a low turret intervening, slightly French and quite hidden by the massively flamboyant Edwardian Jacobean of R. W. Edis' Hotel Grand Central, to which the station was joined by an extensive glazed roof. The railway company lacked the resources to build it themselves so they leased the site, but in other respects it was in effect a railway hotel.

At the turn of the century the Brighton railway finally decided to rebuild Victoria and in 1908 a large pompous Edwardian-Baroque frontage by Sir Charles Morgan replaced the old wooden one. Its prominent vertical rustication and central clock set in a huge scrolly broken pediment could not have contrasted more with its predecessor. The upper floors formed an extension to the Grosvenor Hotel, and for once *The Builder* was full of praise—anything was better than the old, of course—but again lamented the lack of an architect; Morgan had succeeded Dale Banister as the company's engineer. Not to be outdone, the Chatham next year completed a more reticent frontage next door with a marked increase in dignity. The lack of unity in the combined frontages remained as a permanent memorial to the inflexibility of Victorian railway politics.

The Lancashire & Yorkshire Railway essayed two major rebuilding projects in the first decade of the new century. Bolton Trinity Street (1903) was given a plain façade in fierce red Accrington brick behind a large iron *porte cochère*, relieved by a pair of octagonal domed cupolas and a domed pedimented clock tower. Finally, after many alterations and extensions, a new frontage block was erected at Manchester Victoria by William Dawes (1909). Like so many it was notable more for its size than style; four storeys high in ashlar, its numerous bays were broken by pilasters and heavy rustication, the long balustrade above the cornice broken by two huge curved false gables with radial rustication, and a shell-like pediment over the clock on the acute corner to Long Millgate. Massive stone columns broke up part of the long concourse, from which a lengthy subway led to the separate high-level platforms, involving a walk which, if not allowed for, could make the difference between catching and missing a train. A corner at one end of the concourse held a charming little Edwardian refreshment room, verging on the *art nouveau* in some of its detailing. It had a separate roof beneath the main station roof, with a tinted glass dome, decorated inside with liberally applied swag and supported by marble-faced columns. The walls had heavily dentilled and decorated cornices, and were lined with green tiles incorporating more swag on a mosaic frieze. As an illustration of contrasts, the refreshment rooms at Birmingham Snow Hill, which were nearly contemporary, were resplendent with heavy oak panelling and *art nouveau* coloured glass over the doors.

Touches of equal charm and greater delicacy enlivened the concourse at Hull Paragon (1904), where, in contrast to the great teak-panelled booking office in the lofty entrance hall, William Bell introduced a series of little *art nouveau* wooden offices behind the buffer stops. Their 'Queen Anne' touches were simple yet effective, and he repeated them with elaborations in the tea room built at York in 1906, complete with curved bay windows and coloured glass. The principal buildings on the down platform at Northallerton were very similar.

The culmination of Edwardian railway architecture was Waterloo, rebuilt between 1907 and 1922. As Pevsner says, it is the only twentieth-century station in London with architectural ambition, a statement made before completion of the new Euston but still holding good. The vast curving frontage by J. R. Scott, with everything—columns, arches, statuary—in giant size is so hemmed in by the South Eastern's viaduct across the road that it is impossible to stand far enough away to appreciate the whole or even the parts. The arched main entrance flanked by the goddesses of war and peace, with Britannia on the crown, is a memorial to the London & South Western employees who died in World War I.

A small but significant number of important stations were notable for their surprisingly meagre frontages, or in some cases none at all. Leeds suffered particularly, for its Central station (1851) was fronted by a mean little building with a stumpy pediment, and inside it was just as bad. If a lead had been given at Central (jointly owned by four companies, which perhaps was why one was not), it could have stimulated some competitive building in the later stations. As it was, the Midland's Wellington station had its entrance at the back of the company's Queen's Hotel, and New station, as we have noted in Chapter 5, had nothing at all. The Lancashire & Yorkshire did no better at Exchange station in neighbouring Bradford (1888), in which the Great Northern had a share; for all its fine roof it was entered from the approach by a large opening in the wall, and from the street by a smaller one at the foot of narrow stairs.

Similarly William Peachey lavished most of his attention on the roof at York (1877). The frontage, such as it was, did it no justice at all, much less the pile of the adjacent Station Hotel. There was no rival station at York, of course, and doubtless for much the same reason the majority of the principal stations on the London & North Western main line suffered accordingly. Beyond Euston it was, in fact, a line remarkable for its lack of station architecture in the grand manner. Where competition was absent or light, prestige went by the board and the 'Premier Line' was quite prepared to make do with the meanest of frontages. Self-effacement being the least of that company's virtues, economy could have been the only justification for the meagre 'hole-in-the-wall' entrances at Rugby and Stockport Edgeley, for instance, the dowdy little brick entrance buildings at Stafford, Warrington Bank Quay and Wigan North Western, and the partly timber affair at Crewe (but to me amply compensated for by that extraordinary array of bearded heads over the windows on the east side platforms). Only Preston had a façade of any consequence, and there the Lancashire & Yorkshire's separate entrance (it shared the station) was for once the more dignified of the two. Yet within these stations no expense was spared in providing spacious covered platforms and ample accommodation. The Great Northern was the same; Doncaster, its principal junction, had an entrance that gave no indication of the station's importance, or the town's, until the LNER built a new one in the 1930s.

The railway hotel was as much a part of the High Victorian scene as the great station, so to complete this review we must now look briefly at its development as a separate building. The first appears to have been the Crewe Arms (1837), though it did not come into railway ownership until the London & North Western leased and enlarged it in 1864. Like the first Crewe station, it was Jacobean in character, and the extensions were in keeping. Next came Philip Hardwick's twin hotels at Euston (1839), one on either side of the drive to the Arch and, when they were modernised and joined by a link block over the road in 1881, almost obscuring it, ruining its effect. In 1844 a small hotel was built alongside the station at Normanton, possibly by Francis Thompson, though the designer of the station itself was said to have been G. T. Andrews—a feasible combination, as the station was jointly owned by the North Midland (Thompson), the York & North Midland (Andrews) and the Manchester & Leeds. Two other important detached hotels of the early period were the North Stafford at Stoke of 1850 (Chapter 2), and the Great Northern at King's Cross (1854)—a narrow austere block set on a curve and overshadowing the west side of the station. From 1860 the railway hotel boom set in and many more were built. One of particular interest was the Great Eastern Hotel at Harwich (1864), in Free Italianate by Thomas Allom, which, after the transfer of much of the company's Continental traffic to Parkeston Quay, became the town hall.

Where only a forecourt intervened between station and hotel an open-sided covered way might connect the two. The covered way between Manchester Central and Charles Trubshaw's monstrous brown terra-cotta Midland Hotel actually crossed the street and electric trams passed beneath it. The Park Hotel at Preston, a vast red brick edifice by Arnold Mitchell (1882) on a bluff overlooking the Ribble, and one of the best located inland railway hotels, was connected by a covered way and footbridge direct to the station platforms.

The railway actually ran into the Zetland Hotel at Saltburn (1861), though not very far. This pleasant seaside watering place was a child of the railway, owing its development to Henry Pease, ironmaster and director of the Stockton & Darlington, and the station mirrored the character of the growing town. Probably by Prosser but in the style of Andrews, the arched centrepiece, Doric pilasters and bold entablature of the station were in fine harmony with the square it occupied, ranking with Stoke and Huddersfield in this respect. The main platform continued into what was virtually the back door of William Peachey's hotel, the final section having a delightful glass-and-iron roof with classical detailing.

Saltburn was one of the first of many seaside towns created by the coming of the railway. The growth of Southport was stimulated by four separate lines, each at one time with its own station. First came the Liverpool, Crosby & Southport with a simple wooden station in Eastbank Street (1848), superseded by one in Chapel Street in 1851, alongside which in 1854 the Lancashire & Yorkshire built a stone Tudor terminus similar to most of the other stations on its line from Wigan, such as Gathurst and Burscough Bridge. Then in 1882 the West Lancashire Railway built a terminus and large office block in Kensington Road which it named Southport Central. For so small and penurious a company—it had barely 15 miles of route—the station was sumptuous in grey ashlar, 'L'-shaped and faintly Tudor with a rollicking roofline of hipped and pyramidal sections, dormers and gables. The single-span shed was lined with blind arcading, and had a series of circular green-tinted glass lights. The station was repeated on a smaller scale at Preston (Fishergate Hill), and both were designed by our old friend Charles H. Driver. The West Lancashire was quickly followed by the Cheshire Lines Committee's station in fashionable Lord Street (1884)—mild Renaissance in red brick with a projecting clock tower, the interior covered by low overall roofing in glazed bays. The Lancashire & Yorkshire by now owned both Chapel Street stations, and, after absorbing the West Lancashire, decided it ought to concentrate its passenger facilities at one station and at the same time do something to keep up with the CLC at Lord Street. Several internal extensions had already taken place, but about 1900 a complete new frontage was built in a ponderous Italianate offset by an ornate iron *porte cochère*. The interior was spacious and airy, with wide platforms and six spans of glazed and ridged roofing, extended in 1914. Central was converted to a goods station in 1901.

Morecambe also was a railway creation, first of the 'Little' North Western, then of its successor the Midland and to a lesser degree the London & North Western. The Midland's Promenade station was preceded by one with a pointed arched roof in Northumberland Avenue. Promenade, built in 1907, had a mild stone Gothic frontage, very late for the type, embellished with quatrefoils in the gables and a dormer clock on the lofty central booking hall overlooking a large iron canopy with shallow scalloped valancing to match the cornices. Behind was a well executed, spacious glass-roofed concourse. The architect was Wheatley, working under the company's engineer W. B. Worthington, and the building was repeated at Lancaster Green Ayre but without a clock. The rival Euston Road station (1888) was typical of the London & North Western's ideas of going to town —a long vivid yellow-brick façade, which must have been quite startling when it was new, with a large glass-and-iron *porte cochère* repeated on the platform side as an awning. It was a fairly gross piece of work, only the iron cresting and brackets displaying any delicacy.

Threats to the Great Eastern's East Anglian monopoly by the Midland & Great Northern Joint Railway produced a competing station in black-and-white pseudo half-timbering at Cromer Beach, which outclassed the GER's Cromer High (1887); but at Yarmouth Beach the Joint station could not compare with the Great Eastern's stations at Vauxhall and South Town. On the Essex coast, the Great Eastern built a new terminus at Southend Victoria (1889), with a long, loosely composed red-brick façade incorporating two of the striped gables that were then fashionable in the company's civil engineering department, and overridden by a massive flat-roofed wooden *porte cochère*. A coffered ceiling and chaste mouldings added distinction to the small booking hall. The designer was W. N. Ashbee, of the company's staff. The Central station of the London, Tilbury & Southend Railway (probably 1884) was notable more for its large glass-and-iron *porte cochère*, with deep frilly valancing articulating with the school-board style windows of the red brick frontage. The booking hall roof was semi-elliptical on stark latticed girders springing from pilasters, the capitals nicely decorated with stars. Great Eastern striped gables also appeared at Felixstowe Town, by Ashbee (1898), loosely derived from Norman Shaw's 'Queen Anne' style, with straight-sided gables capped by curved pediments to the end sections, flat sash windows and a surprisingly elaborate octagonal glass-sided cupola.

On the south coast the influence of the Domestic Revival was clearly at work on the larger stations in the redesigning of Worthing Central and Bognor Regis by the Brighton Railway. Worthing (1907) was plain to the point of dullness, comprising principally a giant gable containing a large round-headed window, and an ugly iron *porte cochère*. Bognor (1902), on the other hand, looked oddly bunched up, with a three-storey corner block, a solid undulating parapet which broke into mini-gables on all four sides of a near-pyramidal roof, a cupola clock tower, and a quaint little half-domed tea room on the concourse.

When the London & North Western set about rebuilding Llandudno in 1892, it had no inhibitions about styling; what was good enough for industrial towns on the system was good enough here, too. So the ugly flat standard red-brick elevation that formed the frontage, displaying the glazed gable ends of Euston-type roof bays, came as no surprise. (Yet the increasing tourist traffic at Kenilworth induced reconstruction in a red brick late-Victorian Gothic splendour far superior to the company's normal practice, complete with a large iron *porte cochère*, ridge-and-furrow awnings, lantern-lighted entrance hall and an elaborately carved wooden screen to the booking office. Even the base of the signal box was panelled in brick to match.) In the LNWR's partnership with the Lancashire & Yorkshire at Blackpool the latter's characteristics were predominant at the two stations. Central station (1900) had a prosaic frontage in Accrington brick and terra-cotta, with French corner turrets and central clock gable, and umbrella awnings over the platforms; North station (rebuilt in 1898) was a stronger composition in the same materials, but having a low corner clock tower with a high-pitched ogee cupola that was echoed in little angle turrets. The interior, more impressive than Central's, was composed of broad platforms beneath a double span roof of tied arches, their lofty height emphasised by exceptionally deep end screens.

Outside both stations was a series of open excursion platforms for summer-holiday traffic. Other seaside stations had them in varying numbers and at several resorts they virtually formed separate stations with their own distinguishing names, like Southport London Street and Locking Road at Weston-super-Mare. Londesborough Road station at Scarborough was unusual in being a good five minutes' walk from the main Central station and in having a roof. Although there was only one platform and no frontage, the large concourse was fully enclosed with extensive glazing, and barriers were arranged in rows to accommodate under cover as many queueing home-bound passengers as possible.

CHAPTER 8

STANDARDISATION

When all is said and done, they [the railways] could fairly claim that, before the tide of sensibility turned, they contributed far more to the enjoyment of the pleasures of scenery than they subtracted from them; and after the turn of the tide, too few seemed to care very much either way, at any rate as compared with the heroic days of railway development.
L. F. Gregory. *Railways in the Victorian Landscape* (*Country Life*, 22 Feb 1968)

THIS chapter begins where Chapter 4 left off—with the universal spread of brick consequent upon the opening of wider markets by the railways, and the end of the vernacular in building. We have seen how the retreat from Gothic, which marked leading architectural thought from the mid-1860s, gradually found an echo in the large stations, and how new styles were mainly those known as 'Renaissance'—Italian, French or, a little later, 'Free'. We shall see how this trend was accompanied by a large measure of standardisation, and how, as time went on, railway boards considered a style of any sort to be less and less necessary. The last quarter of the century was, with one or two exceptions, a period of consolidation, and new work of any moment was now firmly in the hands of the large companies, making the wide variety of style employed by the old promoters a thing of the past. As might be expected in such highly conventional and capitalistic organisations, the Arts and Crafts Movement, with its suggestions of William Morris and left-wing sympathies, found little favour with the railways. School Board functionalism was often the order of the day until the impact of the Domestic Revival; but that must wait for the next chapter.

Most railway companies' engineers drew up standard designs for components, sections and complete buildings, in some cases probably with a degree of prefabrication—a trend anticipated, as we have seen in Chapter 3, a good deal earlier by the South Eastern Railway and

I. K. Brunel but not so far adopted by many others. Only in exceptional circumstances was individual treatment allowed, and the identity of a company could be established by its standardised stations just as surely as by the colour of its engines and rolling stock.

For a time the railways continued to use brick or stone, which we will consider before passing on to the increase in the use of wooden buildings. Examples of individuality lingered on into the 1870s and 1880s here and there. Extensions to the system by small local companies continued to be a Great Western feature where other railways tended to do it themselves; consequently there was more individuality, as was shown, for instance, by the local stone Tudor buildings at Marlborough (1864) and Malmesbury (1877), by the continuing vernacular on the Pembroke & Tenby Railway of 1863 (Tenby's pierced wooden gables in particular), and by a truly delightful set of stone *cottage orné* stations on the Cheddar Valley Railway (1869–70) at Congresbury, Sandford & Banwell, Axbridge and Lodge Hill. Draycott was in Swiss-chalet style, repeated in timber at Winscombe, while Cheddar itself had delicate iron entrance gates and exquisitely glazed gables in a Brunel-type roof (p 103).

For some time flint withstood the encroachment of brick in its native districts served by the Great Eastern Railway, several stations between Wells and Heacham (1866), and Stow Bedon between Thetford and Swaffham (1869), comparing well with the local tradition. On the other hand the rebuilt frontage of Kings Lynn (1871), a clumsy attempt at French Renaissance, was quite out of place; yet at March a quiet but strong Italianate composition formed quite the most meritorious of the Great Eastern junction stations. Tiny pedimented keystones, rich brickwork and a dainty front awning helped to give unusual interest.

Interspersed with its twin-pavilion stations in the 1860s and 1870s the Midland Railway continued to produce some striking individual designs. Four fine new stations were built when the Tewkesbury branch was extended to Malvern Wells in 1864, Tewkesbury itself having a simple, well proportioned and highly effective composition in Free Italianate to replace the old Birmingham & Gloucester building. Ripple was more cottage-like, with tiny dormers, patterned brickwork and a hipped projecting gable forming a porch; and Upton-on-Severn heavier and less homely in outline, perhaps a trifle misplaced, yet sturdy and commodious. With Malvern Wells (Chapter 4) these stations formed a remarkable quartet on a rural byeway.

Frontage and awning detail, March, GER

Midland work of the 1870s included three town stations presenting particularly good features for their time. Northampton St Johns Street (1872) was an amazingly showy little red-brick terminus for the relatively small traffic, in debased Italianate thrusting out a massive *porte cochère* with Roman columns, blind arcading and a florid balustrade. A more sober touch marked Mansfield Town (c 1875), in local stone with good detailing and an iron-and-glass pitched overall roof —unusual for a Midland station of this size. The new station at Burton-on-Trent was of quite a different character—an incredible place, with a vast brick-and-timber patterned entrance, canopied cab drive, and an odd open-fronted balcony overlooking the long island platform, along much of which ran a narrow black-and-white pseudo half-timbered building frivolously decorated with fancy gables. The platform was roofed by hipped iron-and-glass awnings of the standard type. Half-timbering was used at one or two other Midland stations, notably Irchester and Earby.

The charming French-style buildings at Cromford (c 1860), particularly the little gem on the up platform, with its near-steeple turret, delicately elaborate iron finials and small diamond-paned windows, are thought to be the work of Paxton's assistant, G. H. Stokes. The main building was less striking, but the whole was overlooked from higher ground at the rear by a magnificent chateau of a stationmaster's house. Nearby, Matlock Bath station was built in the 1880s to serve the increasingly popular spa, and to add to the romantic alpine atmosphere of the Derwent gorge no less than five separate Swiss chalet buildings were erected on its platforms, three on one and two on the other, plus a short length of detached awning. Overhanging eaves, herringbone brick nogging and multi-paned windows were all in character.

The extension of the Rowsley line to Buxton and Manchester was undertaken by William Barlow, who, in addition to his work at St Pancras, had a long association with the Midland, first as a resident engineer in 1847, then as consultant from 1858 to 1904. His friend the Manchester architect Edward Walters designed simple one-storey stone stations at Rowsley (replacing Paxton's), Bakewell and Hassop (1863), and Chapel-en-le-Frith Central (1867), which achieved quiet charm by the use of hipped roofs with curly wooden eaves brackets, articulated segmental-arched openings and distinctive parapets chamfered at the ends, behind standard ridge-and-furrow glass awnings. The same pleasing symmetry in red brick appeared on the London Extension south of Radlett (1867). J. S. Crossley used a similar style in timber at Mansfield Woodhouse, and applied the same roof to his pavilion-and-screen buildings at Nuneaton Abbey Street in 1864, on the Ashby & Nuneaton Joint line (1873), and at Whitwell (1875). Barlow was probably responsible for quite different Tudor stations at Great Longstone and Peak Forest, with highly decorative gable treatment at the former.

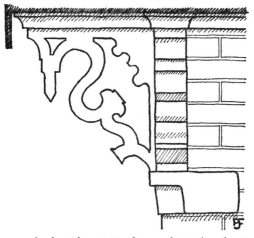

Wooden eaves bracket, Elstree & Borehamwood, MR (London Extension)

The 'ugly, inconvenient stations' that E. L. Ahrons remembered on the Lancashire & Yorkshire from 1876* doubtless included a character-less and much used single-storey brick or stone type, typical of the Oldham–Royton–Rochdale lines of 1863, at Netherton and Meltham (1869), and repeated between Liverpool and Manchester. The tall barracky buildings at Farnworth, Westhoughton and Hindley North probably dated from this period also, while the ultimate in economy was achieved at Lostock Junction, where a new entrance building in 1885–6 had an iron water tank for its roof. Yet however dreary and drab these stations may appear to our eyes, they were at the time of building no worse and often a lot better than the areas they served, while their accommodation was of a notably higher standard than some of their contemporaries in the south.

There was a noticeable improvement in the twin-pavilion buildings at Clitheroe (1871)—replacing a *cottage orné* station of 1850—and Great Harwood (1877), and a more imposing manner was tried in the rebuilding of Sowerby Bridge in 1876—two storeys high with crenellated chimneystacks and a gabled and twin-arched centrepiece. But this recovery had barely started before there was a long relapse into yellow brick on the new Manchester–Whitefield–Radcliffe line of 1879, at Darwen (1883), and on the Bolton avoiding line of 1887–8, among others. Gisburn (1879) and its very prominent station house were particularly unfeeling yellow-brick intrusions in the pleasant Ribblesdale landscape. Larger rebuilding schemes in this material included sloping glass verandahs along the fronts of Ashton Charles-town and Rochdale (1889), and the former also had some nice fanlights; while beyond the large square block at Fleetwood (1883) a striking line of glazed gables stretched along the top of the trainshed wall. C. W. Green, the company's architect, was responsible for the design here and perhaps at the others as well.

The humdrum main line stations on the Great Northern were repeated in even duller fashion on many of its later branches. Some of the Lincolnshire stations were drably typical of the 'middle' railway period, though Skegness could be given full marks for its spaciously proportioned concourse. The worst kind of timber hutting with a dash of brick at Honington, Hubbert's Bridge and Rauceby on the Grantham–Boston line contrasted markedly with the vigorous Tudor in red brick and local stone at the earlier stations of Ancaster and

* *Locomotive and Train Working in the Latter Part of the Nineteenth Century,* Vol 2 (1952), reprinted from *The Railway Magazine,* 1917

Sleaford (1857–9); but better standards were attained between Grantham and Lincoln (1876), where substantial brick house-type buildings were put up. In an uncharacteristic burst of liberality the company even planted conifers and copper beeches behind the platforms and went to the extreme of transforming the similar buildings at Leadenham with stone instead of brick, including the signal box.

Lengthy single-storey stone buildings with a low central turret gave individuality to the stations at Eccleshill, Idle and Shipley & Windhill on the Shipley branch (1875) and Earlsheaton on the Dewsbury loop (1874); twin-pavilion types appeared at Holmfield (1879), Cullingworth and Ingrow East (1884) in the same district, with flat awnings on rectangular brackets. This last feature was typical of the GNR at this time, being seen on the branch to Leicester Belgrave Road (1882), among others. At Leicester itself the Great Northern for once built an imposing terminus, the double-span crescent trussed roof enabling the provision of very wide platforms and a broad concourse for traffic, which never warranted such generosity. The low tower and feeble fenestration in the sizable frontage, however, were unworthy of the interior.

For its incursions into Nottinghamshire and Derbyshire, begun in 1876, the Great Northern built large, monumentally dull two-storey red-brick stations—Daybrook, Pinxton South, and Etwall were examples—with the exception of Basford North, which, like Leadenham, was in light grey stone, picked out with darker dressings to give a striking chequered effect to the chimneys. Smaller stations on the Leen Valley line beyond Annesley (1897–1900) were softened by the use of a grey stone quarried from the deep cuttings.

On the London & South Western's secondary lines in the thirty years from 1856 numbers of vaguely Italianate stations were built, from Colyton (1868) and Lymington Town (1860) to Strawberry Hill (1877) and the mixed-up façade at Bournemouth West (1874). Frimley (1878) sported some apparently surplus valancing as bargeboards. Equally undistinguished, oddly hunched-up stations appeared from Staines to Wokingham (1856). If the patrons of Royal Ascot expected something better, they reckoned without the thrift of the South Western, which deemed wooden extensions quite sufficient for race-goers using them only a few days a year.

It is an odd fact that over the same period of this unexceptional but entirely respectable development the company built some most dreadful stations. *The Builder*, in one of its periodic architect-versus-engineer campaigns, bitterly attacked the rebuilding of the Tudor-Gothic stations at Putney, Mortlake and Richmond in 1887:

> They have now been 'translated' and are the ugliest stations near the metropolis—that at Mortlake being an especially abominable '*contraption*' of iron, wood and zinc. We ought to improve in railway architecture as we have done in other branches of the art. The South Western Railway are retrograding. Have they an official, salaried architect? and is that the reason? or is it mere parsimony and callousness? In any case it is deplorable.

Mortlake and Richmond deserved criticism, but the entrance building on the bridge at Putney had stylish pretensions in its fairly elegant fanlights before it was defaced by a wretched awning and a clutter of kiosks. But by the time *The Builder* wrote, this sort of thing had been going on for over twenty years. West Moors (1866) was like a row of terraced houses taken out of an industrial street and deposited on the edge of Dorset. Daggons Road (1876) was similar though smaller, and Mottisfont (1865), a few miles away, consisted of the poorest kind of Victorian agricultural cottage. There were many more fairly wretched examples in this period: Addlestone (1866), for instance, was merely a pair of long awnings attached to brick screen walls with a little hutch of a booking office at one end. Stations like this gave the South Western its bad name.

Away in North Devon things were rather better. Soundly built stations in snecked rubble, but otherwise possessing little local affiliation, could be found at Torrington and Bideford (1872). The best, probably, were the low rangy plain buildings at Halwill and Ashbury (1879), relieved only by bright rendering, but by their very severity somehow fitting into that bare upland landscape beyond Dartmoor.

The ousting of local materials was well illustrated by the introduction of red brick into the Welsh mountains at places like Frongoch, Trawsfynydd and Maentwrog Road on the Festiniog & Bala Railway (1882), where stone and slate should have been the order; and by the use of blue brick at Nantwich, Whitchurch and Wem (1858) by the London & North Western, which, while not ineffectively used, was hardly at home on the Cheshire–Shropshire border.

Accommodation undoubtedly was vastly improved at the new and rebuilt stations of the Great Western Railway from 1870 onwards, but at the expense of a particularly dismal appearance. Mass-designed single-storey red-brick stations with hipped roofs and shallow eaves were built at random from Camborne and Cullompton to Hanwell,

Honeybourne Junction and beyond. Occasionally the stone example appeared, with quietly contrasted rustication at Hallatrow but startlingly white against dark grey at Briton Ferry. To distinguish stations of greater importance two or three flat-topped French pavilion roofs would be added, adorned by intricate iron trellis-work, as at Ross-on-Wye (1873), Southall and Truro (both 1876), Stourbridge Town and Langley (both 1879), and Winchester Chesil (1885) (p 168). Local stone was used more effectively at Wrexham General and Teignmouth, while Cheltenham St James had an elegant, classically detailed glass-and-iron *porte cochère* added. But at all of them there was no change beneath the roof line and after the 1880s the style seemed to die out. Only at Slough (1879) did the Great Western's idea of French Renaissance really blossom in a more sophisticated manner, with three bulbous pavilion roofs containing elaborately framed bulls-eye windows and surrounded by delicate ironwork. The subsidiary building was a smaller replica, but here again the icing was all on top with plain cake underneath.

A slightly different version, without the pavilion roofs, was used on the new lines of the early 1900s, accompanied by the planting of deciduous trees on embankments and cuttings. They could be found at Westbury (c 1905), Broadway (1904–5), Henley-in-Arden (1907) and Bicester North (1910).

Thomas Prosser appears to have originated the dull but substantial villa-type standard station building for the North Eastern Railway. It could have been transplanted from any Victorian middle-class suburb from the 1860s onward; deep sashes and a central bay window for the stationmaster were its only distinguishing points, and the design was used without change for many years. Cherry Burton was a sample. It came in various sizes and was further varied by Scottish-looking crow-stepped gables on the Pateley Bridge branch (1862) and at Goathland, Egton and Glaisdale in 1865. It could be enlarged by altering the siting and size of its standard components: the two-storey portion, for instance, could be lengthened by the insertion of an extra 'section', and generally a small one-storey pavilion would be added at the opposite end from the house, with a sloping glass verandah over the intervening recess. Pool-in-Wharfedale (1865), though more elaborate than its successors, was among the first, in stone instead of brick, with a dash of scrolly corbelling (p 165). There were good examples of variations on the same theme on the Swinton & Knottingley Joint line (1879); Chester-le-Street was a later two-storey example;

Boroughbridge second station (1875) and Fourstones were one-storey types; and Scholes and Hebburn combined both. A *cottage orné* adaptation in rock-faced stone was built at Askrigg (1878), and Brotton had a French-looking roof studded with scrolly iron finials and a segmental arched verandah on barley-sugar iron columns and capitals.

The North Eastern's engagingly elaborate ironwork of this period was countered by generally poor frontages. High Shields (1879) had a

Coupled iron roof columns, Middlesbrough, NER

clumsy, half apologetic *porte cochère* that looked like an afterthought. Tynemouth's façade (1882) was long and low with round-headed openings, while at South Shields (1879) there were segmental-headed openings, with a rose window repeated on the platform side even though it only overlooked the slope of the overall roof.

After a brief flirtation with Italianate at Grimsby Docks (1853), Broadbottom (1855)—which unlike its name was tall and narrow—and Cleethorpes, where by 1880 much tinkering had produced a long shambling assemblage, the Manchester, Sheffield & Lincolnshire Railway developed its own style of twin-pavilion station, which

Plate 33 (*right*) The St Pancras influence at Sunderland's old station, NER, by William Peachey

Page 153

Plate 34 (*left*) The eccentric interior of Battersea Park's booking hall, LBSCR, in 1966

Plate 35   Pomp and circumstance at Eastbourne, LBSCR, in 1954, showing the characteristic Brighton lantern

Plate 36   The spacious concourse at Norwich Thorpe, GER, in 1956

Plate 37 (*right*) Clock tower at Wakefield Westgate, GN & GCR Joint, in 1966

Plate 38 (*left*) Hydraulic lift tower at Hamilton Square, Birkenhead, Mersey Railway, in 1951

Plate 39 'Domestic Revival' on the Great Eastern at Battlesbridge, about 1910. Note curved wing walls, tile hanging and striped gable, typical GER features of the period

Plate 40 Rural 'Domestic Revival' at Sandling, SER, in 1967

originated at Woodley on the Sheffield & Midland Joint line in 1862 and was to become a familiar feature of new stations for the next twenty years. Essentially it comprised two projecting gabled end-buildings, one of which might be a two-storey house, with a sloping verandah roof on iron columns over the recess between (p 164). The columns might have small decorated brackets, as at Woodley and Deepcar (1865); broad curved ones to form an arcade, as at Reddish North (1875), Chapeltown Central (c 1876) and Wombwell Central (1877); or straight diagonals, as at Dukinfield (1863-4) and Conisborough (c 1884), in two, three or four sections according to size. Shireoaks (1884) dispensed with the columns in favour of deep brackets on the rear wall. Several of the earlier stations were in stone but later they were all brick with window and gable variations, except the rather special job at Mexborough (1871) where only part of the central portion was recessed behind two segmental stone arches.

The same theme was developed by the Great Eastern after its formation by amalgamation in 1862, but considering the depths to which its inherited reputation continued to sink, including insolvency, the stations were surprisingly good. The buildings were recessed at the front as well as on the platform side, with hipped roofs and generally buff or yellow brickwork with contrasting rusticated quoins. At small stations like Pampisford and North Weald the central section was omitted, and others, like Theydon Bois and Clare, had the central roofing carried forward as a verandah and perhaps enclosed with a timber and glass screen. Most had a matching wall backing the platforms instead of the more usual fence, the Braintree-Bishops Stortford stations (1869), such as Dunmow, being in this form (p 172).

Two principal awning styles were widely introduced by the Great Eastern in the 1860s and 1870s. One was flat with shallow double-serrated 'ripsaw' valancing in endless variations—plain at Cressing and Dersingham (1862), and pierced by circles at Palace Gates (1878), by trefoils at Kimberley Park, and rounded at Ely. The other type consisted of shallow ridges and furrows with deep curved saw-tooth valancing. Many in the London area—Hackney Downs and Seven Sisters (1872), for instance—had brick screen walls at the rear, and the brackets were generally decorated with the company's initials, floral patterns or interposed concentric curves giving a whorl effect.

The London, Brighton & South Coast Railway's stations of this period also included the usual rash of middling designs, but they were frequently a good deal larger and generally superior, for country places, to those of other companies. Downright meanness was almost absent and there was more than a sprinkling of merit in some of the larger stations, which was all the more remarkable since this company, too, was nearly bankrupt in the mid-1860s. Buildings akin to those on the South Western beyond Basingstoke were built at West Grinstead (1861) and on the Guildford branch, rendered instead of tile-hung, and good quality chunky red-brick stations appeared elsewhere, such as at Isfield (1858) and Falmer (1865). Goods sheds adjoining the platforms at Billingshurst (1859) and Amberley (1863) were given a row of eye-catching fan windows.

A series of large sedate two-storey Italianate villa-like stations was begun along the Sussex coast at Seaford (1864), Cliftonville (1865, renamed Hove in 1880) and Kemp Town (1869), with round or segmental arched openings and hipped roofs over corbelled eaves. Epsom Downs (1865), in similar vein, was more restrained, and in 1877 the design was revived at London Road, Brighton, followed by Portslade & West Hove in 1881 and Worthing in 1889. Pointed hoods over the main segmental arched windows added piquancy at Polegate (1889) and St Leonards West Marina.

After building some of our best stations in 1848 and 1849 the standard of the North Staffordshire Railway declined abruptly. After it continued with several pleasant but unremarkable country stations like Clifton (1852), Bucknall & Northwood and Ford Green & Smallthorn (1863), it then proceeded to erect a series of uniform single-storey brick stations, Spartan in accommodation and appearance, on the Macclesfield, Bollington & Marple line of 1869 (later jointly owned with the MS & L). The main feature of these stations, a pitched roof brought down low at one or both sides on straight wooden struts to make an integral awning, was repeated in substantial batches on the Market Drayton branch (1870), Normacot (1882), the old station at Fenton (a larger edition), and others (p 171).

The era of wooden buildings was brought about by increasing land and labour costs and even greater competition. For the South Eastern Railway it meant little change; the company simply went on building its 1842 vintage stations with even more determination—Smitham, for instance, in 1897, and Tattenham Corner as late as 1901, though the latter was admittedly larger than normal and spruced up with a central gable. The London, Chatham & Dover copied the South Eastern's wooden models somewhat less prolifically, as at Sheerness-on-Sea (1883), with occasional unconventional ventures like the herringbone boarding at Westgate-on-Sea (1871). The Brighton line, to its credit, rarely built all-wooden stations and those it did have were in the same substantial manner as its brick structures—Petworth (1859) and Wivelsfield (1886) for example—though its timber subsidiary buildings were just as common as on other lines.

The small waiting shelter on the subsidiary platform could often add considerable charm to a station when it was as well designed as some of the North Staffordshire Railway's, such as those at Marchington and Sudbury. The southern lines had good work of this kind, too, particularly the South Eastern and the London, Brighton & South Coast; Frant and Warnham were nice examples of each.

There was a different picture on the South Western, which entered its timber and corrugated iron era in the 1860s. Chard Town (1863) and Andover Town (1865) were in iron, and Sutton Bingham derived a tin-tabernacle air from its low pointed windows. Chandlers Ford (1894), on the other hand, was a jolly little wooden station with a nicely decorated awning and glazed end screen; but Templecombe (1860) had an awful collection of choice South Western wooden shacks, about which the less said the better. Effingham Junction (1885) tried hard to fit itself into the developing commuter belt with an openwork decorated gable and a part-balustrade from which a large brick chimney breast curved upwards; and one hopes that the residents were impressed as they descended the open stairs to the bare wooden platform shelters.

The Midland built somewhat fewer wooden buildings than the other large systems, although wood came into favour at several stations on the Kettering–Nottingham direct line (1879). Diagonal boarding and a hipped roof extended as an awning, with saw-tooth valancing, were the chief characteristics, as at Grimston and Old Dalby. Widenings and new work from the 1880s to 1910 increased the number of wooden buildings, usually with flat roofs and minimal decoration, and as widely spread as Cricklewood, Swinton, Saltley and Stroud.

The North Eastern's wooden stations were particularly Spartan, and distinctive rabbit-hutch waiting shelters were as common as they were on the London & South Western. Longish ranges with little gables and glass screens were built at Airmyn & Rawcliffe, Staddlethorpe and Ferriby. A wooden station notable for its elaboration was built by the Londonderry Railway—later part of the North Eastern—at Seaham Harbour, with gabled entrances, fanlights, iron clover-leaf cresting and a little turret complete with valancing and a tall spike.

To the Manchester, Sheffield & Lincolnshire company goes the credit for some of the best wooden stations in England—on the Chesterfield Loop of 1892—accompanied by glazed ridge-and-furrow valancing and foliated brackets, giving generous platform cover. Originally gabled, those at Chesterfield Central (and possibly Renishaw) were later altered to hipped ends, and the wooden entrance building on the road bridge had a neat French pavilion roof with a square of decorative iron cresting. Kirkby Bentinck (1893) was similar at platform level.

The cheeseparing period on the London & North Western was most pronounced between 1861 and 1891 during the chairmanship of Sir Richard Moon. Among railway officials he was a byword for stern discipline, ruthless efficiency and, above all, economy; a portrait of his hard features almost suggests one of the North Western's severe looking red, blue or yellow brick stations. This company was among the large band of utilitarians when it came to wooden structures, its standard wooden hut being used all over the system as platform building, shunter's cabin, crossing keeper's hut, permanent way shed, ground frame and even on occasions as a small signal box. At a good many stations it formed the subsidiary building, and at not a few it was the sole type of structure, singly or in a range of several placed end-to-end in sectional form; Alsop-en-le-Dale, Napton & Stockton, Wigston (Glen Parva) and Talacre were examples.

The larger standard wooden buildings had horizontal boarding, deep sash windows and full-length flat awnings. They were ungainly to look at, and as time went on the heavy awning tended to pull the whole structure inward. But appearances could be deceptive: despite an outward severity they generally incorporated generous accommodation absent from the hut variety, so that a relatively unimportant station like Lubenham had a full range of offices and waiting rooms. Apart from the tendency to lean, sound structural work was evidenced by the large number that survived unaltered for a century, while a close examination revealed good quality detailing (p 167). A slight touch of the romantic crept into some of the wooden entrance buildings built on road bridges. Stechford (1882), Eccles, South Hampstead, Wolverton and Pleck (opened 1924 but to a much earlier LNW design and possibly moved there) had hipped roofs and gables, tall clustered chimneys set at angles, and—a touch of elegance—small flat canopies on delicate iron brackets. An overall-roofed wooden terminus, much larger than Oxford and Banbury (Chapter 5), was built at Swansea

Victoria—basically a Euston-type roof on iron columns—enclosed at one side by the brick viaduct of one of the Great Western's dock branches, and at the other by lean-to wooden offices.

The most characteristic feature of the North Western wooden station was the extremely heavy aspect given to the awning by its deep valancing, sometimes edged with plain saw-teeth, sometimes decorated. It was used on the more substantial buildings, too, often as a later addition, and on occasions was carried right round almost flush with the walls, as at Aston and Oldbury & Bromford Lane (with unusually deep brackets), and at Chilvers Coton. Pendants and finials were added embellishments at Watford Junction.

Mundane though many of the London & North Western's wooden stations were, they warrant fairly detailed attention not so much because of their profusion but rather for their importance in large-scale standardisation of components. Certainly standard drawings were used, although whether uniformity went so far as prefabrication is hard to say. We know that lineside cottages were built with woodwork and ironwork mass-produced at Crewe*, and no doubt the company's workshops could turn out station components with equal ease.

Equally substantial wooden hipped-roofed buildings appeared on the North Western's neighbour, the Lancashire & Yorkshire, but lacking the finer detail. Several had ridge-and-furrow roofing extended to form glazed awnings to which were added square-glazed ends and valancing following the slopes. The settings of Middleton Junction, Accrington and Radcliffe Central, V-shaped in the angle of a junction, made interestingly curved zigzag vistas. This kind of roof and awning articulation on stone or brick buildings was equally effective at conventional two-platform stations, care being taken to build the opposing structures of equal length, on the Manchester–Whitefield–Radcliffe line, for instance, and at Shawforth (1870) and Hapton. Heavier editions at Burscough Junction (p 166), Birkdale and Blundellsands & Crosby had deep valancing and ball finials, while lighter types, mounted Midland-fashion on large brackets enclosing circles, gave a much needed touch of airy elegance to stations like Oldham Central, Burnley Central and Bury Knowsley Street. This type was particularly suitable at Lytham (1874) to accompany the balustraded ashlar frontage, though elsewhere it did not always match. Denby Dale & Cum-

* Sir George Findlay. *The Working and Management of an English Railway*, 6th edn (1899)

berworth, for example, had ridge-and-furrow work on one side and pitched on the other. Then with the rebuilding of many stations on island platforms a vast ridged awning evolved, hipped at the ends, its ugly maze of trussing spread over the platforms at Mill Hill (1887), Rochdale (1889) and Rose Grove (1897), among others.

The rebuilding of Ferryhill (1875) and Thornaby led the North Eastern to construct complete series of island platform stations. In addition to Copmanthorpe-Church Fenton mentioned in Chapter 6 there were numbers in the Hull area and on the south bank of both Tyne and Tees, the latter with unusual iron valancing.

Distinctive awnings often made up for the lifelessness of the Great Western's latter-day buildings. On island platforms, shallow-pitched awnings with deep cut-away end-gables achieved a satisfying and well balanced appearance. The end patterns varied in an interesting way, too; the deep 'pointed arch' cut-outs at Hanwell (1877), for instance, contrasted with the shallow curves at Stourbridge Junction (1901). Flat-topped awnings with chamfered corners marked the stations rebuilt from Twyford to Cholsey & Moulsford for the quadrupling in 1892–3, while a sloping awning in front of a long glazed clerestory on arcaded columns was a striking feature at Stourbridge Town, Teignmouth and Wrexham General. A few curved awnings in corrugated iron appeared on the Great Western—Starcross, Clifton Bridge, Bewdley and Yatton among them—and even fewer ridge-and-furrow types—Ruabon, Dawlish and Malvern Link in timber; Weston-super-Mare (1884) and Tiverton (1885) in glass-and-iron.

The introduction of one coach push-and-pull trains in 1903, which the Great Western developed on a far wider scale than any other company, led to the construction of small halts that spread over the whole system during the following decade. They gave rise to another, quite different, standard building constructed entirely of corrugated iron and unique in having a concave pagoda-like roof that rapidly became characteristic features at halts and were also used at waiting shelters, lamp rooms and for similar purposes at smaller stations. Colwall had an outsize one in timber with iron cresting along the roof.

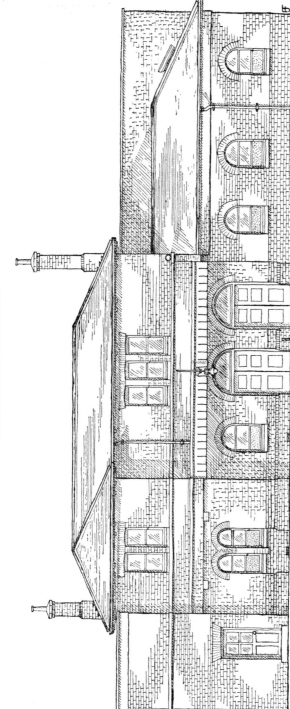

Standard Great Northern: the frontage of Hatfield

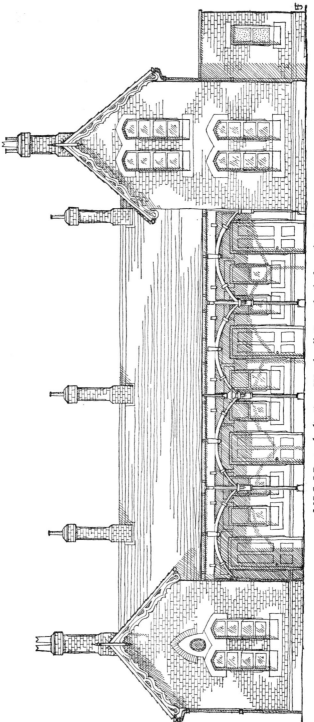

MS & LR standardisation: Wombwell Central, platform elevation

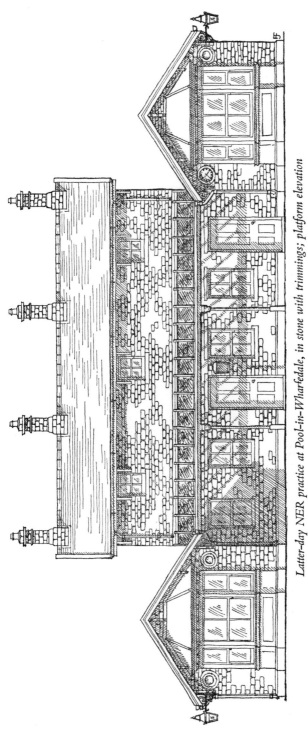

Latter-day NER practice at Pool-in-Wharfedale, in stone with trimmings; platform elevation

STANDARDISED BUILDINGS

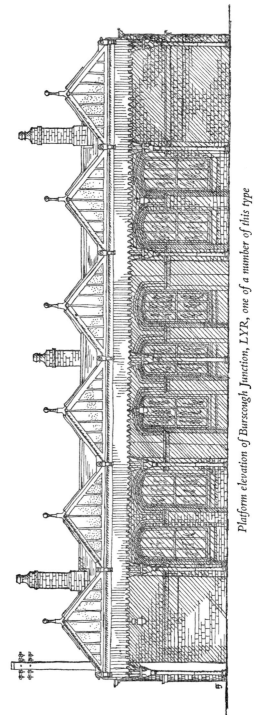

Platform elevation of Burscough Junction, LYR, one of a number of this type

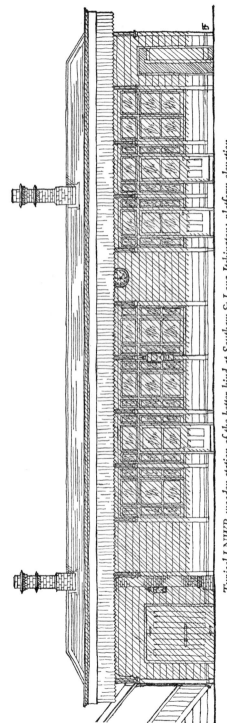

Typical LNWR wooden station of the better kind at Southam & Long Itchington; platform elevation

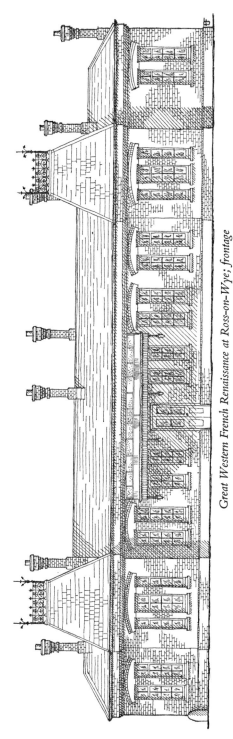

Great Western French Renaissance at Ross-on-Wye; frontage

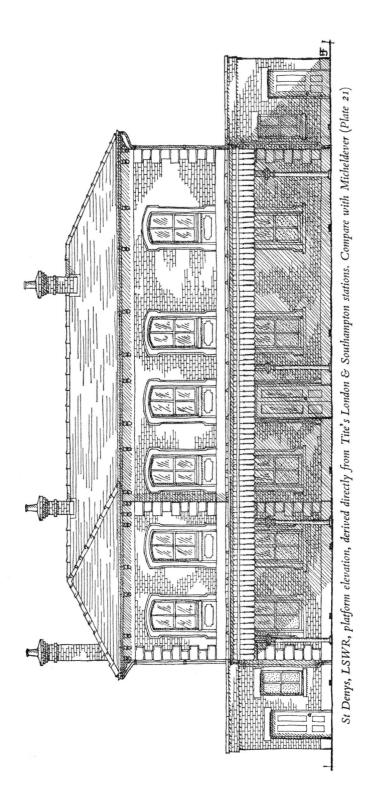

St Denys, LSWR, platform elevation, derived directly from Tite's London & Southampton stations. Compare with Micheldever (Plate 21)

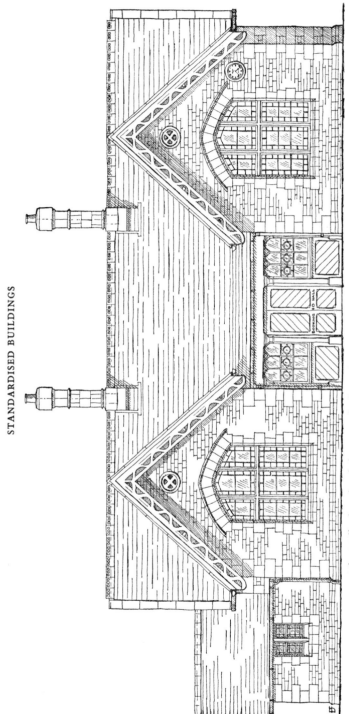

The Midland Railway's 'twin pavilion', Settle & Carlisle style; Little Salkeld, platform elevation

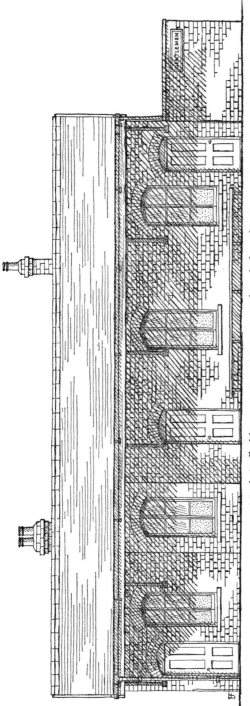

North Staffordshire austerity at Norton-in-Hales; platform elevation

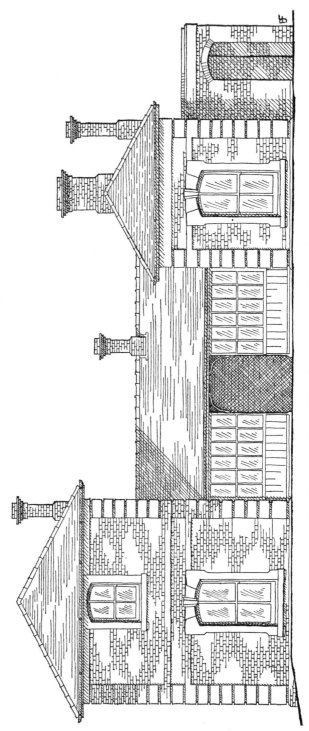

Great Eastern 'middle period' styling at Dunmow; platform elevation

Plate 41   Urban 'Domestic Revival' at Earlswood, LBSCR, in 1967

Page 173

Plate 42   Rustic timber framing mixed with Lake District drystone walling at Foxfield, Furness Railway, in 1966. The overall roof covers one platform only, and adjoins the goods shed on far left

Plate 43 (*right*) Gerald Horsley's charming frontage at Hatch End, LNWR, in 1963

Plate 44 (*left*) Narrow gauge magnificence: the entrance arch at Douglas, Isle of Man Railway, in 1963

Plate 45   Welsh Italianate at Llanidloes, Cambrian Railways, one-time headquarters of the Mid-Wales Railway, in 1955

Plate 46   The massively blank yellow brick frontage at Putney Bridge, Metropolitan District Railway, in 1965

Plate 47 (*right*) Oak fireplace in the Duke of Rutland's private waiting room at Redmile for Belvoir, GN & LNWR Joint line, in 1954

Plate 48 Tenbury Wells, Shrewsbury & Hereford Joint line (GW & LNW), with matching signal box on left hand platform, in 1957

CHAPTER 9

REFORM

THE impact of the Domestic Revival on the railways, though fairly slight, was significant because it led some companies to reintroduce a degree of individuality. With most, however, the new trend simply induced new standard designs. The favourite materials were terra-cotta or glazed brick, and, on some lines, changing ideas were acknowledged by nothing more than use of the semi-elliptical arch. The Great Western at Birmingham Moor Street (1909) and Westbourne Park combined arched openings with curved or steeply pointed gables and brown glazed brick interiors; on the Lancashire & Yorkshire Railway they appeared at Cleckheaton Central (1891) and the new entrance building at Church & Oswaldtwistle in stone, and on the platforms at Bolton Trinity Street (1903) in brown and yellow glazed brick; while they were the main feature of the dark red brick frontage at Wigan Wallgate (1896), articulating with the glass-and-iron *porte cochère*. Wallgate's best features were the careful mouldings and discreet little door and window pediments on the wooden platform buildings.

On its South Manchester line of 1891 the Manchester, Sheffield & Lincolnshire echoed the Norman Shaw tradition with steep tiled roofs, sandstone dressings, gables and cupolas over elliptical headed openings at Wilbraham Road and Levenshulme South; at Fallowfield, however, a larger building on a prominent corner site was also given a hexagonal two-storey section and a triple-arched Tudorish entrance. All three had spacious platform buildings with ridge-and-furrow roofs and awnings, but Fairfield (1892) was a less satisfactory, hunched up design.

The last new railway company in England to have any sort of main line status, the Lancashire, Derbyshire & East Coast of 1896–7, built nearly all its stations in an exactly uniform hard red brick with closely spaced elliptical headed openings, as seen at Edwinstowe, Tuxford

Central and Clowne South—the last built against a matching goods warehouse. The company was taken over by the Great Central in 1907.

The London & South Western tried the same fenestration in an extension to Salisbury station in 1900, where it clashed with Tite's earlier building, yet produced at East Putney (1889) an excellent example of quiet, well proportioned Revival styling. The restrained terra-cotta trim to the openings and the tastefully detailed false pedimental gable obviously were part of a desire to live up to the Forsytean neighbourhood. It was part of a gradual movement towards more interesting designs, marked, among others, by the white rock-faced Purbeck stone of Corfe Castle and Swanage (1885), the slate-grey random stone heightened by raked joints of contrasting dark mortar at Tavistock North (1890), and a series of decent red-brick buildings with hipped tiled roofs and School Board windows on the New Guildford and the Bournemouth New lines. Cobham (1885), Sway and Hinton Admiral (both 1888) were examples; Wanborough (1885) had added tile-hanging. Some, notably Shawford (1882), Swaythling (1883), Longparish and Wherwell (both 1886) were variously given tiny dormer ventilators and quite ornate terra-cotta Dutch gables. These gables blossomed most exuberantly at Wareham (1886), with assorted windows, finials and tablets bearing the company's crest, all completed by an ogee-shaped cupola. The gable treatment was too enthusiastic at Wimbledon Park (1889), however, where it completely overwhelmed the small entrance building. On the other hand the attempt to combine all these features in the rebuilding of Guildford (1884) simply produced incoherence, while Farncombe (1903) was a revival of Tudor styles, and weak at that.

The Midland Railway characteristically embraced the Domestic Revival in a much more emphatic manner. The entrance building at Cricklewood (1884) displayed dark red and orange-pink terra-cotta, with moulded brickwork, elliptical archways and large ball finials on the gables. Others followed at Wigston Magna, Coalville Town, Rotherham Masborough and elsewhere; Gloucester Eastgate was lavishly endowed with pedimented balustrading. Bingley (1892), by Charles Trubshaw (who could well have been responsible for the others), repeated the style in stone. The finest example, with all the trimmings, was the rebuilt frontage building at Kettering, in best terra-cotta with a prominent 'MR', two tall chimneystacks springing from restrainedly flamboyant gables, and that favourite motif of the times, the sunflower, carefully moulded on each.

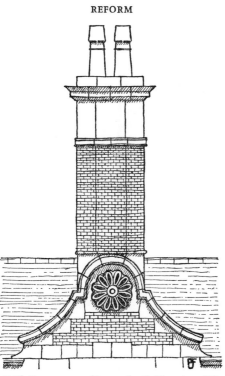

Brick & terra-cotta chimney detail, Kettering, MR

After 1880 the London, Brighton & South Coast Railway was way ahead in giving full scope to the influence of the Domestic Revivalists as part of its continuing policy of building big. Sussex was becoming popular with London commuters, and the stations reflected current changes in taste—in marked contrast to the company's rolling stock, which hardly changed at all. Traditional East Sussex tile-hanging was extensively used to form patterns, though on the large two-storey buildings it blended less successfully than on the Great Eastern's more homely single-storey variety. Rotherfield & Marks Cross and Mayfield (both 1880) were tile-hung, with panelled chimneystacks, stone mullions and an oriel window overlooking the heavy wooden-trussed platform awnings. Mayfield, the larger station, had curved eaves mouldings, striped gables and an elaborate lychgate of a porch glazed with leaded coloured glass. The stations on the East Grinstead–Barcombe line (1882) were built in the same fashion, East Grinstead itself, the largest, being fitted with a glass verandah between projecting end blocks, and a typical Brighton-style glass-sided lantern over the refreshment room with pyramidal top. At Horsted Keynes black-and-white half-timbering, decorated with stylised 'pot plant' pargetting, formed part of the theme. The most lavish half-timbering was on the Chichester–Midhurst branch in West Sussex (1881), at Lavant, Singleton, Cocking and Midhurst, replete with porches and gables in the Mayfield style and quatrefoil designs. Lavant seemed huge, its three storeys towering up above the countryside. *The Builder* enthusiastically complimented the architect, a Mr Myers, on his 'Old English style'. The internal woodwork was in varnished pitch pine, there was a profusion of 'lead fret glazing with cathedral tinted glass freely introduced', and the chimneys were decorated with sunflower motifs. At Singleton a glass covered way connected the subway to the high-level platforms, and the whole place was set off at the head of a beech-lined drive by a circular carriage sweep, for the wealthier patrons of Goodwood.

In 1897–8, in contrast to the long wide platforms generously

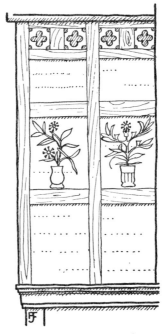

Pargetting and half-timbering, Cocking, LBSCR

covered with ridge-and-furrow awnings, a fussy little frontage was
built on the overbridge at East Croydon, long and low in dark brick
with ashlar trim. Vaguely Italianate, with the LBSCR arms in moulded
brick and a Baroque-mounted clock, it was not a normal Brighton
style except for the inevitable lantern.

Edward Wilson's Liverpool Street Italian-Gothic did little to enliven
the London suburban stations of the Great Eastern Railway in which
it was perpetuated—the Chingford line of 1870-3 had some, Waltham-
stow Hoe Street being an example—although a lively transformation
was achieved at St James' Street station by housing the stair heads from
the street level in low brick towers with curved parapets. Happily
the company was not particularly addicted to all-wooden construction,

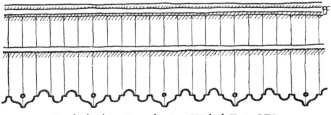

Standardised awning valancing, Wisbech East, GER

though inevitably there were a few examples, such as Sawbridgeworth,
Salhouse, South Worstead and Gunton (1874). When the main line
out of London was widened at the end of the century, well built
wooden platform buildings were provided for such stations as Chad-
well Heath and Gidea Park. Strangely enough, even the traditional
weatherboarding of Essex and Suffolk, which might have been
expected, was conspicuously absent on the railway. Like the Brighton
company, the Great Eastern was not slow in adopting new styles, for
by the 1880s it had recovered its fortunes and was busily burying its
old reputation. Expense was not spared in rebuilding old stations and
constructing new; some may have been a shade flamboyant, but they
were eye-catching compared with the mediocrity of many other railways. Symmetrical buildings in dark red or rustic brick with striped
gables and patterned tile-hung ends, well proportioned chimneys and
stone-capped wing walls produced an agreeable effect that could
easily have been something out of Sussex. Detail differences to prevent
monotony showed at Althorne, Battlesbridge (Plate 39) and Waltham
Cross, for instance. Above the platform the standard flat awning was

the invariable accompaniment and most buildings were one-storeyed, though larger ones like Southminster and Wickford had two. Square stone-cased openings, curved dormers and a five-bay saw-tooth awning made up the frontage at Wisbech East, while mullions, a curved-top centrepiece and a segmental-arched entrance were added at Cheshunt (1891) and Highams Park.

Like the Metropolitan Railway, the GER built the Churchbury and Hainault Loops (1891 and 1903) as speculative lines in the hope that they would encourage housing development; but the Great Eastern was less fortunate as the new estates did not materialise until after the 1923 grouping of the railways and little attempt was made to provide visually attractive stations, though they were spacious enough. On the Churchbury Loop only Southbury's immense ogee gable, false pediment and splayed scrolly chimneys were at all notable. Hainault and Fairlop were described as 'palatial stations within ¼ mile of each other and scarcely a house in sight', and the latter part of the statement was true enough. Both were built on arches, and, although it did not form a true frontage, the main platform building at each had a gabled rear 'façade' echoing Norman Shaw, yet doing nothing more than look out over fields. Also of this period, Forest Gate's entrance building on a tricky corner site had an appropriate semi-elliptical dome to match the window hoods; and the centrepiece at Barkingside had a touch of Queen Anne in the windows and a delightful little Baroque cupola.

Major rebuilding produced good work and a fair variety. Reconstruction at Stratford produced a new main building composed of large-gabled end blocks, elliptically headed tripartite windows and a recessed entrance with windows and panelled doors offset by broken and triangular pediments. As a final flourish a pair of curved dormers displayed plaster cherubs and assorted foliage overlooking an arched glass-and-iron *porte cochère*. Edward Wilson rebuilt Colchester in 1896 equally in the spirit of the time. Three well separated red-brick and tiled pavilions formed the frontage, the central one having a fine Baroque pediment, little angle lantern turrets of classical grace, and a cupola-cum-ventilator on the ridge. Newmarket (1902) received a strangely 'free' centrepiece to its lengthy single-storey frontage— stone-mullioned windows in banded brickwork broken by a glass verandah at top transom level, the semi-circular heads peering out above being set in radial voussoirs between five pairs of chubby three-quarter round columns under a shallow cornice.

In 1890 the Manchester, Sheffield & Lincolnshire acquired, with the small Wrexham, Mold & Connah's Quay Railway in North Wales, four new stations at Buckley Junction, Hawarden, Caergwrle Castle & Wells and Wrexham Exchange. Red terra-cotta trimmings and cresting, Minton-tiled floors and twisted iron columns combined with yellow brick to create garish buildings quite out of key with the local vernacular. Wrexham Central (1887) looked more like a wooden mission hall.

The parent company did much better with black-and-white pseudo half-timbering of the 'Stockbroker Tudor' kind, complete with over-hanging gable and rustic touches, which nonetheless made satisfyingly attractive near identical stations, not out of place, at Blacon and Saughall on the Chester–Hawarden line (1892); but when this style was tried more ambitiously at, of all places, Wigan, the result was one of the most exotically ridiculous wooden stations to be erected in England and Wales. Named Wigan Central, its long 'L'-shaped mixture was formed of gabled end and corner buildings in the Blacon style, half brick and half timber with quite pretty little ogee cupolas, flanking a longer wooden pavilion. The pavilion dominated the rest, its large gambrel roof surmounted by a domed balustraded cupola perched on the gabled apex, and linking these three features were plain sections having tall coupled chimneystacks styled, no less, in diamond-patterned Tudor.

The Great Central is generally recognised as having achieved the ultimate in standardised stations on any continuous stretch of line. At its opening, the London Extension of 1899 had twenty-two of them between Annesley in north Nottinghamshire and the junction with the Metropolitan Railway at Quainton Road in Buckinghamshire, all built on the island platform principle. The only exceptions were Carrington, sandwiched between two tunnels, and Arkwright Street, on a viaduct, in Nottingham. Entrances were above or below, generally at a bridge, and the booking office was on the platform beneath a short awning, except at Hucknall, Loughborough, Rugby and Brackley (all suffixed 'Central'), of which the last three were bigger stations with larger awnings. Excluding these three, the layout and strictly functional appearance of the buildings were identical. The entrances at Rugby and Brackley had a touch of the Revival in their well proportioned semi-circular arched openings, the latter particularly pleasing. Carring-ton not only had a different layout but an entrance building in the black-and-white Blacon style with an attractively tile-hung upper storey.

The company's stations built in the new century failed to sustain the improvement at the end of the old. On the St Helens branch (1900) they were functional in the School Board style, while Oldham Clegg Street (jointly owned with the LNWR) was rebuilt in 1900 with a gabled windowless dormer and a squat, even more useless-looking flat-topped tower. New work ended in an even less prepossessing manner in particularly gaunt red brick at Barnetby (1915) and the four-storey Mansfield Central (1917).

Striped gables evidently were thought to be quite sufficiently *avant-garde* for the turn of the century, and they were the only features of many stations to identify them with their time, as at Poulton-le-Fylde (1896) on the Lancashire & Yorkshire and London & North Western Joint line, Stainforth & Hatfield on the Great Central (1913) and Kirkstall (c 1900) on the Midland. Interspersed with such stations, however, were some individual buildings of real merit. The L & Y's rebuilt Nelson station (1892), for instance, notably achieved a restrained dignity by combining a tall Mansard roof and widely spaced pedimented dormers with a bold cornice, string course and ashlar facings behind an elegant flat canopy on simple iron columns. The same company rebuilt Hebden Bridge as a cheerful smaller edition, while at Northorpe North Road (1891) the island platform had four small separate buildings—each almost identical in fine-coursed ashlar with pilaster strips and splayed chunky chimney shafts moulded at the bases—which were remarkably styled and detailed for their date. Likewise the South Western's new three-storey building fronting Lavender Hill at Clapham Junction was an instance of the infrequent use by this company of white terra-cotta striped quoins, large pediments and a cupola-and-spiked turret.

Even the Great Northern achieved some comparatively mild distinction at Enfield Chase (1910), a new station in a compact but rather heavy Edwardian style but immensely better than the characterless old terminus, which was relegated to goods traffic. Enfield Chase was built when the Enfield branch was extended to form the Hertford Loop, on which the only other station worth noting was the neat brick island platform building at Hertford North, with its cream terra-cotta detailing and moulded corbels for the awning brackets. It was a pity it was so sadly betrayed by the wooden shed that served as an entrance building. But the supreme effort on the Great Northern was its worthy attempt at local harmony with the Parker-Unwin garden city scheme at Letchworth. As rebuilt around 1903, the characteristic GNR entrance building was given a strong Arts and Crafts flavour by mellow bricks and tiles, herringbone nogging in the gable ends, leaded lights and bottle glass in the windows, and a dentilled canopy beneath a six-light flat-topped dormer.

When the South Western Railway briefly embraced the Arts and Crafts movement on the Meon Valley line, it built its best twentieth-century stations. The influence of Edwin Lutyens was suggested by the Tudor mullions, gently moulded gables, good overall proportions and fine workmanship at Droxford, Tisted, Privett and other stations in that delightful valley. In time they were easily absorbed into the landscape, the essence of the good country station. At least one London & South Western suburban station hit the same happy note—Barnes Bridge (1916). The platform buildings were nondescript timber erections, but they were reached by a covered ramp from a charming little entrance, barely more than a porch. Its corbelled cornice, round-topped openings and tasteful ironwork created a very fair attempt to tone with the riverside Georgian of Barnes Terrace.

Despite the proliferation of wooden buildings, the South Eastern Railway built a small number of nondescript single-storey brick stations with round-headed openings and hipped roofs, among them North Camp (1863), Folkestone West (1881), Orpington (1901) and Crowhurst (1902). Stone quoins, dressings and a cornice were added as a concession to the Georgian of Blackheath (1864); Northfleet (1891) imitated the general style in wood. This company's new building policy over the twenty years up to 1900 showed a most curious paradox in designers' thinking, indicated by the contemporaneous erection of the familiar long-outdated wooden structures, mediocre Italianate buildings of the kind just described, and some excellent Domestic Revival stations verging on Arts and Crafts, starting with Nutfield in 1883. Here the timber-framed brickwork, steeply tiled roof, simple flat awning and dentilled eaves were more than signs of an awakening to new ideas; they were an outstanding example of a style being applied to the overall design of a station, including not only the subsidiary building but the signal box as well. Such complete co-ordination was rare, and did not find an imitator until the LNER rebuilt some of the stations between York and Northallerton in the 1930s. Sandling followed the same theme in 1888 (Plate 40), incorporating a gabled entrance porch, and at both stations the use of awning valancing was eschewed rather than spoil the comfortable simplicity of the design. Eltham Park, dated 1890 on the ornamental rain water heads, was in dark red brick and pebble dash with a cosily hipped roof, but spoiled by an unsympathetic, fussily dentilled gable. High Brooms (1893) varied the fashion with a giant centre gable enclosing a large semi-circular window, seen again with more variations on the Chipstead Valley line at Kingswood & Burgh Heath (1897) and Tadworth (1900). Kingswood had three storeys and a flat platform awning surrounded by a light wooden balustrade, serving as a terrace for the tea rooms on the upper floors.

In 1899 the South Eastern and the London, Chatham & Dover Railways ended their bitter forty years feud by forming a joint Managing Committee to control the combined systems. Hitherto the better of the Chatham company's small stations were more notable for substance than style, like the red-brick two-storey domestic Gothic of Eynsford (1862), the Maidstone–Ashford line stations of 1884—Harrietsham, Lenham and the rest—and the single-storey structures between Otford and Maidstone (1874) at Kemsing, Borough Green & Wrotham, West Malling and Barming. Borough Green and Barming were rebuilt around 1880 as two-storey buildings with dormer windows at back and front, but retaining parts of the old. The Revivalists found no home on the Chatham, only Bellingham (1892) receiving a touch of extravagance in its little Jacobean gable and nicely arched openings, and with the advent of the Managing Committee new stations continued for a time to be in the South Eastern's reformed manner.

They opened a branch to Bexhill in 1902 with a jazzy edition of High Brooms in the detached entrance building at Sidley, where red brick and cream terra-cotta created a startling chequerboard effect beneath the eaves and on the gable, and the platform buildings were Arts and Crafts timber-framed pavilions. Bexhill West itself was large (too large for the traffic, which never reached expectations), low and excessively showy. Vertically striped gables vied with the horizontality of bright red brick and cream terra-cotta quoins, high arched windows surrounded by pargetting, overmuch swag and other terra-cotta moulding in the main gable, and a small Baroque clock tower looking down on a cupola-cum-ventilator over the waiting room behind. An exceedingly roomy station with a well lit concourse and ample ridge-and-furrow platform awnings all extensively glazed, it was the SE & CR's answer to the Brighton company's Bexhill Central of 1901.

After such excitements things calmed down at Merstham (1905–6) and Rochester Bridge (1908); the latter was given utterly crude windows, which completely shattered the otherwise pleasant neo-Queen Anne effect created by the central gables and quoins. Black-water (1910) was quietly functional, apart from its large curved false gable; but the effective first-floor treatment and hipped pantiled roof of Godstone (1914) was spoiled by a blank wall below, as though the designer forgot to put something in. Sir Reginald Blomfield is thought to have designed the new down-side building at Tunbridge Wells Central in 1911. Its two large arched entrances in brick, stone cornice and hipped tiled roof would have created a quietly attractive effect but for the overbearingly elaborate false gable that masked the lower part of an angular clock turret. Then in 1915 the last major work of the Committee displayed complete *volte face* with the rebuilding of Whitstable & Tankerton in classical form—heavy stone cornice, brick parapet and coupled pilasters—but Georgian sash windows; with Tunbridge Wells it gave a foretaste of the post-war commercial styles.

To accompany the electrification of the North Eastern's suburban lines north of the Tyne, William Bell embarked on a brief courtship with the Revival School, although its greatest impact was on his prize-winning head office at York, designed jointly with Horace Field. A design for Carville appears not to have been carried out, though *The Builder* in 1892 fully described the arched portico, small tower and white glazed interior. Perhaps the directors considered the 1879 standardised building perfectly adequate for shipyard workers. Manors was rebuilt in 1909 with a giant gable and a cupola-cum-clock tower, and rather more glamour was bestowed on the day trippers to Whitley Bay (1910), where Bell built a much taller clock tower adorned by fashionable festoons of terra-cotta fruit and flowers and an ogee-shaped top. Ball finials and more terra-cotta decoration embellished the three accompanying pavilions. Extensive glazed awnings were erected at these and other rebuilt stations like Wallsend and Monkseaton (1915), where there was little or no attempt to provide a frontage.

The same year saw much greater enlightenment by the London & North Western. In 1909 a new station was opened at Nuneaton Trent Valley, the clean lines of its neo-Georgian façade, circular windows and clock tower presenting a complete contrast to the elaborate Tudor of Livock's old station. Simultaneously work was under way on widening the lines out of Euston to Watford for the electrification of 1914–22, and Gerald Horsley was responsible for a number of the stations. He had been a pupil of Norman Shaw and the hand of the master was particularly apparent at Harrow & Wealdstone (1910) in the skilful contrast between dark red brick and white terra-cotta string courses in the tower, although the letters 'LNWR' set in circular orifices in the parapet concealing the booking hall dome were not the happiest of embellishments. Cream terra-cotta was sparingly applied to the neat entrance at Queens Park, Headstone Lane and the Harrow Road entrance to Willesden Junction, but lavishly at Bushey & Oxhey, where a cupola was graced by a clock and a smoking locomotive weathervane. Horsley undoubtedly achieved his best in the elegant neo-Georgian of Hatch End (1911), where red brick and white stone quoins made an appealing contrast (Plate 43). Door and window arches, chimney bands, beribboned swag and another cupola, clock and weathervane completed the composition, while the platform side had two pleasant Queen Anne gables. In his *First and Last Loves* (1952) John Betjeman called Hatch End and Harrow 'halfway between . . . a bank and a medium sized country house'. The new frontage block at Walsall, by H. J. Davis (designed in 1922 but opened by the LMSR), concluded this lamentably small revival with a booking hall of rare elegance. Its free classical vein included loosely coupled columns and pilasters and fine wood panelling.

Less appealing work in the same vein on the London, Brighton & South Coast Railway was carried out at Norbury, where the general effect of unequal sized gables and circular windows was of a struggle for recognition. Far better, the essay in Edwardian neo-Georgianism that replaced Mocatta's station at Horley in 1905 imparted a quiet dignity unknown on the Brighton since Mocatta's day, and even more effective was the slightly more elaborate example at Earlswood (Plate

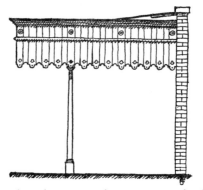

Typical South Eastern Railway awning, Wokingham

41). New buildings at Bosham and Three Bridges failed to achieve quite the same charm.

Seen from the train, the most distinctive late Brighton feature was the flat awning with deep plain-edged 'loping' valancing (to use Ian Nairn's description*). It first appeared in the late 1860s but only became widespread around the century's turn, generally decorated with a thin vertical slot shaped like a double keyhole. Columns and

LBSCR 'loping' valancing, Emsworth

brackets were suitably plain and simple, with circles in the spandrels, and some of the awnings had elliptical tops, as at Baynards and Isfield. Curved-topped awnings were also a distinguishing feature on the South Eastern, with fairly consistent adherence to attractive wavy-edged valancing perforated in a variety of patterns; likewise on the South Western, but without valancing, as at Surbiton and Lymington Pier. Larger stations on the latter system had very good, well glazed awnings—in contrast to such blank frontages as Basingstoke (1896)—with large end-gables decorated with triangular beading or semi-circular cut-outs, very much in Great Western fashion.

* *The Buildings of England: Sussex*, with Sir Nikolaus Pevsner

CHAPTER 10

THE SMALLER COMPANIES
AND JOINT LINES

THIS chapter deals with stations on lines that were not among the 'top ten' pre-grouping companies, or lines that were jointly owned by two or more other railways and have not so far been mentioned. Most of them were developed in the second half of the nineteenth century and many of their stations were of substantial but unimaginative appearance. Take, for instance, those small one-storey brick or stone stations in South Wales, built by the Taff Vale and Rhymney Railways, in which yellow brick or lighter stone banding usually formed the main relief. The Taff Vale rebuilt a few of its larger stations later in a more stylish manner. We have met Cardiff Queen Street in Chapter 7; but Pontypridd, rebuilt in 1907, was also remarkably ornate for this company, in ashlar with a panelled parapet and dentilled pediment mounted on an elaborate false gable over a series of rusticated semi-elliptical openings and interposed pilaster strips. The generous island platform roof covered no less than seven equally elaborate buildings. Terra-cotta and a general Free Renaissance air marked the reconstructed Aberdare station. Both companies, together with the later Barry Railway, made extensive use of timber buildings, as did the Brecon & Merthyr and Neath & Brecon Railways at Pontsticill Junction and Colbren Junction respectively, the latter with an interesting curved roof, frilly bargeboards and well moulded stone chimneys.

Brecon station (1871), headquarters of the Brecon & Merthyr, was a large two-storeyed red-brick edifice that did not really 'belong', despite fanciful bargeboarding and finials. The open-ended awning was the best touch. The stone one- and two-storey buildings at Talyllyn Junction (1869) and Talybont-on-Usk (1863), however, suited their hilly surroundings well, smacking strongly of some of the stations on the connecting Mid-Wales Railway (1864), such as Builth Wells and Talgarth, or the attractively rendered variations at Three Cocks Junction, Builth Road and, on the Aberystwyth & Welsh Coast Railway, Llanbedr & Pensarn (1867). These two lines joined with the Oswestry & Newtown, Oswestry, Ellesmere & Whitchurch and Newtown & Machynlleth Railways to form the Cambrian Railways. (It may be thought strange, incidentally, that with close on 300 miles of line the Cambrian is treated as a smaller company compared with, say, the North Staffordshire, which had only about 200. However, the latter formed not only an important link in a trunk route but was virtually a single entity from the start, hence its inclusion in earlier chapters.)

The Cambrian's constituents bequeathed it four remarkably large stations that hitherto had housed their respective head offices. Ellesmere (1864), Oswestry (c 1866) and Llanidloes (1864) were all two-storey red-brick structures with strong Italianate features in their round-headed openings, the latter two having attractive bay windows and stone dressings (Plate 45). Welshpool (1860) was the most remarkable of the four, in a purposeful French Renaissance style with stumpy pavilion-roofed end towers, gables, dormers and iron cresting. The platform was covered by a deep lean-to awning with valancing on the ends but not the edge, similar to those at Oswestry, Machynlleth and Aberystwyth. Similar awnings but with distinctive naturalistic cut-out end brackets were used at Newtown (1869), Towyn (1863), Barmouth, Portmadoc and Afon Wen (all 1867). The most memorable among Cambrian stations was the series of *cottage orné* buildings from Scafell to Machynlleth and on the Llanfyllin, Kerry and Mawddwy branches, some in brick with stone dressings, others all of stone, of which Cemmes Road was the most decorative. This consistency in stock designs owed much to the personalities common to these small companies—Benjamin Piercy the engineer and David Davies and Thomas Savin the contractors. The Cambrian itself rebuilt Frankton in the 1880s, using the same basic plan dressed up in red brick and terra-cotta with crested Dutch gables, ball finials and decorative glazing bars, almost a copy of something from the London & South Western Railway of this period.

Sir John Fowler left different but equally distinctive features on the sub-surface Metropolitan and Metropolitan District Railways in London, where he erected elliptically arched overall roofs between the retaining walls of the cuttings in which the stations of the Inner Circle lay, with characteristic radial glazing bars in the end screens. King's Cross, Edgware Road (1863), Bayswater and Notting Hill Gate (both 1868) were thus on the Metropolitan, among others, while Euston Square, Great Portland Street and Baker Street were truly 'underground' in tunnels, the curved roofs over the platforms being broken by vaulted alcoves fitted with thick glass lights and ventilation gratings in the streets above. A month after the opening some of the glass was already being removed to let out more smoke, and in 1871-2 special vents were made into the Euston and Marylebone roads to try further to alleviate the nuisance. Surface buildings were mostly variants on an Italianate theme, except Paddington (Bishops Road), which was French Renaissance in company with the Great Western Hotel. Great Portland Street had a pair of circular domed pavilions, and apart from Edgware Road they all had imitation stonework and mouldings in cement rendering, to *The Builder's* disgust.

Common entrance buildings were built where the Metropolitan and the District met, despite their notorious rivalry. Gloucester Road was a two-storey square Italianate structure in brick with white bands and a dentilled string course, the two company names appearing in green and white mosaic; and South Kensington was a low single-storey block with a plain columned entrance, above which the name appeared in ornate iron lettering. Wide shallow segmental roof trusses were used for the rebuilding of Farringdon and Aldersgate, while at Earls Court (1878) and Fulham Broadway (1880) the District favoured straight pitched roofs, the latter with Euston-type end screens. J. Wolfe Barry, the District's engineer, was responsible, though the design work for Fulham Broadway and Putney Bridge was by a Mr Clemmence. Putney had ridge-and-furrow awnings strikingly like those of the Metropolitan on its country extension, and a huge, seemingly two-storey frontage in yellow brick, with much dentilling, rustication and blank panels in the upper portion, which in reality was a screen wall at the rear of the elevated platform (Plate 46). The Moorish minarets at the District's Blackfriars were uniquely bizarre.

Station frontages in central London later tended to become mixed up with office and shop development, some being expressly rebuilt for this purpose, like the Moorfields block at Moorgate by Delissa Joseph in 1898 and Charing Cross and Temple by H. W. Ford in 1913. Large staid buff-brick buildings were erected by the Metropolitan at Ruislip and Uxbridge (1904), with red bands, terra-cotta and tiled roofs, but better than the ugly frontage of Rickmansworth (1887) with its even uglier iron *porte cochère* decorated with giant circles like the ungainly brackets under the hipped ridge-and-furrow platform awnings. The remaining stations out to Aylesbury, built between 1889 and 1892, had straight-gabled ridge-and-furrow awnings on neater foliated brackets, and were particularly commodious in anticipation of the residential development that followed.

East of the capital, the London, Tilbury & Southend Railway's stations chiefly had dull brick, slightly Gothic buildings—Pitsea and Laindon (1888) for example—with flat awnings and elaborately monogrammed brackets. East Ham's frontage had a lively 'Free Renaissance' parapet and Woodgrange Park some very fine though plain brick mouldings. Wooden valancing, particularly round the down-side ticket collector's hut, provided some of this line's most visually exuberant detailing at Westcliff-on-Sea.

Apart from its towers at James Street and Hamilton Square (Chapter 7), the Mersey Railway's other stations were notable more for their ample accommodation than appearance, though Birkenhead Central did have little Baroque-styled gables over its dormers and Green Lane a row of nicely arched terra-cotta openings and a low tower. In the late 1880s the Mersey's neighbour, the Wirral Railway, built new stations at Birkenhead North, Wallasey Grove Road and New Brighton in red brick with dark sandstone trim in a mildly Tudorish styling typical of the Domestic Revival. The company's arms were prominent on the gables in terra-cotta, and flat wooden awnings were carried on bulbous wooden pillars. New Brighton (1888) had a lofty booking hall with a wooden dentilled dado and open rafters. West Kirby (1896) could have passed off as a later station on the Great Central, the similarity in the large round-headed windows, timbered gables and well proportioned clock tower being so marked.

Sandstone buildings typified many of the stations on the local railways serving the Lake counties, ranging from the dark red ashlar of Ulverston in the south and the small plain Maryport & Carlisle Railway stations in the north to the pink rock-faced stone of the Cockermouth, Keswick & Penrith company's stations and the honey-coloured stone of Cockermouth itself. Tudor flourishes were sparingly added to the M & CR's headquarters at Maryport (1860), the junction station at Bullgill and at Papcastle (both 1867). Dalton (1846) on the Furness Railway had Gothic touches and Ravenglass (1849) attractive random walling with dressed stone trim. Blencow, on the CK & PR

(1865) and Woodend (1857) on the Whitehaven, Cleator & Egremont Junction Railway, each had a Midland-type twin-pavilion building in front of the simple house that was the more usual on the latter line, as at Winder and Rowrah (1862); as an alternative the Furness & Midland Joint line stations had the pavilion building added at one side, as at Borwick (1867). Two much larger stations broke the CK & PR's series of standardised cottage buildings: Keswick's two-storey building, with extensive ridge-and-furrow awnings, was connected to the company's hotel by a short glazed passage-way bearing portraits of famous painters in coloured glass, while Cockermouth was almost as spacious with an elaborate timber and glass screened waiting area on the platform. Even that late arrival the Cleator & Workington Junction Railway used sandstone in its ugly overhanging building at Working- ton Central (1879) and, as recently as 1910, at Moresby Parks—another structure in the style of Woodend. Finest of all was the new station at Ulverston, built in 1873 to replace the stone trainshed of 1854. It was strongly Italianate in composition with a large two-storey block at one end, elaborate iron cresting surrounding the top of the pavilion roof, and a handsome clock tower with large corner urns on the parapet. A central sandstone tower also graced the Furness Railway's main offices at Barrow (1866), with a platform round its campanile- like turret.

Grey random limestone was entirely fitting at the homely cottage stations of the Ulverston & Lancaster Railway (1857) at Silverdale, Arnside, Kents Bank and Cark & Cartmel, with rustic wooden shelters; light grey stone was also used at Brigham on the Cockermouth & Workington line (1847), which was rather gaunt with steep roofs, and at the Cleator & Workington Junction's station at Seaton (1887); and Sandside (1876) on the Furness Railway had deep overhanging Swiss chalet roofs.

The local brick used in the old Barrow station of 1863, with twin- arched entrance and a ridge-and-furrow roof, needed the slightly Italianate touch to give it life, but its successor of 1882 was a much enlarged edition of one of the Furness Railway's distinctive timber- framed structures, painted in contrasting colours to give a rustic effect. The lofty ridge-and-furrow roof had round-headed glazing in the end screens and a deep concave awning over the outside platform. It was as curious a choice for industrial Barrow as its precursor at the foot of the Old Man at Coniston (1869), where the roof had an arched end-screen springing from the platforms, gabled drystone walls and a large pent-roofed wooden *porte cochère*. On a much smaller scale, Foxfield's overall roof covered only one side of the island platform, where it joined the goods shed, the rustic wooden building being matched by the adjoining signal box (Plate 42). Seascale, Kirkby-in-Furness and subsidiary buildings at a number of other stations had more restrained rustic-styled timber buildings. Yellow brick with red banding was quite inimical to the environment of the Lakeside branch (1869), yet it was used on the stations at Greenodd, Haverthwaite and Lakeside itself, the last distinguished by a slender pointed tower and ridge-and-furrow overall roof. Conversely the quiet resort of Grange-over-Sands, which owed its growth to the Furness Railway, had a pleasant hipped-roofed stone station (1872) matching well with the Grange Hotel opposite.

The Furness provided some of our most delicate railway ironwork in brackets enclosing the FR monogram at Dalton and Ulverston (where the lamp brackets also were monogrammed), and floral designs at Grange and Whitehaven (Corkickle and Bransty). They supported hipped Midland-style ridge-and-furrow awnings on slender columns, though wooden brackets spoiled the effect on the down platform at Cark.

The monopoly of the North Eastern Railway ensured that only a few smaller companies could operate independently between the Humber and the border. Among the colliery lines of Durham the South Shields, Marsden & Whitburn Colliery Railway operated a unique public passenger service from 1888 between its surprisingly large and elaborate station at South Shields Westoe Lane—all brick

Iron awning bracket, Dalton, Furness Railway

dentilling and curved gables—and the imitation stone, faintly Tudor station at Whitburn Colliery. Further south the Derwent Valley Light Railway opened with a string of neat 'sports-pavilion' wooden stations in 1913; and on Humberside the Hull & Barnsley Railway (1885) mostly built stations of large stock designs in red brick with School Board windows, assorted gables and hefty chimneys, only Willerby & Kirk Ella being permitted the frivolity of bargeboards and valancing. The terminus at Hull Cannon Street was little more than a wooden shed, one of the sorry band of temporary stations that became permanent.

Monogrammed bracket, Shanklin, Isle of Wight Railway

Two stations on the Isle of Wight Railway warrant mention. Sandown (1864) had a plain two-storey rendered main building, and, beside it, a smaller gabled and finialled building enlivened by a giant eight-light mullioned window, later removed. Bembridge (1882) was an ambitious terminus for a $7\frac{1}{2}$ mile branch serving less than 2,000 inhabitants, its two-storey buff-brick building composed of seven bays with gabled dormers and heavy chimneystacks—all very solidly Victorian, if lacking a recognisable style. Ventnor West (1900) on the Isle of Wight Central Railway was well built in uncoursed stone with large School Board windows and a patterned tiled roof typical of its date.

We have noted in their appropriate chapters those joint-line stations that clearly showed the style of one of their owners. Now we must complete the picture by looking at those with some individuality, derived from independent origins or a largely independent management. For both these reasons the three phases of building on the Birkenhead Joint Railway owed nothing to either of its owners—the LNWR and GWR. From the original company came the *cottage orné* of Halton and Norton (1850) and the Jacobean or Tudor rock-faced sandstone of Helsby, Ince & Elton, Little Sutton and Ellesmere Port (1863)—the last endowed later with preposterous brick chimneystacks. The second and third phases were the work of the joint-line's engineer, R. E. Johnston, beginning with weakly neo-Gothic in brick at Hooton, Bromborough, Neston South and Hadlow Road (1863), but followed by sedate Domestic Revival buildings at Bromborough, Ledsham, Bebbington & New Ferry, Rock Ferry and Birkenhead Town when the line was widened in the 1890s. Striped gables and sandstone mullions set the latter stations apart, the last two being further distinguished by Brighton-style lanterns.

The stations of the Midland & Great Northern Joint line's components can be divided into two parts, west and east of Kings Lynn. From Peterborough to Sutton Bridge (1866) they were small, substantial but unimaginative, all in red brick except Eye Green, which was in yellow with red dressings, and Wisbech North, a wooden twin-pavilion station. Stations between Lynn and Bourne clearly showed the hand of more than one company. Walpole, for instance, on the Lynn & Sutton Bridge Railway, had in effect three brick buildings—a two-storey house, plain single-storey offices with central gable, and an even plainer waiting room added later. Gedney, on the other hand, built by the Spalding & Norwich company, was styled in the Thompson manner of the Eastern Counties Railway with a lean-to 'apron' and end blocks. East of Lynn two small lines built between 1878 and 1882 combined to form the Eastern & Midlands Railway. Their buildings were small, generally brick and had only slight differences. Hillington, for instance, had twin pavilions with plain gables and a hipped-roofed timber-framed extension; North Walsham Town had striped gables. Brick to dado height, with timber and extensive glazing above, was a feature of later buildings at South Lynn, with the deep flat awnings that were also to be seen at Sutton Bridge (all timber) and Melton Constable (all brick); 'GNR' in the brackets denoted the source of the design. The Cromer branch of 1887 had quite extensive stations, notably Sheringham's hipped ridge-and-furrow awnings on severe Great Northern-type buildings, and the ridge-and-furrow overall roof at Cromer Beach. Debasement of Italianate was well illustrated by the Eastern & Midlands Railway's headquarters at Norwich City station, where red brick was given superficial grandiosity by adding a giant pediment, raised corner blocks and extensive surface frills from blind arcading to blank mini-porticos.

Three stations on the Manchester South Junction & Altrincham Railway (LNW and MSL) were of more than ordinary interest. Deansgate (1896) occupied an acute-angled site with a curved entrance on the corner. The twin doorways were Gothic-arched, complete with mock portcullis; and crammed into the short parapet were brick castellations, two stone shields, a pointed false gable and a clock. Beneath the frieze the words 'Knott Mill Station' (its name until 1971) appeared on a terra-cotta scroll. Old Trafford had a curious twelve-sided building at street level with a circular pavilion roof and iron cresting proclaiming the word 'Station' behind a low stone parapet with large ball finials, looking like some hefty fairground roundabout. The rest of the stations were of London & North Western pattern, Altrincham & Bowdon (1881) having quite attractive polychrome brickwork in the lintels and curly eaves brackets. The large iron *porte cochère* and platform awnings contained elaborate ironwork, and the long frontage was set back behind iron railings with red and yellow brick pillars and, in the middle, a free-standing clock tower.

Ilkley, Burley-in-Wharfedale and Otley (1865), on the Otley & Ilkley Joint line of the Midland and North Eastern companies were single-storey Italianate buildings in ashlar, given dignity by contrasting stone pilastered windows at each end. They were similar to the neighbouring Midland station of Guiseley. Ilkley, larger and longer, had a raised central section and stone corbelling under the eaves; Ben Rhydding (1866), quite different, had an unusual 'up-and-down' stepped parapet that perhaps owed something to the local Hydro.

In 1862 the Somerset Central and Dorset Central Railways joined forces as the Somerset & Dorset, later coming under the joint ownership of the Midland and London & South Western companies. The two original lines worked closely with each other, as was evidenced by their very similar small, simple, foursquare stations with either upward or downward canted awnings and plain saw-tooth valancing. In the north they were in creamy-grey rock-faced Mendip stone, and further south in red brick. One of the larger buildings, at Masbury (1874), was two-storeyed with dormer windows, and its stationmaster's bay sported a stone tablet engraved with what purported to be a likeness of Maesbury Castle. Since the real thing was no more than an Iron Age hill fort, its portrayal as a medieval castle was rather more than artist's licence. Pylle (1862) had what was surely a unique stone goods shed flanking the platform, for one end contained the station house. Glastonbury (1854) was wooden with valancing along the eaves and generous awnings, and contained the company's offices; Bason Bridge (1856) was a much smaller repetition. Highbridge had stone dressings and a war memorial tablet in the wall; Bridgwater (1890) had round-topped openings in an otherwise plain brick exterior.

Stations on the originally independent Shrewsbury & Hereford Railway (LNW and GWR), opened 1852–3, were well built in brick or stone, and were either plain, with shallow hipped roofs and distinctively patterned glazing bars, or tending towards Tudor. The original Church Stretton station, Woofferton and Dorrington were in the first category; and Onibury, Condover and Bromfield in the second, with Ludlow claiming special interest by its angled chimneys and low-arched main window to the frontage. Tenbury Wells station (1861), on a branch, was among the largest of the Tudor stations, a quietly dignified composition with a matching signal box attached to the subsidiary building (Plate 48). Very deep, effectively decorated iron brackets were a notable feature of the extensive saw-toothed awnings at Craven Arms & Stokesay.

South Elmsall and Carcroft & Adwick-le-Street (1860) in Yorkshire had rock-faced grey stone buildings with low hipped roofs bracketed at the eaves and, in each case, a short square conical turret topped by a tall iron weathervane. Considering that they served the colliery district traversed by the West Riding & Grimsby Joint line of the Great Central and Great Northern companies, their styling was quite remarkable. Hemsworth was rebuilt about 1912 in the London Extension idiom of the Great Central.

The Great Northern and London & North Western Joint line stations were essentially GNR in character, but Melton Mowbray North (1879) deserves special mention for the delightfully moulded and carved brick pedimented window hoods, gables and even ball finials that enlivened the long low frontage. Fluted brick pilaster strips with more decorative work flanked the central doorway and windows; brick coats of arms in the Redmile style (Chapter 11) were fashioned in the gables.

The Great Northern and Great Eastern had a long joint line from March almost to Doncaster. South of Lincoln the stations were mainly single-storey in typical Great Eastern style of 1882; northward the line was part of the Great Northern's original route of 1849 to Gainsborough, extended to Doncaster in 1867, on which the stations were typical of that company and nearly all alike. Some exceptions were the confused composition of gables and Tudor chimneys at Saxilby and the pleasant round-headed windows set in buff brick amid the hollies and fir trees of Gainsborough Lea Road. Detached sections of earlier origin south of March contained two particularly outstanding stations, both in their different ways a delight. Godmanchester (1847) was Jacobean with a plain wooden awning on wooden brackets containing trefoils, a modestly dignified station typical of the good building then being practised by the railways. Chatteris (1848) had a three-bay arcaded brick portico beneath a simply panelled parapet with matching arched windows behind, and to the platform another arcade of five bays. Deep stone mullioned windows, corner pilasters and a decorative panel marked the stationmaster's office.

Three companies owned the largest and most individual joint railway, the Cheshire Lines Committee. It may not have possessed any locomotives, like the Midland & Great Northern and the Somerset & Dorset did, but it had its own distinctive rolling stock, signals and stations, none of which could have been mistaken for any other. The influence of the Great Northern Railway was notably absent but features of the other two partners—the Manchester, Sheffield & Lincolnshire and the Midland—were prominent in CLC stations. Cheadle, Northenden and Baguley (1866) were the first to display them, their general building design being unmistakably attributable to the MSL—one- and two-storey brick pavilions with a single-storey section between, the steep roof brought forward on iron columns and shallow curved brackets to make a waiting shelter, but superimposed by most elaborate bargeboarding that was equally unmistakably Midland-inspired. On the Manchester–Liverpool main line buildings of this kind were standard, but without the bay window of the earlier ones, differing from each other only in their bargeboarding, which varied not just between stations but between gables on the same building. Door and window openings were debased Gothic in coloured brick. Examples were Irlam, Sankey, Widnes North and Hough Green, all of 1873, Irlam having the later addition of a curious, partly detached hipped glass awning leaving an open space between it and the main building. Hunts Cross (1873) comprised a very tall four-storey building against the road bridge, with peaked dormers, a

CLC bargeboards at Widnes North

decorative iron balcony at first-floor level and stairs down to the platform. Garston (1874) was even more elaborate: stone crow-stepped gables, iron cresting and stone mullions without; four flights of iron-banistered stairs around a square well, open raftered roof with central pendant finial, and white tiled walls within. St Michaels and Mersey Road & Aigburth, dating from 1864 before the Midland secured an interest, had round-headed openings but retained the bargeboarding and general MSL style; St James (1874), on the edge of an inner Liverpool residential district that was still fashionable and essentially Georgian, had a special five-bay arcaded frontage in rusticated ashlar. Half-hipped gabled roofs with perforated eaves valancing and various other trimmings gave Cressington & Grassendale station a suitably special air for the two private estates whose names it took. Actually situated in Cressington Park estate, developed c 1850, it was reached via the private entrance lodge.

Warrington Central (1873), the CLC's principal intermediate station, also received special treatment. In brick with stone trim, the long one-storey frontage of twenty bays had Italianate round-headed rusticated openings, some single, some coupled with pleasantly patterned glazing bars. In the middle a giant triangular pediment was flanked by short balustraded parapets, solid further on, with a large pitched *porte cochère*. At the east end a solitary terminal block had an ornamental dormer and a French pavilion roof. It must have been one of the least-observed frontages, as most passengers used the stairs to Horse Market Street.

Stations on the Chester line were severely practical house-type structures with adjoining offices, all brick except for Delamere and Mouldsworth (1870) in rock-faced stone. Knutsford (1862) had an interesting ridge-and-furrow awning with curved outer gables, while Northwich was rebuilt in yellow brick in 1897 with an enormity of a false gable over an intricately patterned iron canopy. Chester North-gate terminus (1874) was indifferent in red brick, and was notable only for its strictly utilitarian two bay glass-and-iron shed. To serve north Liverpool a new line was opened in 1879 with the faintest of Domestic Revival styling, anticipating by twenty years the last practices of the Midland, in brick with sandstone dressings as at Gateacre and West Derby.

By a curious accident of history the four CLC-styled stations on the Manchester South District Railway (1880) belonged to the Midland. The original independent company was authorised to make 'arrange-ments' with the MSL, but after a disagreement in 1877 it fell into the Midland's hands during construction. The separate entrance buildings at Didsbury and Withington had CLC features, though the ridge-and-furrow platform awnings favoured Midland practice, with curved outer ends like Newark's and glazed end-screens. But Heaton Mersey and Chorlton-cum-Hardy were pure CLC designs in the main-line style and—the final twist—Chorlton eventually became CLC property when a short section of line at the west end was transferred to it, but not before it had become more obviously hybrid by the addition of a Midland awning.

One joint station that cannot be ignored was Market Harborough, at a junction of the London & North Western and the Midland. The symmetrical two-storey Queen Anne frontage, in pleasingly reserved red brick with stone pilaster strips, moulded door and window casings

Iron balustrade, Hunts Cross, CLC

and curved pedimented hoods, owed nothing to the traditions of either of its owners but kept up well with the Georgian vernacular of the town. A moulded wooden dormer set in the slightly concave hipped roof added a nice touch of fantasy.

Neither must the narrow gauge be disregarded, for, although the limited resources of these small lines rarely allowed flourishes, some modest touches did appear on occasions. The shorter Welsh lines generally kept to small stone structures, though the Corris Railway aspired to an overall roof at Corris and a surprisingly large though plain coursed-stone building at Machynlleth. Standard gauge neighbours sometimes provided ideas for design; Bryngwyn and Tryfan Junction (1877) on the Welsh Highland were replicas of the little stone and yellow brick buildings on the Caernarvon–Afon Wen line, though South Snowdon (1877) relapsed into objectionable red brick and Beddgelert (1923) even further into corrugated iron. As befitted the premier Welsh narrow-gauge line, the Festiniog Railway's stations were nearer to main-line standards. Minffordd and Duffws displayed distinct Cambrian characteristics, the former two-storeyed in slate with ashlar quoins, tiled roof, bargeboarding and an ample waiting shelter alongside. Tan-y-Grisiau and Portmadoc also were two-storeyed, with 'apron' type lean-to shelters in front. Blaenau Festiniog was merely a long narrow shelter against the rear wall of the platform, with a small office section at one end, but Penrhyndeudraeth, though wooden, was commodious, with a large roof extending outward to form a canopy on wooden pillars.

English narrow-gauge lines had wooden hut type stations in the main. The Ravenglass terminus of the Ravenglass & Eskdale Railway in its 3ft days boasted a wooden shed whose close-boarded gables and end-screens had scalloped edges; and the Southwold Railway's station at Southwold (1879) was well above the average in brick nogging. The Lynton & Barnstaple (1898) went in for an attractive chalet-bungalow style called *Nuremberg*, which had prominent sloping roofs and deep eaves-height projections. At Woody Bay, Blackmoor and Lynton such stations achieved minor distinction and a sympathy with their settings.

For sheer grandiosity on the narrow gauge we must turn to the Isle of Man. Douglas (c 1890) eclipsed many an important standard-gauge station on the mainland, showing Dutch gables and a French-styled tower, long platforms extensively roofed over and a highly original, separate entrance arch with Baroque turrets and a pedimented clock

(Plate 44). Port St Mary's massive gabled building (1896) had black-and-white timbering on one wing, yellow brick detailing in the other and a gabled waiting shelter in front—the most freely Domestic Revival-cum-Tudor imaginable. It completely dwarfed the low platform and single 3ft gauge line. Castletown (1874), in grey rock-faced stone, and Port Erin (1903), in brick and terra-cotta, were twin pavilions, again unusually large, as were the half-timbered Peel (1907) and the pebble-dashed rendering of Ramsey (1879).

CHAPTER II

SPECIAL STATIONS

SOME stations were built for special people or special places. Taking the first category, a number of stations designed or embellished to suit powerful personages have already been referred to, but most special of all, of course, were the royal stations.

The lengths to which the South Western Railway and Sir William Tite were prepared to go in order to accommodate Queen Victoria in proper style at Windsor & Eton Riverside, and simultaneously outdo the Great Western, has been described in Chapter 3. Eventually the GWR decided to provide something better than its Brunel-type shed, and in 1897 opened an enlarged edition of one of its French-styled stations at Windsor & Eton Central. The two, quite separate, elliptical glass-and-iron roofs over the cab drive made the station look like a miniature Paddington, surmounted at the front (facing the castle) by a vast screen gable of red brick and white stone bands with a Queen Anne styled hood over the company's arms and a clock—a ponderous affair seemingly supported by the thinnest of stone soffits and a slender glazed screen. A private waiting room on the main platform was essentially a standard building, the only concessions to royalty being stone facings instead of brick and a pair of crowns bearing the ciphers of Victoria and—a diplomatic addition in 1902—Edward VII. A cherry-red brick three-storey office building adjoining the platform had the usual French turrets and, for good measure, pedimented first-floor windows and small iron balconies on the third.

Tite's Gosport station was supplemented by a private station inside the Royal Dockyard for the Queen's journeyings to Osborne on the Isle of Wight. It was unusually functional, merely a long curving platform and single line covered by a glass roof on screen walls with round-headed openings and latticed iron windows. A simple covered way led from the middle of the platform to the landing stage. Across the Solent, Whippingham station was specially built for Osborne, but it was also open to the public.

The most convenient station for Sandringham was Wolferton, where the Great Eastern obliged with a selection of their best Domestic Revival designs, by W. N. Ashbee, in a spreading frontage clearly divided into public and private sections. The former's pseudo half-timbering and 'sports pavilion' aspect, with overhanging eaves, gables and cupola-clock, played definite second fiddle to the older royal building in carstone, with brick dressings, striped gables and rustic 'lych-gate' styled *porte cochère*. It housed three royal waiting rooms, and a standard flat awning sheltered the platforms. As a final touch, the platform lamps were topped by gilded crowns.

When occasion demanded—usually the use of or need for influence by one side or the other—the nobility and gentry got special consideration, too, particularly if one happened to be the company chairman like the Earl of Yarborough, for whom a delightful Jacobean station was built near the gates of Brocklesby Hall on the Manchester, Sheffield & Lincolnshire Railway's main line. Brocklesby station (1848) had a lively roofline, gables on four sides, and stone-mullioned windows in brick walls. Prince Albert used it when he stayed with the Yarboroughs before laying the foundation stone of the company's new Grimsby dock in 1849.

The great railway contractor Sir Morton Peto employed John Thomas to build him an extravagant neo-Jacobean house at Somerleyton in Suffolk, begun in 1844, and a half-timbered thatch-roofed village to go with it. It seems likely that Thomas also designed the station on the Norfolk Railway (1847), in brick with generous stone trim, a low square tower, diamond-panelled parapet and latticed windows, and Peto's crest over the entrance porch. A chaste wooden awning perfected the platform elevation, an effect completely opposite to that of the heavy standard wooden awning used by the London & North Western at its late-Victorian station at Waverton (1899), styled in sandstone similarly to the local estate buildings of the Duke of Westminster at Eaton Hall, Cheshire. The main features were twisted Tudor chimneys and four spiked finials on each roof.

Belvoir Castle and the Duke of Rutland were the justification for the Great Northern and London & North Western's joint Domestic Revival extravaganza at Redmile (1878–9). The Great Northern's engineer, Fraser, articulated his standard ridge-and-furrow awning into a series of gables along the platform elevation, while the long low frontage displayed extreme versatility in carved and moulded brickwork, from festoons of swag on the huge square chimneystacks to sunflower motifs over the windows and a giant coat of arms on an end gable. The ducal waiting room, lavishly panelled in wood on walls and ceiling, was dominated by a vast oak chimneypiece. In the centre, framed, was a carved depiction of the chase, with Belvoir Castle in the background, and the whole elaborate erection was supported by two pairs of muscular unclothed instrument-playing caryatids (Plate 47).

The other extreme was represented by Easton Lodge, between Bishops Stortford and Braintree, where the Great Eastern built the Countess of Warwick a standard small wooden station.

Some quite ordinary stations had special apartments set aside for local notables. The standardised London & North Western station at Berkhamsted (1875), for instance, had a 'permanent suite of rooms with octagonal hall and external verandah' for Earl Brownlow's use, *The Builder* approvingly noted, discreetly tucked away near the rear entrance. Likewise the Midland maintained more than usually well appointed first-class waiting rooms at Rowsley, with leather sofas, armchairs and travelling rugs, for the occupants of Chatsworth and their guests.

Schools were sometimes felt to warrant special treatment. When the younger Charles Barry built the new Dulwich College, he also designed a special Tudor-Jacobean station for the Brighton Railway at North Dulwich (1868) quite unlike anything else on that line, with a three-arched entrance on coupled columns, splendid fretted parapets and tall clusters of six to ten chimneystacks. Yet in 1902 an amusing, almost comical, derivation of the same company's large Italianate building was erected at Christ's Hospital, partly for the school and partly in anticipation of housing development which failed to materialise. Capricious red-and-white chequerwork that filled the bargeboarded gables was repeated over round-headed windows below, and a smaller subsidiary building was built to match.

Railway companies were not particularly regardful of the past, but at least two that built stations to serve the more serious tourist attractions had their localities in mind and found the same solution. Neath Abbey station (1863) was provided by the Swansea & Neath Railway with elaborately half-timbered bargeboarded buildings; Furness Abbey, alongside the Furness Railway (to Wordsworth's disgust), also had a half-timbered station in the company's then current style, with a slender pointed turret. Neither was a discredit to its surroundings.

At one time there existed a fair number of completely private stations to which the public was not admitted. Somewhat surprisingly two were on the small Maryport & Carlisle Railway: Dovenby (1867), a stone house-styled station adjoining the grounds of the Ballantine-Dykes at Dovenby Hall; and Crofton (1843), outside the Ionic gateway to Crofton Hall and more stylish, as one would expect from its earlier date, with Tudorish triple gables and two platforms lending an air of greater importance for its patron, Sir Musgrave Brisco. A more modest single-platform station was built by the London & South Western Railway at Avon Lodge, on the Ringwood–Christchurch line, for Thomas Turner of Avon Castle; and, as part of a deal over land with Sir Barrington Simon, the Freshwater, Yarmouth & Newport Railway built him a small private station at Watchingwell on the Isle of Wight. There were others, too—Tir Celyn on the Cambrian's Mid-Wales line, and Black Dog Halt on the Great Western's Calne branch. Some were later made public. Trains usually called by prior agreement, or were simply signalled to stop, the latter practice giving the name to Westmoor Flag Station on the Hereford, Hay & Brecon line of the Midland Railway. Built for a local landowner, G. H. Davenport, it was the most substantial station on the line—the others were wooden—in red-brick Italianate including a small arcaded waiting shelter. Hall Dene station (1871) was the private station of Lord Londonderry, close to Seaham Hall near Sunderland, and when he sold his Londonderry Railway to the North Eastern in 1900, it remained his property. It was quite a large single-storey building in red brick with white terra-cotta bands and decorative bargeboards. A separate private platform, just long enough for one coach, was provided for Lord Hastings at Melton Constable on the Midland & Great Northern Joint line.

Private stations were sometimes built to serve factories. Irlam Halt on the Cheshire Lines served the Co-operative Soap Works, and Daimler Halt (1917) the motor-car works of that company close to the London & North Western's Coventry–Nuneaton branch. It later became a public station. Port Sunlight originally was a factory station, its weatherboarding and low hipped roofs intended to tone with the model estate. Even rural industries were provided for: Briery bobbin mill near Keswick had a special halt on the Cockermouth, Keswick & Penrith Railway. The curiously named Salvation Army Halt on the

Great Northern's Hatfield–St Albans branch served the Army's printing works. There were several special platforms for railway employees at places not otherwise accessible, from the rural Sugar Loaf Summit on the LNWR Central Wales line to the South Western's carriage sidings at Durnsford Road near Wimbledon. Some large hospitals had their private branch lines for conveying coal and supplies, one or two with passenger stations, such as Cheddleton Asylum on the North Stafford-shire's Churnet Valley line and Netley Hospital on the London & South Western Railway near Southampton. The Whittingham Hospital Railway, which ran from the Preston & Longridge Joint line at Grimsargh, carried passengers free between its two stations. The hospital terminus, situated on a curve, even had a glass overall roof.

The London Necropolis Company built a private branch to its cemetery from Brookwood on the London & South Western's main line, with two suitably designed stations. The South Western obligingly made a special entrance at its own station, which was repeated in the 1903 rebuilding, while at the London end the Necropolis Company erected a special station next to Waterloo. After several moves to allow for enlargement of the main station, the final form (1902) comprised two platforms beneath hipped awnings—one for mourners and one for coffins—which were reached by a covered way leading from an ornate entrance arch, heavily corniced, with ornamental gates and an iron parapet bearing the words 'Cemetery Station'.

After the Crystal Palace was moved from Hyde Park to Sydenham Hill, the London, Brighton & South Coast Railway built a new station, opened in 1854, which was fully equal to the occasion. Crystal Palace Low Level had a faintly French Renaissance frontage with unequal pavilion roofs and an elegant five-bay iron *porte cochère*. The usual Brighton lantern rose over the iron-ribbed booking-hall roof, and, below, a low crescent-shaped twin-span roof formed the trainshed between heavily buttressed brick screen walls sporting blind acarding and massive end-blocks. Three 'grand staircases', with huge stone-capped newel posts and copings, ensured rapid entry and exit for the crowds. *The Builder* considered that while the design—by a Mr Gough —left little to be desired, it could have done with 'more light after sundown and shelter from piercing winds'.

The London, Chatham & Dover Railway reached the Palace by constructing a new branch line from Peckham Rye, completed in 1865. Its Crystal Palace High Level station outdid the Brighton's in style and location. Banks and Barry were commissioned to build it right alongside the Palace, to which it was connected by a subway, and for £100,000 they provided an amazing structure, each corner occupied by a broad square tower with four French turrets apiece like miniature castles. Blind arcading with glazed upper sections appeared in the long side screen walls, and end walls were provided as well, with four square openings to admit the trains. There were to be no complaints about draughts here! Platforms were built on both sides of the centre tracks to ensure rapid alighting and boarding, and two circulating areas were built on bridges above them. The whole was enclosed by a two-bay roof, crescent-shaped like the Low Level station, on a central brick arcade. Heavy rustication, banded brick and tile work and an elaborate parapet completed the external adornment of this, the Chatham's most extravagant station. The Great Northern's station at Alexandra Palace (1873) was much less dramatic, anti-climactic, in fact; the dumpy little buff-brick building beside the broad entrance staircase was completely overshadowed and dominated by the huge bulk of the 'Ally Pally'.

Sport was served by special stations, too, racegoers being provided for by the Great Western at Cheltenham and Newbury Racecourse stations, for instance, and by Aintree Racecourse on the Lancashire & Yorkshire Railway. Old Trafford cricket ground and Manchester United football club had a station on the Manchester South Junction & Altrincham Railway, which started an intermittent life as Manchester Art Treasures Exhibition in 1857 and eventually became Warwick Road; and in 1901 the Great Central provided Nottingham Golf Club with a halt at Hollinwell & Annesley. They were all wooden stations. Even shooting was not forgotten at Shooting Range Platform on the LSWR Bodmin branch and by the South Eastern & Chatham at Milton Range Halt.

Port stations grew with the development of railway shipping interests, their layouts becoming more elaborate as demand increased. By the 1870s and 1880s passengers had seldom far to walk from train to boat, which was usually moored alongside. Folkestone Harbour station (1850) had a typical South Eastern entrance building in rendered brick and two long covered platforms. At Holyhead, built in 1880, separate arrival and departure platforms beneath Euston-type roofs flanked the inner harbour quays, 'V'-fashion, the new hotel occupying the apex and enclosing on three sides a commemorative iron clock. There were minimal buildings at Portsmouth Harbour (1876), though the wooden platforms were amply covered by glass awnings; but

Iron awning bracket, Folkestone Harbour, SER

extensive wooden buildings in typical London, Brighton & South Coast style—complete with two pyramidal turrets, pitch pine interiors and the inevitable lantern—formed the Continental section of Newhaven Harbour station (1886). The Furness Railway's Ramsden Dock station at Barrow (1881) also bore its owner's stamp, being extravagantly gabled with a long overall roof. Liverpool Riverside (1895), belonging to the Mersey Docks & Harbour Board, was a long brick shed looking like a transit warehouse and in keeping with the more utilitarian ideas of the early twentieth century. Heysham (1904) was composed of wooden Midland Railway buildings and screen wall beneath a ridge-and-furrow roof on latticed girders, and Fishguard Harbour (1906) was equally and unmistakably Great Western under a lofty pitched roof; both were plentifully glazed. The swansong of the South Eastern & Chatham and the apotheosis of harbour stations, Dover Marine was opened first for military traffic in 1915 and had as its main elevation a massive chunky Baroque inner end-screen in rock-faced stone with arched openings admitting the tracks. Inside all was lightness and grace, from the glazed roof to the slender elliptical trusses. Low, rather austere brick platform buildings were reminders of the old Chatham days.

Pier stations were built of wood for lightness, again in their owners' distinctive styles, like the South Eastern building at Port Victoria (1882), the South Western's at Lymington Pier (1884) and the Great Central station on New Holland Pier, which was probably rebuilt when extensive renewals took place in 1922. Two harbour stations had no trains: Dartmouth, the Great Western's 'station' for the Kingswear ferry, comprised a wooden booking office and waiting room with the company's French pavilion roof and cresting; Hull Corporation Pier, built by the Manchester, Sheffield & Lincolnshire in 1880 for its New Holland ferry service, was a more imposing two-storey brick building with ashlar dressings and a moulded gable enclosing a clock. Two 'non-railway' pier stations, built by the Furness Railway at Ambleside and Bowness for its Windermere steamers, were typically rustic wooden station-type structures; while the third, Lakeside, was a proper station on the branch from Ulverston (1869—see Chapter 10), with an elaborate two-storey iron-and-glass covered landing stage alongside. The upper floor formed a tea room whence Victorian excursionists might admire the scenery in fitting style.

CHAPTER 12

FIXTURES AND FITTINGS

VISIT a closed station and realise how doubly forlorn it is without the seats, lamps, noticeboards and other miscellaneous accessories that once gave it life. Platform seats alone had tremendous variety. They were not only ideal for displaying the station name along the back-rest, but also for showing off the company's initials on the iron ends. The Great Western, Great Eastern, London, Tilbury & Southend and South Eastern Railways in particular adopted this latter practice, while the North Staffordshire exhibited its knot motif and the Furness Railway its life-sized squirrel emblem. Proprietary pseudo-rustic knobbly iron seats were favoured by the Midland, springy park-bench types by the London & North Western.

Furness Railway iron seat end, with squirrel emblem, Grange-over-Sands

Although cheap mass-produced cast iron of this kind was coarse compared with the hand-worked wrought iron it superseded, a good deal of the railways' ironwork was worthy in its own right. The delicate ironwork on the hydraulic lifts at Manchester Victoria and the almost filigree brackets of the entrance canopy matching the Venetian windows at Leamington Spa Avenue readily come to mind, and, as we have seen already, many an ordinary building was transformed by outstanding ironwork. The rare quality of geometric patterns and floral flourishes at Pudsey Greenside and Lowtown stations (1871), for instance, or the brackets at Derby Friargate, did much to enhance these humdrum Great Northern stations, as did the frilly valancing at Hightown and curious iron lacework at Heywood on the Lancashire & Yorkshire. A really magnificent specimen of the moulder's art was a Great Eastern knife-board seat at Huntingdon East: the ends con-

Iron frill beneath eaves, Heywood, LYR

tained the company's crest (itself a combination of the arms of nine towns or counties) set in a tight pattern of swastikas and diamonds, and the back-to-back sections were formed by a pair of finely decorated iron plates. Equally notable cast-iron work could be seen in delicately monogrammed initials in roof and awning brackets, including those of forgotten lines like the Eastern & Midlands Railway at Yarmouth and Cromer Beach stations and the Bedford & Cambridge at Gamlingay and Potton, whose initials lingered on a century or more after their original owners had disappeared.

The Midland Railway forsook its usual simple bracket at Hellifield in favour of one snugly enclosing its wyvern symbol, a decoration more often found on a stone plaque on the frontage, as at Skipton. At Bala the letters 'F & B', for Festiniog & Bala Railway, appeared on a stone plaque on the façade. Although initials were the more common, sometimes coats of arms adorned a station: early examples were those of the joint owners of Carlisle, the Lancaster & Carlisle and Caledonian Railways, the crest of the East Lancashire Railway on the iron gates at Bury Bolton Street, and the Manchester & Birmingham's insignia in the London & North Western booking hall at Manchester London Road.

Waiting-room benches, too, formed convenient places for initials. The Midland had a fondness for Gothic lettering and a meticulous regard for ownership: 's & m j l', for instance, appearing on the waiting-room benches and in the awning brackets at Marple, stands for Sheffield & Midland Joint Line.

A lengthy chapter could be devoted to the countless shapes and sizes of platform lamps. Country stations were lit by paraffin lamps in iron-framed lanterns hung beneath awnings or fitted to wall brackets or posts, but principal stations generally were gas-lit from the beginning. Lamp posts ranged from some early elegant fluted examples from the London & North Western to the Midland's robust hexagonal variety, the South Western's twisted pattern and the old rail used by the Great Eastern in its later days. For its London Extension the Great Central adopted a slender spiral design terminating in a wing-shaped crossbar. The crossbar on some of the North Eastern's posts bore its initials, and most lamp posts and roofing columns carried the name of the foundry. Handyside of Derby and Mabon & Sons of Ardwick produced ironwork for countless stations, along with small local firms like Smith & Sons of Whitchurch, who cast the nice trefoil brackets at that station and at Nantwich.

Lanterns were even more diversely designed than posts; generally square or hexagonal in cross-section, they had tapered sides ranging

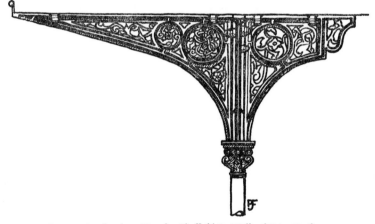

Iron awning bracket, Marple, Sheffield & Midland Joint Railway

(left) *Glass-topped oil lamp, Harmston, GNR*

(right) *Cage-type iron oil lamp, Wrenbury, LNWR*

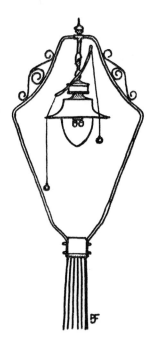

(left) *GWR Gas lamp at Goring & Streatley, with Sugg-type lantern substituted*

ASHBURY

(right) *Standard LSWR twisted iron lamp column and lantern, Ashbury*

from near-upright to the almost pointed hexagonal lantern of the North Western. The iron ventilator on top might be formed as a finial, pointed on the Midland, butterfly-shaped on the London & South Western, or as a plain 'pepper-pot' on the North Eastern, whose lanterns often simply sat in a square iron hoop on a wooden post. Elsewhere lanterns might be suspended in an iron cage or vertical hoop, the Great Western being partial to a broad square type hung in a squashed-out hoop on a fairly plain post. Later on and after the grouping the ugly Sugg 'top-hat' type of gas lamp began to supersede the glass lantern.

Enamel sign, Cholsey & Moulsford, GWR

Large stations were treated appropriately. Big circular-section all-glass lanterns, rounded at the bottom, hung from the roof at York or, crowned by an iron coronet, drooped mournfully from double iron brackets and posts of excruciating elaboration at Liverpool Street. Large globes were popular, slung in iron cradles to illuminate High Street Kensington on the Metropolitan Railway, for instance, or fitted on cruciform iron standards at Cannon Street. Rarely among the progressives, the South Eastern Railway surprisingly was the first to install electric lighting there and at Charing Cross.

No station was complete without its crop of notices to inform, exhort or order the passengers about, generally in cast-iron letters on a wooden board. Vitreous enamel signs were later adopted on some lines, the Great Western going in for dark blue lettering on a white ground, the Midland the opposite, the Hull & Barnsley white on black and the North Eastern brown letters on a distinctively shaped cream coloured plate edged in brown—made by the Patent Enamel Company and looking not unlike British Railways' 'double sausage' nameplates. Etched window glass was a widely used method of indicating the use of offices, and the Great Central used a standard frilly-edged cast-iron sign throughout its London Extension. A notably enduring piece of publicity could be seen in the booking halls at two Victoria stations—the London, Brighton & South Coast's in London and the Lancashire & Yorkshire's in Manchester—in large wall maps of the systems in glazed tiles. The North Eastern installed tile maps more widely and made them more elaborate. They were found at medium-sized stations like Tynemouth and Beverley, and even indicated cathedrals, castles, abbeys, parks and battlefields, with insets showing the layouts at Tyne Dock, Middlesbrough, the Hartlepools and Hull docks.

By far the most fascinating thing about notices was their terminology, since niceties of grammar were secondary to economy in words. One

Standard GCR London Extension cast-iron sign, Brackley

could be told how to cross the line in an infinite variety of phrases. The Great Western could bluntly state that passengers were 'not allowed' to cross except by the bridge, yet add a polite 'request' for them to use it. At Helmsley on the North Eastern, where there was no footbridge, passengers were warned to 'SEE THAT NO TRAINS are APPROACHING before you attempt to CROSS the LINE', and the Wrexham, Mold & Connahs Quay Railway felt it imperative to stress that trains might be approaching from both directions. There was perhaps a degree of class distinction at Hockley where the Great Western warned that 'Workmen must not CROSS the RUNNING LINES but go through the SUBWAY. By Order'. Were the short cuts prohibited by this instruction the result of habitual lateness among the passengers or by the trains, one wonders?

The station exit was always the 'Way Out', which left no doubts, and the 'Premier Line' was much addicted to an ungrammatical notice 'To Cross the Line & Way Out'. The Midland indicated at Ashchurch the way 'To the Tewkesbury Train', suggesting there was only one and seemingly forgetting that in 1864 it had extended the branch to Great Malvern. The odd emphasis given by enlarging certain words was notably curious at Brockholes where the Lancashire & Yorkshire proclaimed in large letters 'TO TRAINS FOR', followed below in much smaller letters (and distinguishable only from a much shorter distance) by the apparently single sentence: 'Huddersfield Passengers Must Not Cross the Line'.

Railways were sternly on their guard against the vandals of their day. The well known exhibit at the Museum of British Transport prohibiting 'skylarking' was matched by the Cheshire Lines notice at Liverpool Central warning that 'These closets are intended for the convenience of passengers only. Workmen, cabmen, fishporters and idlers are not permitted to use them'. There were the elements of a Whitehall farce at those North Eastern stations where the gentlemen's lavatory displayed a discreet notice declaring that 'THE USE of this WATER CLOSET can be had on PAYMENT OF ONE PENNY at the BOOKING OFFICE'. It must have been cheaper than fitting Messrs Lockerbie & Wilkinson's patent locks.

The most important signs, of course, gave the station's name. On many early stations it was engraved in the stonework or, more often, painted on wooden boards, which were gradually superseded by screwed iron letters, though the Brighton and South Eastern companies were slow to change. These nameboards were supplemented by small

Cast-iron nameboard on concrete posts, Ancaster, GNR

glass panels on platform lamps, which illuminated them at night, and sometimes the panels were placed in platform windows, as at some of the London suburban stations of the Great Northern. Eccles, on the LNWR, had the name etched into the windowpanes, but this was unusual. Many junction stations were noted for their large nameboards offering a wealth of information about connecting services, of which the Great Western's were most prolific. 'Old Hill, change here for Halesowen, Windmill End branch and Dudley' was a fairly short example that lingered on well beyond the withdrawal of the branch trains—at Halesowen at least thirty-six years after public services ceased. Mighty boards with gigantic sans-serif lettering suspended from the roof were a familiar sight at Rugby and Crewe, but earlier London & North Western nameboards had attractive, chubbily seriffed lettering, as on the board behind the buffer stops at Banbury Merton Street. Earlier Great Western names were cast integrally into an iron board in rather ugly seriffed letters. Handsome Roman lettering marked the Cheshire Lines' distinctive nameboards, and the North Eastern adopted free-standing letters attached to the board by wooden or iron pegs. The Midland characteristically produced a double board, each one angled to the track so that it could easily be read from trains in either direction. In its later days the Great Northern went in for some particularly indestructible cast-iron boards on concrete posts with ball finials, and around the same time the South Western tried some entirely cast in reinforced concrete. As befitted its rural character, rustic lettering was used at Aspall and other stations on the Mid-Suffolk Light Railway.

Station clocks were most important, and generally came from well known makers. John Walker's clocks from London could be seen all over the Midlands and the South, though the London & North Western tended to stick to Joyce of Whitchurch or Potts of Leeds. Some clocks were quite ornate, but again often from stock designs, so that identical two-faced clocks with decorative crenellations could be found as widely separated as Birkdale on the Lancashire & Yorkshire and Denbigh on the London & North Western. Some lines, such as the Midland and Great Northern Joint, added a nicely individualistic touch by painting the station name on the clock face.

The growth of traffic, not to mention promptings from the Board of Trade, gradually forced railways to provide more footbridges from the 1850s onward. At first they were open, frequently lattice-girder, structures of the type found so often on the Great Northern and

Two-sided platform clock, Denbigh, LNWR

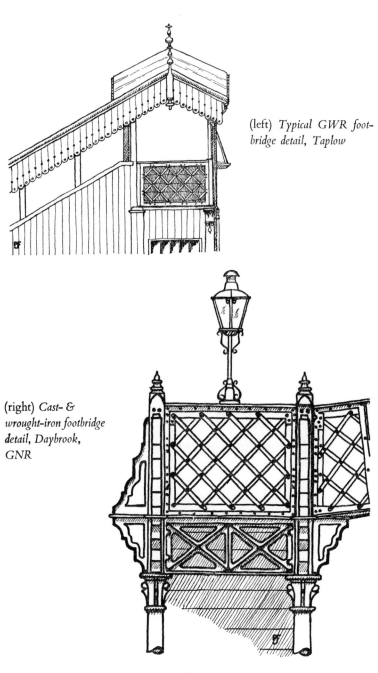

(left) *Typical GWR foot-bridge detail, Taplow*

(right) *Cast- & wrought-iron footbridge detail, Daybrook, GNR*

Midland systems with varying degrees of decoration, but occasionally made of wood, to which the South Western was partial. Flanged plate girder footbridges came later. The North Eastern Railway widely used a distinctively arched cast-iron bridge, while the Midland & Great Northern had some rare braced girder bridges trussed like a roof principal. Where covered bridges were needed, the Great Northern, Great Eastern and Metropolitan would simply add a corrugated iron roof, but the North Western was more considerate and usually glazed the sides as well. The GWR built some curious hybrids with covered stairs but an open bridge deck, or one side enclosed but not the other, yet applied extravagant valancing and finials to match the platform awnings.

The water column standing at the end of the platform was a very familiar item in the station scene, its supply coming from a nearby tank or tower which, at the earlier stations, generally matched the station buildings. Haydon Bridge on the Newcastle & Carlisle Railway and Penrith on the Lancaster & Carlisle had stone water towers designed to blend with the stations, and later at St Pancras and Christ's Hospital they were very much a part of the whole design, in the latter case an impressive example virtually forming part of the frontage. Fine stone corbelling marked the tower at Cirencester Watermoor, equally good brickwork the circular tower at Knutsford, and door and window openings added a touch of near-elegance at Llandovery, to quote three examples.

As we have already noticed at Nutfield, Kenilworth, Tenbury Wells (Plate 48) and Foxfield, signal boxes could match the station buildings, but comparatively rarely. At Dovecliffe, on the Manchester, Sheffield & Lincolnshire Railway, the station building was so plain that its harmonious relationship with the adjoining signal box, which was entered from it, was quite coincidental. Carlisle No 4A box, however, was carefully designed to fit in with the Tudor styling, and was really more of an upper room, with an oriel window overlooking the platforms. Signal 'boxes' ran right through the broad buildings at Nottingham Victoria and Midland stations and Leicester London Road, with a bay window in each end at platform level, so inconspicuous as to be hardly noticeable. Other stations could be quite dominated by a signal box, particularly the lofty specimen at Leominster and the box slung across the lines between the awnings at Stalybridge; while one was actually built on top of the awning at Bath Spa, and also at Bournemouth Central, to give the signalman a good view. At the other extreme, wayside stations like Betchworth and Marsh Gibbon & Poundon had to be content with signal levers in the booking office or, at more than a few LNWR branch-line stations, in the open on the platform.

War memorials are even less common. There is the monument at Euston, the commemorative arches at Waterloo and Stoke, and the elaborate plaques and plinths at Manchester and Sheffield Victoria stations, erected by dutiful companies to record their employees who fell in World War I, but more touching are local memorials like the modest brass tablet at Mexborough provided by railwaymen themselves and the small plaque to the memory of six of the station staff at Attenborough subscribed to by grateful passengers.

In addition to all these fixtures and fittings, there were a vast number of other miscellaneous but nonetheless useful items deemed necessary by Victorian railway managements, which in our own utilitarian age are now so fascinating that they are rapidly becoming collectors' pieces. Their variety in purpose and design was as infinite as that of the stations themselves, from the dated drinking fountains thoughtfully installed by the Midland to the lion-headed cast-iron umbrella stands, initialled 'LYR', found in many a north country waiting-room—first-class, of course.

Iron booking-office grille, Ferryhill, NER

EPILOGUE

In 1916 a leading article in *The Builder* on 'The Railway Stations of London' concluded:

> . . . the energies of the Victorians were directed to strewing the country with cinders and not to designing architectural monuments of civic interest.

I hope this book has shown that comment to be not entirely true.

Cast-iron bridge parapet, Middlesbrough, NER

SOURCES AND ACKNOWLEDGEMENTS

MY principal sources have been the stations themselves, supplemented by the photographs of the late R. E. G. Read and Professor C. L. Mowat for locations I have not visited personally or where I arrived too late to beat the demolisher.

Much material on early stations has been gained from contemporary literature such as the railway guides of the 1830s and 1840s like *Osborne's Guide to the Grand Junction Railway* (1838), *Roscoe's London & Birmingham Railway* (1839) and J. C. Bourne's *Great Western Railway* (1846), though detailed descriptions tend to be sparse, not comparable with those in Francis Whishaw's *The Railways of Great Britain and Ireland* (1842) which are in a class of their own. A. F. Tait's *Views of the Manchester & Leeds Railway* (1845) and *Views of the Liverpool & Manchester Railway* (1848) comprise series of fine lithographs showing stations.

Three periodicals have been especially prolific sources: *The Illustrated London News* (1842–1900) and *The Builder* (1843–1923), both particularly valuable for contemporary details, illustrations and names of architects; and *The Railway Magazine* from 1897 to the present day for articles and photographs of stations long since gone or altered. The more recent *Railway World* and *Journal of Transport History* have also been useful; much of the account of David Mocatta's work in Chapter 3 was drawn from David Cole's article in the latter (Vol III, No 3, May 1958).

General railway books containing sympathetic accounts of railway structures are *The Railways of Britain* by Jack Simmons (1961) and *The Railway Age* by Michael Robbins (1962); London stations are given specific treatment in *London Railways* by Edwin Course (1962) and *London's Termini* by Alan A. Jackson (1969), while Jack Simmons' *St Pancras Station* (1968) is a complete history of that remarkable place. Christian Barman's *Early British Railways* (1950) is an excellent short account of the motivations of the railway builders.

Railway architecture itself is not well served; Christian Barman's *An Introduction to Railway Architecture* (1950) is the most sensitive essay yet to have been written on early English stations; *The Railway Station* by Carroll V. S. Meeks (1957) is the standard work on the development of the large city station, on a global basis; *Railway Station Architecture* by David Lloyd & Donald Insall selects sixty stations for possible preservation, some of which have now been destroyed; and *Railway Stations: Southern Region* by Nigel Wikeley & John Middleton (1971), a collection of first-class recent photographs, suffers by confining itself to the region and not to the more logical Southern Railway, so that it stops abruptly at Salisbury yet includes three ex-Great Western lines.

The Architectural Review has been a valuable architectural periodical, particularly for the articles on 'Unit Stations' by J. L. Martin (1946), 'All Change' by David Lloyd & Donald Insall (1966) and 'Railway Thompson' by O. F. Carter (1968). The annual reports of the Victorian Society have also included references to stations from time to time.

Historical background, opening dates, etc have been taken mainly from the large number of railway histories and chronologies, now too numerous to mention apart from two which deserve special acknow-ledgement. George Dow's three-volume *Great Central* (1959-65) contains considerable material on that company's stations and those on lines in which it had an interest, not to mention the numerous period illustrations and the comprehensive index. *A History of the Southern Railway* by C. F. Dendy Marshall, revised by R. W. Kidner (1963), has a particularly useful list of opening dates of stations, as amended by H. V. Borley. Additionally the *Regional History of Railways of Great Britain* series—still in course of completion—provides concise information on lines and some stations, although the value of the indexes varies between volumes.

The most useful general works on Victorian architecture have been Henry-Russell Hitchcock's masterly *Early Victorian Architecture in Britain* (1954), *Victorian Architecture* edited by Peter Feriday (1963) and Robert Furneaux Jordan's *Victorian Architecture* (1966). Sir Nikolaus Pevsner's classic *Buildings of England* series has been useful for tracing some elusive station architects, mainly in the later volumes. G. F. Chadwick in his *The Works of Sir Joseph Paxton* (1961) gives valuable background on Paxton's railway associations and ridge-and-furrow roofing, but otherwise the relatively few biographies of railway engineers say little about their station work.

Other sources are mentioned in the text.

In addition to those mentioned in the Preface, I am grateful to the following for their kindness in providing information from their own researches or verifying points of doubt: The Director of the Sunderland Public Libraries for establishing that Thomas Moore designed Monkwearmouth and for details of Prosser's Sunderland station; J. H. Barratt, Staffordshire County Planning Officer, for similar evidence that H. A. Hunt designed Stoke; John Boyes for the story behind Maldon East; Charles E. Lee for confirming that the Surrey Iron Railway does not appear to have had any direct connection with the entrance building at Mitcham and for verifying that Sir John Fowler designed the Chatham's roof at Victoria; Philip Stevens for patiently unearthing newspaper accounts of Sancton Wood's activities on the Leicester–Peterborough line; Oliver F. Carter for so freely making available his researches into Francis Thompson, his collection of Sam Russell's lithographs of the North Midland of 1840 and for solving the Ambergate rebuilding puzzle; Dr L. G. Booth for details of the work of John and Benjamin Green on the Newcastle & North Shields Railway; and Gordon Rattenbury for taking photographs of stations in South Wales and helping to dispel a little of my ignorance about the history of that complicated area.

I also have to thank the Librarians and staff of Birmingham, Blackburn, Exeter and Manchester Public Libraries, J. Chambers, R. A. Dane, J. M. Dunn, J. M. Fleming, M. D. Greville, Dr J. R. Hollick, K. Hoole, Edward Hubbard, David Lloyd, R. S. McNaught, R. W. Miller, J. E. Norris, Peter Norton, Michael Reading, L. T. C. Rolt, Peter Stevenson, A. P. Voce and Geoffrey Webb for their kind assistance on various occasions.

I have a particular debt to those who have let me inspect plans, photographs and printed material: the Curator and staff of the Museum of British Transport, and in particular Jeoffry Spence, for access to their photographic collection; the Regional Architect of the former North Eastern Region of British Railways, York; the Chief Civil Engineer and his plan room staff, London Midland Region of British

Railways, Euston; the Archivist and staff of the former British Railways Historical Records at Paddington and at York, particularly for access to their set of *The Illustrated London News*; and A. E. L. Cox, a director of *Building*, for allowing me to consult his complete file of *The Builder*.

Finally I must thank E. & R. E. Pye, Ltd, of Clitheroe, for their careful photographic work.

GLOSSARY

ASHLAR Large smooth squared blocks of stone with fine joints.

BARGEBOARD A board following the slope of a gable, fixed to and hiding the ends of the purlins, usually decorated.

BLIND ARCADING An arcade of arches attached to a wall but not piercing it.

BOSS A projection covering the intersection of ribs in a roof.

CAMPANILE Italian for a bell tower, often detached from a building, but here used loosely to describe an Italian-style tower.

CAPITAL The top of a column, in classical architecture decorated according to four 'orders'. *See fig 1.*

i   ii   iii   iv   v

Fig 1   The Classical Orders: (i) & (ii) Greek & Roman Doric; (iii) Corinthian; (iv) Ionic; (v) Tuscan

CARYATID A column or pilaster (qv) carved in the form of a female figure.

CLERESTORY A central elongated raised roof section, often with glazed sides.

CORBEL A projection from a wall to support a beam or bracket.

CORINTHIAN See CAPITAL.

CORNICE Projecting moulding along the top of a wall, arch, etc.

COTTAGE ORNÉ An elaborate rustic style introduced by the romantic movement of the late eighteenth century, typified by fancy bargeboards, finials, glazing bars, overhanging eaves, half-timbering, etc.

CRENELLATIONS Alternate indentations in a battlement-style parapet.

CRESTING Ornamental work along the ridge of a roof or turret.

CROCKET Carved projections at regular intervals on a spire.

CUPOLA A small dome, generally circular or polygonal, crowning a roof or turret.

CUSPS Pointed projections in window tracery (qv).

DADO Lower part of an interior wall up to waist height.

DENTIL Small, regularly spaced blocks beneath a cornice (qv)—see fig 2.

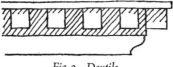

Fig 2   Dentils

DORIC See CAPITAL.

ENTABLATURE The horizontal section supported by a column, incorporating architrave, frieze and cornice.

FENESTRATION The arrangement of windows in a wall.

FILIGREE Ornamental work of great delicacy, resembling lace.

FINIAL A decorated vertical ornament on top of a gable, parapet, turret or other vertical projection; sometimes pendant on a gable, etc.

GAMBREL ROOF See fig 3.

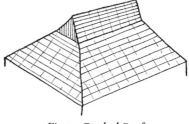

Fig 3   Gambrel Roof

HAMMERBEAM A horizontal bracket projecting from a wall to carry an arched brace or strut supporting a roof.

232

HIPPED ROOF   Roof with sloping ends instead of vertical gables.
IONIC   See CAPITAL.
IN ANTIS   A portico (qv) recessed into a building with columns in line with the front wall.
LANCET WINDOW A very slender pointed arched window.
MANSARD ROOF See fig 4.

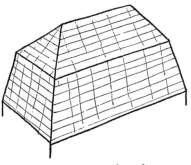

Fig 4   Mansard Roof

MULLION   A vertical upright dividing a window.
NOGGING   Brick panels in a timber-framed building.
OGEE   See fig 5.

Fig 5   Ogee arch or gable shape

ORIEL   A bay window projecting from an upper floor only.
PALLADIAN   A style derived from the great sixteenth-century Italian architect Palladio, whose work was based on Roman classicism. In England, used in eighteenth-century domestic work and mainly confined to the decorative features.
PANTILE   A 'double' roofing tile, S-shaped in section.
PARGETTING   Decorated external rendering, here generally incised.

PAVILION   A projecting section of a building, usually one-storey and gabled.

PEDIMENT   In classical architecture, the upward reversal of an entablature (qv) at its extremities to form a low triangular or curved gable on top of a portico (qv); also used on small scale over doors and windows; used by Victorians in various other positions. A broken pediment has a gap in the apex.

PILASTER   A square column projecting slightly from a wall, but not free-standing.

PITCHED ROOF A roof, triangular in section, having straight 'pitches' meeting at the ridge.

PORTE COCHERE A large porch to accommodate vehicles.

PORTICO   A roofed area, open-sided or enclosed and often on columns or arches, forming the entrance and centrepiece of a façade.

QUEEN-POST ROOF TRUSS *See fig 6.*

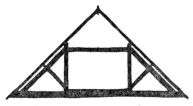

Fig 6   Queen post roof truss

QUOINS   Dressed stones or brickwork, usually alternating large and small, giving prominence to the corners of buildings or door or window openings.

ROCK-FACED STONE See RUSTICATED.

ROUNDEL   Small flat circular moulding applied to a surface as decoration.

RUSTICATED   Large squared blocks of stone with wide deep joints to give a bold appearance and provided with a variety of surfaces, eg rock-faced: rough-hewn straight from the quarry, or carved thus in simulation.

SEGMENTAL ARCH *See fig 7.*

'SCHOOL BOARD' WINDOW A type of plain window associated with many of the late nineteenth-century Board Schools. *See fig 7.*

Fig 7   A School Board type of window beneath segmental arch

SOFFIT	The underside of an arch.
SPANDREL	The triangular space between the curve, the vertical side line and the horizontal top line of an arch or bracket, or between two arches.
STRING COURSE	A projecting horizontal band in a wall, often moulded.
SWAG	Carved or moulded ornamental festoons of fruit and flowers.
TERRA-COTTA	Very hard decorative tiles or bricks, usually moulded and often glazed.
TRACERY	Continuation of mullions (qv) in a Gothic window up to decorative ribwork in the upper portion.
TRANSOM	A horizontal bar across a window or opening.
TUSCAN	See CAPITAL.
VALANCE	Decorated boarding suspended from the edge of a canopy or awning; occasionally along the eaves of a roof.
VOUSSOIRS	Wedge-shaped stones or bricks used to form an arch.

GENERAL INDEX

For stations, see separate index on *page 242.*   Illustrations are indicated in *italic* type. Railway companies are indexed under owners as at 1921.

INDEX OF STATIONS

Illustrations are indicated in *italic* type. Company ownership is shown as existed in 1921.